S0-ARO-568

WITHDRAWN

WITHDRAWN

The FIRST AMENDMENT
and CIVIL LIABILITY

The FIRST AMENDMENT and CIVIL LIABILITY

Robert M. O'Neil

LEMONT PUBLIC LIBRARY DISTRICT
50 East Wend Street
Lemont, IL 60439-6439

INDIANA UNIVERSITY PRESS
Bloomington and Indianapolis

This book is a publication of

Indiana University Press
601 North Morton Street
Bloomington, IN 47404-3797 USA

http://iupress.indiana.edu

Telephone orders   800-842-6796
Fax orders   812-855-7931
Orders by e-mail   iuporder@indiana.edu

© 2001 by Robert M. O'Neil

All rights reserved

No part of this book may be reproduced or utilized in any form or by any means, electronic or mechanical, including photocopying and recording, or by any information storage and retrieval system, without permission in writing from the publisher. The Association of American University Presses' Resolution on Permissions constitutes the only exception to this prohibition.

The paper used in this publication meets the minimum requirements of American National Standard for Information Sciences—Permanence of Paper for Printed Library Materials, ANSI Z39.48-1984.

Manufactured in the United States of America

Library of Congress Cataloging-in-Publication Data

O'Neil, Robert M.
   The First Amendment and civil liability / Robert M. O'Neil
      p. cm.
Includes bibliographical references and index.
   ISBN 0-253-34033-0 (cloth : alk. paper)
   1. Freedom of speech—United States. 2. Liability (Law)—United States.
3. Authors and publishers—Legal status, laws, etc.—United States. 4. Libel
and slander—United States. I. Title.
   KF4772 O54 2001
   342.73'0853—dc21
                                        2001002832

1   2   3   4   5   06   05   04   03   02   01

3 1559 00137 2422

To — **hazel, elinor, otis and robert peter**

the next generation

contents

preface

Like most books, this one had serendipitous origins. While on vacation in the summer of 1990, I came upon a newspaper account of a bizarre lawsuit. Harrison Ford was soon to star in the film version of Scott Turow's best-selling novel *Presumed Innocent*. To prepare for his unfamiliar role as a Midwest prosecutor, Ford spent a day shadowing the Wayne County, Michigan, district attorney. The venue was appropriate; some of the scenes would be filmed in Detroit, even though Turow never identifies the city in which his tales of crime are set. The core of the experience was a "charging conference," during which Ford and the real-life lawyers would review a recently discarded case file. Though the file involved a homicide, the prosecutor's staff had found insufficient merit to justify pressing criminal charges. A self-defense plea on the part of Ronald Wnuk, the arrested suspect, had seemed to them dispositive.

Chief prosecutor John O'Hair, Ford's mentor for the day, had a quite different view of the now dormant file. The case seemed to him well worth taking to court, a step which was still within the permissible time limit for homicides. Charges against Wnuk were immediately reinstated. After a protracted trial, a jury eventually acquitted Wnuk. That might well have ended the saga, had Wnuk not somehow learned of the circumstances that had caused him to be placed back in jeopardy. He then filed a $9 million suit against Harrison Ford, the studio, and the county. Wnuk's legally plausible claim was that but for the charging conference which the real-life prosecutors had arranged to prepare Ford for his screen role, he would have soon fallen beyond the reach of the criminal process.

Though it seems to have been quietly dismissed some months later, this novel lawsuit posed fascinating issues about the extent to which, and conditions under which, the news and entertainment media might be held liable for causing harm or injury. There have, in fact, been a host of lawsuits seeking redress for imitative or so-called copy-cat actions, inspired or provoked by a film, a broadcast, a book, or a magazine article. Most of these cases have, however, occurred during the past decade; at the time Mr. Wnuk sought to hold Mr. Ford legally liable for his distress, there were few precedents.

Until quite recently, commentators had virtually ignored issues of *civil* liability, viewing threats to free expression as chiefly the product of *governmental* action, not implicated by private resort to the courts. When in the early 1960s I served as a law clerk to Justice William J. Brennan, Jr., the focus of his remarkable First Amendment jurisprudence was wholly public. Yet change was imminent; the very next year he wrote for a unanimous Court in the *New York Times* libel case, which first made clear that private lawsuits could and sometimes did abridge free expression. In this spirit, the few lower courts that considered potential media or entertainment liability before the 1990s ruled that the First Amendment's guarantees of free speech and press would not permit imposing damages on those who created or published catalytic material, however direct the link might be, and however grave the consequences.

Yet in the very year the Harrison Ford case was filed, a subtle change began to occur, virtually unnoticed even by normally attentive media and entertainment lawyers and scholars. An article appeared in Larry Flynt's *Hustler* magazine on the subject of auto-erotic asphyxiation. A misguided Texas teenager tried the technique which the article described—masturbating while being suspended or gagged so as to cut off the blood supply to the brain. He died in the process. His mother and a young friend who had discovered the lifeless body sued *Hustler* in federal court for substantial damages, insisting the magazine was legally liable for causing the boy's death.

A sympathetic jury returned a large verdict in the family's and friend's favor. Though the federal appeals court eventually reversed the judgment, finding the article protected by the First Amendment, the panel was not unanimous. Judge Edith Jones, who has lately been mentioned as a possible Supreme Court nominee, filed a blistering dissent. She rejected *Hustler's* First Amendment claim, insisting that a "pornographic" magazine, and especially the suspect article, was not what Thomas Jefferson and James Madison envisioned when they convinced the new nation to protect free speech and press. She also argued that the targeted article posed for readers an unacceptably grave risk of just the sort of tragedy that befell the hapless young reader. Remarkably little note was taken either of Judge Jones's dissent or of the adverse judgment in the trial court. The case had come to an end, *Hustler* was seemingly free to publish such material, and Mr. Flynt's continuing battles with the law found different venues.

It was not, in fact, until the late 1990s that alarm bells began to sound. Two cases then brought an end to an era of complacency. A brutal murder in a Washington, D.C., suburb was traced to a hired assassin who had used a book called *Hit Man: A Technical Manual for Independent Contractors*—though in one respect he had failed to follow the book, since its promotional claims promised success "without getting caught." The victims' family sued the publisher, Paladin Press, claiming that one who issues instructions for such a heinous crime is as fully culpable as the person who pulls the trigger. The district judge, a former prosecutor, dismissed the case on free speech grounds; in his view, "words do not kill—only people kill." The federal appeals court, however, saw the case very differently, and sent it back for trial.

Though recognizing that normally such claims must be tested by the Supreme Court's standard for "incitement," the higher court felt this case was different, partly because the publisher had stipulated its intent to have the book used for such brutal killings. The appeals court also suggested, rather like Judge Jones, that the Framers had not intended to extend free speech guarantees to such marginal material as a hit-man manual. The appellate judges promised, however, that such a ruling could never apply to films, novels, or other "legitimate" entertainment material.

That promise soon proved illusory. When victims of a brutal slaying allegedly inspired by the film *Natural Born Killers* sued producer Oliver Stone and the film studio, a Louisiana appeals court confidently cited the *Hit Man Manual* ruling in holding that the suit should go to trial. The Louisiana and United States Supreme Courts declined to intervene at this early stage in the litigation. Although the suit was eventually dismissed by the trial court, the precedent remains in full and ominous force. Its ominous portent is magnified by the critical comments of novelist John Grisham, a close friend of another victim of the same killers, who has publicly suggested that imposing liability in an occasional extreme case may be warranted as an antidote to irresponsible or avaricious producers.

Thus by the end of the decade, there were few places for the news or entertainment media to hide. The First Amendment could no longer be invoked as a secure shield. A new branch of law of free expression had emerged in a remarkably brief time—from nearly total neglect of threats posed by civil damage suits, as recently as the late 1980s, to a time barely a decade later, when apprehension about damage suits had, for many in the media world, overshadowed concern about government regulation or intervention.

The perspectives which this book offers have come, in substantial part, from direct involvement in some of the principal cases. The Thomas Jefferson Center for the Protection of Free Expression, which I direct, filed friend-of-the-court briefs at the appellate level in the *Hit Man Manual* case, and in the appeals court in the suit brought by Planned Parenthood against anti-abortion activists who posted threats on the so-called Nuremberg Web site (discussed in Chapter 3) and the case filed by Dean Sharon Yeagle against Virginia Tech's *Collegiate Times* libel cases (discussed in Chapter 2), among others. Along the way, there have been many opportunities for current media comment on these and other cases that presented potential issues of civil liability. While this field seems relatively calm during the summer of 2001, new suits have already been filed and will reach judgment in the months ahead, probably compounding the uncertainty and media anxiety in the post–*Hit Man Manual* period. Without the slightest doubt, a topic which a decade ago would not have sustained even a meager article now demands book-length treatment.

In the analysis of these issues, I have been most ably advised and assisted by University of Virginia Law students in courses on Free Speech and Press, Free Expression in Cyberspace, and First Amendment and the Arts, a number of whom have done major papers on civil liability topics. An especially dedicated and effective summer of research by U. Va. Law students (and recent graduates) Tarah Grant and Jonathan Riehl and University of Richmond student/graduate Jessica Galazka marshaled the material which made the writing process both imperative and feasible. A year later, law students Grant Penrod and Hailey Vaughan, our current researchers, carefully read and checked the page proofs. At each stage of the creative process, my Thomas Jefferson Center colleague Amy McClung read and reacted to early drafts, final drafts, and completed copy, with an uncanny sense not only for stylistic perfection but also for substantive cogency. Josh Wheeler, the Center's Associate Director, not only has been my colleague in our myriad professional activities, but has contributed countless insights during our shared litigation of civil liability questions, as well as on broader First Amendment matters. My wife Karen, a lifelong teacher and more recently a college counselor and department chair, has been by far my most thoughtful and conscientious guide and companion teacher in this as in so many others areas.

Robert M. O'Neil
Charlottesville, Virginia
July 2001

The FIRST AMENDMENT
and CIVIL LIABILITY

1.
First Principles and Basic Tensions

During the March 1995 taping of a Jenny Jones television program on "secret admirers," Scott Amedure revealed that he was attracted to Jonathan Schmitz, another male guest on the show. Amedure then described, in Schmitz's presence, some of his sexual fantasies. Though this segment was never broadcast, it was hardly forgotten. Three days after the taping, Amedure was shot to death in the doorway of his home in a Detroit suburb. Schmitz was soon charged with the killing and was convicted of second-degree murder. While that case was on appeal, the Amedure family retained Geoffrey Feiger, a Michigan lawyer who had achieved prominence as the principal attorney for Dr. Jack Kevorkian and who would later run a futile campaign for governor. Feiger filed suit in a Michigan state court seeking millions of dollars in damages from Warner Brothers, the producers of the *Jenny Jones Show*.

The central claim in this suit was that the producers had negligently caused Amedure's death and should therefore be liable to the victim's family, as would any other commercial entity that had caused the killing of an innocent person. Specifically, Feiger (himself a sometime talk-show host) argued that before creating such volatile situations as the "secret admirer" segment, producers had a legal duty to conduct psychological background checks on guests who might be surprised or overwhelmed; it turned out that Schmitz was a severe manic-depressive.

The trial attracted much national, indeed international, attention during the winter and early spring of 1999. The day that Jenny Jones herself testified drew especially intense public scrutiny. (Jones's testimony revealed that she had a surprisingly limited grasp of how the segment had been planned and arranged.) In early May, the jury returned a verdict in the Amedures' favor of $25 million—$5 million for Scott's pain and suffering, $20 million for his death, and a few thousand dollars for funeral expenses. The judgment immediately evoked intense controversy. Feiger was jubilant: "This industry has got to clean itself up because these people care nothing about the people they use and abuse." Warner Brothers' lead counsel issued a dire warning: "This will have a profoundly chilling effect not only on talk shows but on all media."

Most free-speech advocates and First Amendment experts saw the verdict as another example of blaming the messenger for an unwelcome message; New York media lawyer Floyd Abrams called the ruling "unwarranted" and insisted that the impact of programs such as the *Jenny Jones Show* was basically "a matter of public taste" and not a proper province of the courts. But some media experts took a different view. Dean Ken Bode of the Medill School of Journalism at Northwestern University, former host of PBS's *Washington Week in Review*, saw potential value in such a stunning verdict: "If the way to get their attention is the checkbook, perhaps that will restore some propriety." Former Secretary of Education and federal drug czar William Bennett was more pointed: "It's a good thing for the public to look the entertainment companies in the eye and say, 'We've had it.'"

There was ample reason to credit Bennett's view of how "the public" felt. Commenting on the Amedure verdict, Andrew Kohut, director of the Pew Research Project for the People and the Press, said he was "reasonably sure" that "the public would be on the side of the plaintiff in this case because they feel the media don't care enough about the consequences of their actions." In fact, the popularity of such confrontational talk shows had already declined sharply, partly in response to the very incident which gave rise to the lawsuit. Some major sponsors had withdrawn their support of what had, through the mid-1990s, been not only one of the most popular but also one of the most lucrative television formats.

Of the programs that had once freely used scenarios such as "secret admirer," only that of Jerry Springer continued to rely on ambushing unsuspecting guests. A month after the Amedure verdict, Jerry Springer in fact agreed to appear before the Chicago city council. No stranger to such forums—he had spent some years on the Cincinnati City Council and served as vice mayor of Cincinnati—Springer had agreed to address suggestions that unruly guests should be handcuffed and hauled off to jail and that the program itself really needed to be licensed by the city as a curb on its more violent strain. Springer's final reply was that "with all due respect, this is your show," strongly implying that the producers and the host were doing no more than reflecting on the air the realities of an increasingly violent society. To some degree, the subject of the Chicago hearing was already conjectural; by that time, Springer's producers had announced they were taking steps to reduce "violence, physical confrontation or profanity" in their programming.

In a sense, the worst was yet to come. One year to the day after the Amedure verdict, Jerry Springer taped a segment called "Secret Mistresses Confronted." The principal guest was Nancy Campbell-Panitz, who (on her birthday) graphically recounted her marital problems and her deepest emotions. She became, on the program, the target of cruel humiliation at the hands of her German ex-husband and of the woman he later married after he left her. The audience cheered Campbell-Panitz as she left the stage and seemed to savor her predicament. Less than a day later, her body was found in the house that had become a major item of contention among the three parties. Sarasota police called the death a homicide, for which the ex-husband and the new wife emerged as prime suspects.

The Campbell-Panitz tragedy in the spring of 2000 evoked far less media coverage than had the Amedure slaying five years earlier. The decline in interest may have reflected a higher threshold for shock and violence—after all, the Columbine High School and Paducah grade school killings and several other brutal events had intervened. The diminished level of public interest may also have reflected different expectations about levels of confrontation on the programs of Jerry Springer and Jenny Jones, since Springer remained the unrequited "bad boy" of the talk shows. Whatever the reason, it is no longer certain that even a post-taping fatality will make the front pages these days. Yet the degree of public ambivalence about such confrontations, and the potential for legal liability on the part of those who create and broadcast them, remain durable and perplexing elements of the current media scene.

The central question for us, however, is who (if anyone) other than the killer bears legal responsibility for such tragic events. Two sets of legal principles converge uncomfortably in such a situation. On the one hand, when the actions of a commercial entity cause injury or death to an innocent person, we usually assume that such an entity may be held liable for damages if the victim seeks such redress. On the other hand, when literary or artistic expression leads to harmful results, we tend to believe that creative persons, including authors, editors, publishers, and producers, should be immune because they are engaged in a highly valued calling for which civil liability would be wholly inappropriate.

In a few rare situations, to be sure, expressive activity may directly cause injury, even death. Several examples come to mind. Christo, the French sculptor and designer who creates vast tableaus, once covered a hillside with ornamental concrete objects shaped like umbrellas. One of the objects became detached, rolled down the hill, and crushed a bystander. Several years later, a Japanese video-game producer discovered that the bright and rapidly flashing lights and loud noise of the games caused some children to become nauseous and even to suffer mild seizures. There have been sculptures containing an extremely sharp metal edge, such as a knife or blade, placed on display within reach of the arms or fingers of unwary visitors. These are the relatively easy cases, ones in which liability for claims of civil liability arise for reasons that are wholly unrelated to the content or message of the work. In such situations, it is the *medium* that is the source of the harm, and thus a basis for liability, not the *message* or theme of the work. But when it is the *content* that can be said to generate risk and harm—for example, a graphic painting the distressing imagery of which makes some viewers nauseous—we have a very different situation.

The law that defines the scope of potential liability for expressive activity turns out to be remarkably thin and surprisingly unhelpful on most such questions. That is largely because the whole question of civil liability has strikingly recent origins. The first major treatise on First Amendment law, written by Harvard law professor Zechariah Chafee, Jr., appeared in 1920; a second edition appeared in 1940. The title, *Free Speech in the United States*, accurately reflected the book's comprehensive scope. The subject of civil liability claimed but a single paragraph of some 566 pages of text, on page 548, almost an afterthought that noted the latent tension between the law of libel and freedom of expression. The entire balance of the book addressed those myriad issues of criminal law and administrative regulation that constituted the universe of free speech in the period between the two world wars.

Three decades later, Yale law professor Thomas I. Emerson followed Chafee's example with the only other truly exhaustive treatise, *The System of Freedom of Expression*. By the late 1960s, issues of civil liability claimed substantially more than Chafee's lone paragraph. Libel and slander now merited an entire chapter. But there was relatively little else that needed be said about potential damage claims, since criminal prosecution and government administrative sanctions still dominated the field. Few of the other civil-liability issues on which this book will focus even existed for Emerson in 1970, much less for Chafee in 1940.

Had either of these eminent scholars and First Amendment experts ever been asked their views on the constitutionality of the Amedure/Jenny Jones verdict, they would have found the question little more familiar than it would have been a century and a half earlier for James Madison and Thomas Jefferson. The speed with which such issues have assumed center stage in the arena of free expression is a reflection of the changes that have occurred in a society which generates litigation, rather than in the courts which respond to those forces by resolving disputes. A series of specific issues now merits our closer attention.

Why Should Speech Be Free At All? We take freedom of expression so much for granted that its rationale is seldom even considered, much less fully explored. Every so often, and surely in a context such as this one, we need to step back and revisit basic principles. The foundations of free expression in the United States reflect some intriguing paradoxes. Our First Amendment is by far the oldest and most durable of the world's guarantees of free expression. It has been in existence for nearly 210 years in precisely its current form. Despite persistent efforts to amend it—to make possible the jailing of flag-burners, for example, or to confer on broadcasters the same rights that newspapers enjoy—the basic text has remained intact.

Curiously, given such longevity and immutability, the First Amendment has appeared in court only in the past eighty years or so, which constitutes little more than the most recent third of its total life span. The lateness of the emergence of free-speech litigation is a subject that invites much speculation, and it certainly deserves more than the sentence of passing comment to which we are confined here. For the moment, however, the surprising recency of First Amendment case law makes more understandable the even later appearance in the courts of civil-liability claims involving free expression.

As a starting point, it may be worth asking a question courts seldom pause to consider—Why does our Constitution protect free speech at all? Professor Thomas Emerson, in his admirable treatise, sought to answer that question as few scholars ever have. He offered several premises for our deep national commitment to free speech. First, he observed, "freedom of expression is essential as a means of assuring individual self-fulfillment," noting that "the proper end of man is the realization of his character and potentialities as a human being." Second, Emerson argued that "freedom of expression is an essential process for advancing knowledge and discovering truth"—a value that might well have ranked first on Thomas Jefferson's list.

Third, for Emerson, "freedom of expression is essential to provide for participation in decision making by all members of society"—another value that Jefferson and Madison often embraced with their conviction that a functioning democracy needed above all an "informed citizenry." Finally, "freedom of expression is a means of achieving a more acceptable and hence a more stable community, of maintaining the precarious balance between healthy cleavage and necessary consensus"—a value that was always basic to Justice William Brennan's faith in "robust debate" as a key to democracy and self-government.

To this list other values might well be added. Professor Vincent Blasi, one of the few scholars to revisit basic functions of the First Amendment, sees free speech as assuring a vital "checking value" against the exercise of excessive power by government or, for that matter, by large private concentrations. Still other values could be noted, including the contributions that artistic and literary expression make to the quality of life, in ways not fully reflected in Emerson's essentially political taxonomy. But this list serves at least to set the stage for the complexities that follow in a real world where speech turns out to be less free than the framers of the Constitution might have expected it would be. Actually, the First Amendment turns out to protect both more and less expression than the bare text of the Bill of Rights might imply. We need now to examine each of the major variants, since they are vital to an understanding of where civil liability fits in the constitutional constellation. Several propositions follow.

"Freedom of speech and of the press" may in some ways protect more expression than one would expect. In several important respects, the Supreme Court has given a rather expansive interpretation of First Amendment freedoms. In 1958, it faced for the first time the question of whether the clause about freedom of speech and freedom of the press included the right to associate with others for political purposes. The immediate issue was the legal status of membership records of controversial groups such as the NAACP,

which law-enforcement officers had demanded and which civil rights organizations wished to keep confidential. With no directly applicable precedent and no governing provision in the Bill of Rights, the Supreme Court boldly and unanimously declared that the First Amendment contained a "freedom of association" that served to insulate membership lists, as well as individual affiliations, from probing grand juries and police subpoenas. Although the starting point was understandably political groups, the right to associate with others for the advancement of shared goals and interests would soon extend beyond politics.

A few years later, again in the civil rights context, the justices declared with equal confidence that freedom of speech included a right to take issues of public interest to the courts for adjudication and resolution. Here too, the implications of a liberal guarantee of expressive freedom proved sufficient without explicit textual or precedential support: If organizations such as the NAACP could not seek legal protection for their causes and their members without fear of restraints, then the very survival of the group and its causes could be placed at risk.

Perhaps most remarkable among these judicial expansions was the 1969 declaration that "freedom of speech" included "symbolic" expression—in this case the wearing by high school students of black armbands as a form of non-verbal protest against the Vietnam War. As with freedom of association, the justices neither needed, nor cited, directly applicable authority for such a view, either in legal precedent or in the writings of the framers of the Constitution—though in the case of symbolic protest, it seems safe to assume that a generation which championed the Boston Tea Party would expect the Bill of Rights they later wrote to shield such silent but portentous non-verbal messages.

Finally, at least some of what we normally consider "conduct" or "behavior" has received First Amendment protection. This view emerged most clearly in the flag-desecration cases of 1989 and 1990, which involved acts even less like pure speech than the silent display of black armbands by the anti-war students in the 1960s. Very near the close of his remarkable career, Justice Brennan declared that, while not all "action taken with respect to our flag is expressive," that view was appropriate here because prosecutors had targeted "the likely communicative impact of [the flag-burner's] expressive conduct." This was not the first time this concept had been invoked, however. In the case of an anti-war draft-card burner named O'Brien, the justices recognized that much human activity could involve both speech and conduct. The Court then provided guidance, which still controls such cases, for dealing with such hybrid situations. When government seeks to target the expressive element and does so more broadly than is necessary to serve legitimate public interests, the entire conviction may be invalid. Conversely, government may incidentally punish some speech if the focus of its sanctions is not on expression and if the sanction is no broader than is necessary to serve valid public goals. The doctrine set forth in *United States v. O'Brien* has thus turned out to be a very mixed blessing but does nonetheless recognize the degree to which "speech" may mean more than the spoken and written word.

Although one might fairly use the term "expansive" to describe the Court's embrace of freedom of association, public interest litigation, nonverbal protest, and expressive conduct, there is a rather different way of describing how First Amendment law has been reshaped in the last half-century. While the framers gave us no definitions of "speech" or of "press," they did imply, if only by recognizing such liberties through an explicit Bill of Rights, their expectation that protection would be the norm and that denial of protection would be the exception that would be justified by special needs and conditions. Given our limited insight into the Jeffersonian and Madisonian rationale for including such freedoms in the Constitution—albeit as something of an afterthought—we may assume that they meant the courts to construe these safeguards liberally and generously. Thus, in contrast to the protections of freedom of speech and freedom of the press contained in many other constitutions and in national legal systems where such liberties are implicit without textual designation, ours is a structure in which freedom of expression is the norm, or at least the presumption, and the denial of protection is the exception. That being the case, we are now about to learn that the exceptions are nonetheless crucial,

Sometimes words that constitute "speech" and "press" are unprotected by the First Amendment. In two basic respects, words and images that are clearly "speech" for most purposes turn out not to be protected against all legal claims or sanctions. If a plagiarist is sued for having infringed the copyright of another author, it will do the infringer little good to argue—quite correctly— that his offense consisted entirely and exclusively of the use of words. Here the copyright law always trumps, and the infringer loses. Indeed, courts may even order an infringing book or tape or disc off the shelves in extreme cases— a remedy we would be quick to reject as a "prior restraint" if it occurred anywhere else.

Courts do occasionally ponder this curious tension between the law of intellectual property and the law of freedom of expression, noting the anomalous balance. The path of reconciliation between these interests relies directly on early history and constitutional text. Before there was a Bill of Rights and a First Amendment protecting speech and press, the framers included in the body of the Constitution a clause that empowered Congress to protect the works of authors and inventors by conferring certain exclusive rights in those works. The clear implication of such power—indeed the only workable interpretation—is that courts may enjoin some expression that would otherwise be protected and may award to the aggrieved creator redress in the form of money damages in order to protect that monopoly.

There are several tradeoffs which at least mitigate this inevitable tension. Copyright clearly does not protect *ideas*, only the tangible *expression* of them. Thus, an author or artist may not prevent others from using a concept, only his or her particular applications or expressions of it. And if an author or artist independently creates that very same expression without copying the work of another, the parallel work is fully protected, and despite its similarity it may not be charged as an infringement. Copyright also requires something more than the mere labor to create a work; "sweat of the brow," even profuse perspiration, will not suffice. Time, energy, and effort do not provide a legally adequate substitute for originality on a creator's part, else we would have far more serious tensions between copyright and free speech than current law creates. Moreover, the author's monopoly exists only for a "limited term," after which the material passes into the public domain, where everyone may freely use it.

Perhaps most important of the conditions imposed upon copyright, even during the period of protection, is the concept that others may (even without the copyright owner's permission) make "fair use" of a protected work—not only for limited purposes such as quoting a few lines in a book review but also more broadly in the case of parody or satire, as in the case of the Two Live Crew parody of the protected song *Pretty Woman*, which the Supreme Court unanimously ruled to be fair use and, accordingly, exempt from any liability on the part of the parodists. Where we would be without a rather generous concept of fair use is an intriguing but totally hypothetical question, since in the real world the scope of fair use goes far to mitigate the tension and create a workable balance between two sets of interests, both of which are of a very high order.

Not all spoken or written words constitute "speech" or "press" for First Amendment purposes. Some exceptions or exemptions to First Amendment protection may seem obvious, but they require closer scrutiny. A person who is charged with extortion for sending a ransom note to the family of a kidnapped infant could hardly escape prison by pleading—quite correctly—that his crime consisted entirely of words. Much the same is true of most criminal fraud; although the charge and proof of guilt rely almost totally on words, a free-speech claim would be ridiculed. Most conspiracies involve a trail of words leading up to the acts of homicide or theft or arson; some of the co-conspirators, in fact, may have committed no acts but simply uttered words as their share of the enterprise. A number of other criminal charges—for solicitation, inducement, aiding and abetting, most notably—consist almost entirely of words. Yet even the most ardent First Amendment champion does not claim that free speech is abridged when a person is sent to jail or fined because the words used in such contexts have led to a finding of guilt.

The hard question is just where one ought to draw the line between words that are protected as advocacy and those, often superficially quite similar, which are not. Some scholars, such as University of Illinois-Chicago Dean (and former Duke University professor) Stanley Fish, would push that line fairly far away from protection. In his latest work on this subject—*There's No Such Thing as Free Speech . . . and it's a good thing, too*—Fish argues that, as an increasingly legalistic society, we have moved that line too far toward protecting inappropriate levels or types of expressive activity. He writes that "free speech is just the name we give to verbal behavior that serves the substantive agendas we wish to advance. . . . The label 'free speech' is the one you want your favorites to wear." Fish insists that "courts are never in the business of protecting speech per se, 'mere' speech (a nonexistent animal); rather, they are in the business of classifying speech (as protected or regulatable) in relation to a value—the health of the republic. . . . That is the true, if unacknowledged, object of their protection."

The views of Fish and others who share his doubts evoke a passionate reply from scholars such as Professor Franklyn Haiman, who devoted several decades to teaching courses on free speech at Northwestern University and was deeply immersed in real-life tests such as defending the right of American Nazis to march in Skokie, Illinois. In his recent book *Speech Acts and the First Amendment*, Haiman warns of the risks of drawing the line between what is protected and what is not protected in a way that invites denial of protection to expression (however odious) that may genuinely reflect and embody ideas.

None of us could gainsay that some such line must be drawn, unless we were to extend First Amendment protection well beyond what the framers presumably intended. We understand the easy cases at both extremes—the extortionist on one end and the political agitator at the other. What is difficult is the confusion between those poles, with which we will simply have to live with a degree of unavoidable discomfort.

Not all words that are "speech" or "press" for First Amendment purposes are protected. Even within the ambit of recognized "speech" and "press," certain types of expression have been ruled not to merit full First Amendment protection. Most notable of the exceptions is the category somewhat tortuously defined as obscenity. In 1957, addressing that issue for the first time, the Supreme Court declared that literary and artistic material which meets the test it had devised for obscenity does not deserve First Amendment protection. The reason? In part, the justices relied upon the universality of disdain among civilized societies for material which "appeals predominantly to prurient interest and goes substantially beyond customary limits of candor in representation of nudity, sex or excretion."

The Court also observed that "implicit in the history of the First Amendment is the rejection of obscenity as utterly without redeeming social importance," in part because such material was wholly devoid of the sort of "ideas" that the free speech and press clause was designed to protect. With minor variations, the obscenity test first articulated by the Supreme Court in the late

1950s remains in force to this day, and obscenity thus remains one of the principal categories of unprotected expression.

A quarter-century after its obscenity ruling, the Court even more decisively relegated child pornography to the realm of unprotected speech. A compelling societal concern for the welfare of young people, who are potential victims of commercial exploitation, has led to unequivocal condemnation of such material in all forms. Indeed, while the mere possession of *obscenity* in the privacy of one's home may not be made a criminal act, the same is not true for child pornography, the mere existence of which is deemed so potentially harmful as to be inherently unlawful. The extent to which the Court was committed to the banishment of child pornography became clear a decade later.

In the late 1960s, the justices ruled that even otherwise unprotected obscenity may not be seized from, or its use made unlawful in, the privacy of the possessor's own home. That judgment might have invoked the Fourth Amendment's protection against unlawful searches and seizures, though the majority preferred to create, under the First Amendment, a qualification to the exception it had earlier created for obscenity. But when it came to child pornography, no such exception was appropriate. Mere possession, even in the privacy of one's home, could be punished to serve the compelling interests in protecting young people from abuse and exploitation.

The ultimate test of how far child pornography falls outside "speech" is now in the courts. On the eve of the 1996 presidential election, Congress adopted the Child Pornography Prevention Act. One provision makes unlawful the creation and dissemination of "virtual child pornography," consisting of images which, though closely resembling those of real children, are not child-based and thus could not have involved the abuse or exploitation of actual young victims. This law was quickly challenged on First Amendment grounds in several major test cases. The federal courts of appeals split sharply on the constitutional issue. Two courts sustained the new law, noting that potential harm to children could come (as the Supreme Court once observed in a footnote) from using images of youthful sexual liaisons to lure or entice vulnerable minors into posing for such imagery. Computer-generated images would, in the view of those courts, pose no less a risk than images that were child-based or child-derived.

One federal appeals court took a sharply different view, noting that when the Supreme Court created the exception for child pornography, it strongly implied that imagery derived from any source other than exploitation of real children remained protected by the First Amendment. A third view emerged along the way—one that held that during debate on the bill, Congress had made clear its intent not to include cartoons, sculptures, and works of art which might seem to meet the statutory definition but were not "virtually identical" to photographs of real children, and thus would pose a comparable risk to the welfare of minors.

The Supreme Court agreed early in 2001 to hear one of these cases and thus resolve the conflict among lower federal courts. The case is being argued in the 2001 term and will be decided the following spring or summer. Two lines of precedent converge on what now appears to be a collision course. On one hand, the Court has been not only consistent but unanimous in its condemnation of child pornography as material that is undeserving of any First Amendment protection. On the other hand, the Justices were no less unanimous in their 1997 declaration that speech on the Internet was as fully protected as expression in any other medium. Ironically, it is the very qualities of digital communication, which the high Court deems so clearly deserving of protection, that create the potential for such new complexities as "virtual child pornography." The resolution of this tension may afford insight into the most basic process of defining what "freedom of speech" now means in areas the framers could not possibly have foreseen.

Some words and images that are clearly "speech" or "press" are partially, but less than fully, protected. Increasingly in the last decade or so, the Supreme Court has recognized certain categories of expression that claim partial, but less than complete, First Amendment protection. Sometimes these categories are described as "low-value speech" to reflect their relative disfavor. Their origins are quite diverse and defy easy generalization. When the Supreme Court ruled in 1942 that "fighting words" did not deserve First Amendment protection, it relegated to a similar fate "the lewd and obscene, the profane, [and] the libelous." The reason for this striking disparagement? "Such utterances," explained a unanimous Court, "are no essential part of any exposition of ideas, and are of such slight social value as a step to truth that any benefit that may be derived from them is clearly outweighed by the social interest in order and morality." That same year, the justices also consigned advertising to the nether world, finding no redeeming expressive value in commercial marketing messages.

The passage of time would temper, though never obliterate, these distinctions. Libel eventually achieved partial protection, although, as we shall see in Chapter 2, a cause of action for falsely debasing the reputation of a private person remains essentially unimpaired by the First Amendment. Commercial speech has also achieved partial protection, although advertising of an unlawful product or service or claims that are false or misleading still enjoy no immunity under the First Amendment.

Meanwhile, other categories of expression have joined the "low-value speech" club. In sustaining a city's ban on nude dancing in the early 1990s, the Court characterized the proscribed activity as "expressive conduct within the outer perimeters of the First Amendment, though we view it as only marginally so." Nearly a decade later, sustaining a similar local ordinance, a sharply divided Court made clear that the majority still regards such marginal forms of entertainment as barely protected. Curiously, during the very same term, the justices invalidated a federal ban on cable broadcasting activities of "sexually explicit" channels, though it did so at least in part because Congress had provided a means—individual subscriber requests to block certain channels —that seemed both responsive to the problem and less intrusive than the signal scrambling which the challenged law imposed. Moreover, the 1997 Supreme Court ruling which struck down the "indecency" ban in the Communications Decency Act might be seen as redefining the parameters of "low-value speech" in the sexually explicit context, although in fact the decision said much more about the Internet as a medium than about any particular message.

Scholars do not completely agree on what constitutes "low-value speech" or just why it has been devalued. For our purposes, it is probably enough to note the existence of a broad consensus that some words and images, which would technically seem to be "speech" or "press," have received less protection under the First Amendment than has mainstream political and literary expression.

Even where words and images are fully protected, their actual or probable effect may warrant regulation in certain situations. Finally, there are words which may sometimes forfeit First Amendment protection because of the context in which they are used or the consequences they create. Justice Holmes, the architect of the Supreme Court's "clear and present danger" test, illustrated that standard by writing in 1919 that "the most stringent protection of freedom of speech would not protect a man in falsely shouting fire in a theater and causing a panic." The standard for restricting political advocacy has evolved considerably since Justice Holmes's time. In 1969, the Supreme Court unanimously decreed a substantially more protective test, reversing the conviction for breaching the peace of an Ohio Ku Klux Klan official and agitator named Brandenburg. Under the formulation which remains the controlling test to this day, government may "forbid or proscribe advocacy of the use of force or law violation [only] where such advocacy is directed to inciting or producing imminent lawless action and is likely to incite or produce such action." Four years later, the Court added a crucial corollary—that a statement charged as incitement must be "directed to [a] person or group of persons" and must be likely to produce "imminent disorder." This formulation has come to be known as the Brandenburg-Hess standard, which will be analyzed more fully in a later chapter. Nothing less than such proof warrants punishing advocacy.

As though to confirm the Court's heightened commitment to free expression, in 1971, it reversed the conviction of a California anti-war protestor named Paul Cohen, who had entered the Los Angeles County Courthouse wearing a jacket on which he had written in large letters "Fuck the Draft." Noting that "one man's vulgarity is another's lyric," the Court ruled that government may not punish, as a breach of the peace, the public display of a single word; "censorship of particular words" the justices explained, could become "a convenient guise for banning the expression of unpopular views."

In reaching this quite remarkable conclusion, the normally conservative Justice Harlan observed that the charge against Cohen invoked none of the recognized exceptions to First Amendment protection. Cohen's deeply offensive public message was clearly not obscene, nor did it amount to fighting words. There was no evidence whatever of a breach of the peace, either intended or likely to occur—much less incitement to imminent lawless action. The claim that others in the courthouse had become a "captive audience" foundered on the ease with which an offended onlooker could avert his or her eyes. Nor was there any valid concern for judicial decorum; in fact, when Cohen briefly entered a Superior Court room, the bailiff asked him to remove his jacket and he readily complied.

In short, none of the recognized reasons for denying full First Amendment protection to Cohen's vulgarity applied to this case. The notion that speech is protected until and unless it falls within one of those exceptions is basic, and never better illustrated than in Cohen's bizarre case. Such a presumption of constitutional protection—placing the burden on the prosecutor or the plaintiff—is a remarkable, if insufficiently recognized and appreciated, dimension of American laws of free expression. It is also basic to much of the discussion that follows here.

Speech that is protected from criminal sanctions is typically beyond reach of civil damage claims and awards. Finally, given the focus of the chapters that follow, we should apply what we now know about free speech under the criminal law (which has been the focus of most of the First Amendment cases) to the obviously different context of civil liability. The time was when courts would treat criminal sanctions—jail terms and fines—as the only sort of penalty that made a difference to the exercise of free speech and other interests.

As late as the early 1960s, government lawyers still argued that imposing a burden through a criminal penalty was fundamentally different from denying a benefit or any other civil sanction. Justice Brennan saw, in a 1963 religious liberty case, the opportunity to refute that distinction once and for all. "It is too late in the day," he wrote, "to doubt that the liberties of religion and expression may be infringed by the denial of or placing of conditions upon a benefit or condition" even though no criminal sanction ensued.

The stage was now set for a case, the very next year, in which Justice Brennan was for the first time to set First Amendment limits on the power of states to award damages for injury to reputation and thus to bring civil sanctions clearly within the scope of First Amendment protection. The libel plaintiffs, Alabama public officials who were the subject of an unflattering account in an editorial advertisement carried by the *New York Times*, argued that First Amendment guarantees did not constrain civil damage awards but applied only to fines and jail terms.

"What a state may not constitutionally bring about by means of a criminal statute," wrote Justice Brennan for a unanimous Court, "is likewise beyond the reach of its civil law of libel." Indeed, he added, "the fear of damage awards . . . may be markedly more inhibiting than the fear of prosecution under a criminal statute." The very case illustrated the soundness of the parallel; while a sizeable libel judgment would not bankrupt the *New York Times*, it could destroy a marginal publication. Even for the major media, such a risk could cause a degree of self-censorship potentially devastating to the values of "uninhibited, robust, and wide-open . . . public debate" so vital to a healthy democracy.

The decision in *New York Times v. Sullivan* did not, however, resolve all issues of civil liability beyond defamation. The Court soon made it clear that claims for invasion of privacy were subject to the same First Amendment standards. Then, in a titanic struggle between evangelical preacher Jerry Falwell and Hustler publisher Larry Flynt, the same safeguards were extended to civil claims for intentional infliction of emotional distress, at least in the case of a prominent plaintiff such as Rev. Falwell.

Finally, in a case that involved a civil rights–based boycott of Mississippi retailers, the justices strongly implied that similar protection applied also to liability claims against advocacy or exhortation. The *Brandenburg v. Ohio* decision had limited criminal sanctions to "direct incitement of imminent lawless action." It remained unclear for a time whether civil damages could be awarded against an advocate—for example, the organizer of a boycott—on the basis of speech that would not satisfy the rigorous Brandenburg-Hess standard. In the 1982 decision in *NAACP v. Claiborne Hardware*, the justices seemed to resolve that issue in favor of recognizing comparable protection from civil damage awards. The case is complex and confusing, as we observe more fully in Chapter 4, but for the moment we note *Claiborne*'s strong implication that advocacy which lay beyond reach of criminal sanctions would seldom if ever support civil damages.

The commitment of the United States to protect controversial speech is unusual, if not unique, among developed nations. Most nations with which we like to compare ourselves also proclaim the value of free expression. Many even have bold and eloquent textual guarantees, though in the case of the Russian Constitution, for example, the words may mean little against hostile or repressive political forces. When it comes to nations that are closer to our own values, the differences are subtler but unmistakable, and they usually redound to our favor. France, for example, insists upon the authority to force Yahoo! and other Internet service providers to remove certain messages and objects from their systems. Germany and Italy followed suit, also insisting that their territorial integrity and values may shape the content of U.S. networks and providers.

German law has, for most of the post–World War II era, dealt harshly with the legacy of Adolf Hitler and with nascent anti-Semitism. To this day, for example a German citizen may not check out from a public library a copy of Hitler's *Mein Kampf* without special permission and an approved purpose.

Other unsettling messages, which in this country would enjoy full First Amendment protection, may be the subject of civil and criminal sanctions under German law in ways we would find abhorrent, sensitive though we are to the challenges that German lawmakers face even today.

The contrast may be most revealing with that nation whose border we share for over 3,000 miles, most of whose citizens have full access to U.S. mass media. Canada protects free expression, and in a few areas (travel to Cuba and nude dancing, for example) it seems even more tolerant than are we. But four specific examples illustrate a subtly if critically different approach to free speech and press. When it comes to "violent pornography"—material which demeans and may even be harmful to women—U.S. courts have insisted that no such new category of unprotected expression may be created, however appealing or sensitive it may appear. Yet in 1992, the Supreme Court of Canada sustained a strikingly similar law under the relatively new free speech and press provisions of its recently revised Charter.

The Canadian courts have also sentenced virulent and outspoken anti-Semites to long jail terms for acts so clearly subversive of civility that their avoidance is "demonstrably justified in free and democratic society" (a phrase which few in the U.S. would doubt accurately characterizes twenty-first–century Canada).

When it comes to coverage of criminal trials, U.S. law for the past quarter-century has been very clear that trial judges may not gag the news media unless it is clear beyond doubt that prejudicial publicity poses a grave threat to the fairness of justice in a pending case and that "no less restrictive alternatives are available." Thus, a gag order will hardly ever pass muster with our courts. Canadian law views the balance a bit differently and imposes fairly substantial restraints on certain pre-trial or even during-trial publicity. During a celebrated criminal case a decade ago in St. Catherine's, Ontario, bundles of the *Buffalo News* were impounded by Canadian customs officers at the Peace and Rainbow Bridges because they contained accounts of the trial that U.S. reporters had observed, but about which Canadians were not yet free to read. The Ontario prosecutor also secured the curtailment of a Canadian Web site which had posted documents and testimony that were still unavailable under Ontario law—though it took curious Canadians only a few seconds to locate U.S. Web sites containing the same information.

The last of these contrasts may be most revealing, and it certainly relates most directly to the subject of this book. As we learn more fully in Chapter 5, U.S. courts take the view that any person is fair game for the media in a public place—however much he or she may wish he had worn something different on a given day or embraced a different companion or behaved with greater decorum. So long as the image is accurate and taken without breaking into a private space, there is no actionable invasion of privacy.

Canadian law strikes the balance rather differently. A few years ago, a woman sued a Canadian magazine which had published a photograph of her seated a decade earlier on the steps of a dingy Montreal apartment building. She claimed that the much later use of this picture without her permission, accurate though it was, invaded her privacy and gave her a cause of action for damages. The provincial law of Quebec recognized such a claim, though it might have fared less well in other provinces. Canada's Supreme Court held that such an action could proceed, notwithstanding Canada's strong national commitment to free speech and press and despite the absence of any U.S. parallel. The only clear exception in Canadian law covers people who have been photographed without their consent at sporting events and in large crowds; sitting on the steps in full view of the street is a different story, as the magazine's publisher learned to his dismay.

This contrast, however subtle it may be, illustrates a profound difference in philosophy. We tolerate, as Canadians do not, the hateful speech of anti-Semites, sexually explicit material that demeans women, potentially prejudicial coverage of criminal cases, and images photographed in public places without consent. Who is to say which approach is preferable? It should be enough to observe that they are different.

2.

Libel: The Value of a Reputation

Oprah Winfrey has never been one to duck controversy. At the height of the scare over mad cow disease in Europe, she planned a program that would probe potential implications for anxious U.S. consumers. A segment entitled "Dangerous Food" aired on April 16, 1996. It featured the views of several experts on the quality and hazards of American beef. The program opened with an anguished report of a British woman whose granddaughter was in a coma, apparently a victim of tainted beef. The focus then shifted back to the United States. Interviews which had originally been taped for this segment reflected views of experts on both sides, among them U.S. Department of Agriculture officials, who would have provided balance for the program. But the actual broadcast gave primacy to the views of one Howard Lyman, a former cattle rancher turned vegetarian who is now a highly vocal critic of the beef and cattle industries and their practices.

Lyman had become convinced that American beef cattle were regularly being given feed which contained the remains of recently deceased animals, thus posing precisely the risk that had created the mad cow disease crisis in Western Europe. In response to a question about U.S. practices, Lyman warned: "We're following exactly the same path that they followed in England." Winfrey herself then joined the fray, adding just after Lyman's conclusion: "It has just stopped me cold from eating another burger. I'm stopped."

Just as many authors and publishers have learned what an immense economic benefit Oprah Winfrey's endorsement of a book may confer, the beef cattle industry was about to learn that her disdain can have a comparably detrimental impact. Demand for domestic beef plummeted in the days following the broadcast, apparently in reaction to the ominous statements about cattle and their feed. Several months later, a group of Texas cattle producers brought suit in federal court in Amarillo, naming Harpo Productions, and Oprah Winfrey and Howard Lyman personally, as defendants. The suit claimed that the comments on the April show were not only libelous under common law but also violated a specific Texas statute that was designed to grant relief against "false disparagement of perishable food products."

After a preliminary hearing on the legal issues, a district judge dismissed many of the plaintiffs' claims. He ruled that the Texas statute did not apply because cattle were not "perishable" and that Winfrey and her fellow defendants did not "know" (as the law required) that the most harmful statements on the program were false. But the judge held the rest of the issues for presentation to a jury.

During the protracted trial that followed, Winfrey set up temporary residence in Amarillo. She taped her program daily before large and attentive northwest Texas audiences. Huge and vocal crowds greeted and cheered her as she entered and left the federal courthouse each day. Despite the highly technical nature of the legal issues, the implications for free expression could hardly be avoided. One evening during the trial, Jay Leno asked his *Tonight Show* audience: "Can you imagine how stupid we would look to the rest of the world if we let O.J. [Simpson] and Louise Woodward go free but threw Oprah in jail for insulting a cheeseburger?" When a verdict finally was returned in her favor, an exultant Winfrey emerged from the courthouse and proclaimed to a crowd of supporters and journalists: "Free speech not only lives, it rocks!" The cattle producers did not press their case further.

About the same time as the "Dangerous Food" segment aired on network television, a very different type of case was in the making in Southwest Virginia. Sharon Yeagle was a student personnel administrator at Virginia Polytechnic Institute and State University (Virginia Tech). One of her tasks was arranging for the participation of Tech students in the Governor's Fellows Program and garnering favorable public and media attention for those students' achievements. The daily campus newspaper, *The Collegiate Times*, had scheduled an article about the program, including Dean Yeagle's role. The caption under her photograph, as it appeared in the mock-up or dummy version of the paper, included the phrase "Director of Butt Licking." Such an irreverent caption would normally, of course, be replaced by an appropriate name and title before the paper actually went to press. Unfortunately, the editor responsible for that final stage neglected to make the change in this case. Dean Yeagle was thus presented next morning, to the Tech campus and the world, with the unflattering title her picture had been given during the newsroom mock-up.

Though the student editors apologized profusely to Dean Yeagle and ran an abject retraction the next day, she was not mollified. Believing that her reputation had been seriously harmed, she brought a libel suit in Virginia state court against the *Collegiate Times*. She pressed two specific claims—first, that such an caption effectively accused her of the criminal act of sodomy, and second, that it falsely implied she had curried favor with superiors "by disingenuous behavior," the latter casting serious aspersions on her integrity as well as her professionalism. On both grounds, she claimed, her reputation had been sullied to a degree that warranted legal redress. Southwest Virginia's two largest law firms squared off in the case, one representing the affronted dean and the other defending the student editors on a pro bono basis. The trial judge dismissed the case and Dean Yeagle appealed, eventually taking her claims to the Virginia Supreme Court. By this time, other groups had become interested in the case and filed friend-of-the-court briefs in support of the newspaper.

Yeagle v. Collegiate Times was as novel as it was intriguing. Virginia's high court eventually agreed with the trial judge and dismissed the suit. The justices noted that the article as a whole was clearly complimentary to Dean Yeagle and to her role at the university. Its aberrant caption did not provide the basis for a libel suit. The offending phrase, while understandably likely to cause umbrage and embarrassment, "could not reasonably be considered as conveying factual information about Yeagle" and for that reason was not libelous. This judgment was not unanimous, however. Two justices believed Dean Yeagle should have her day in court. The *Collegiate Times*, they noted, had acknowledged that the phrase they inadvertently used would imply a disingenuous currying of favor with superiors. To make out a case of libel, the dissenters insisted, an accusation or insinuation need not be direct but could also be indirect, as it was here. Since "the phrase is a factual assertion regarding Yeagle's job performance [and] . . . prejudices Yeagle in her profession," she ought to be able to present her case to a jury. But since a 5-2 majority clearly prevailed, that was in end of the case—and a source of immense relief to the incautious student editors.

A third libel case entered the equation at about the same time. During the 1996 Olympics in Atlanta, security guard Richard Jewell was the first person to report a bomb that had been planted downtown in Olympic Park. On the basis of this alert, the area was cleared, and because it was nearly empty when the bomb detonated, a possibly massive loss of life was averted. At first Jewell was the hero of the day, acclaimed by Atlanta leaders and the media alike. Quickly, however, rumors about a police report turned Jewell from hero into villain as the prime suspect in the bombing. His life became a nightmare, to the point where his attire, his weight, and even his treatment of a pet dog became fodder for gossip columns and talk shows.

Jewell soon brought libel suits against the *Atlanta Journal-Constitution* and several broadcast outlets, chiefly Atlanta-based CNN. When Jewell was eventually cleared of any possible charges of wrongdoing in connection with the bombing, he and his lawyer assumed the libel suit would prevail. Indeed, one of the media did settle a claim that seemed a poor risk to take before a local jury. But the newspapers hung tough, refusing to settle, and late in 1999, a Georgia trial judge dismissed the libel suit. This court ruled that Jewell was a "public figure," and as such would have to meet a far higher burden of proof—effectively, would have to demonstrate that the newspaper had known the story of Jewell as suspect was false but had printed it anyway. Given the source of the story, a police report, meeting that standard would have been virtually impossible. Though his had hardly been a household name before the bomb incident, the Georgia court concluded that Jewell's readiness to give eleven interviews right after the event had transformed him into a "public figure" for libel law purposes, and it effectively denied him any prospect of redress.

Presumably Richard Jewell, Sharon Yeagle and Paul Engler of the Texas Beef Group have never met. Should their paths ever cross, however, they would soon discover a shared puzzlement about the vagaries of libel law. The Virginia dean, the Texas cattlemen, and the Georgia security guard suffered genuine and substantial harm to their good names as a direct result of widely publicized words of others—words which not only caused them psychic injury but quite as clearly impaired their professional stature. In all three cases, the words were false in certain respects. All three victims seemed confident, in taking their claims to court, that the law of libel would provide relief. Yet these three plaintiffs learned—for markedly different reasons—that libel remedies are somewhat more elusive than they may appear to laypeople whose reputations have been harmed by the false words of others. Those vagaries are the focus of this chapter.

The wrong that libel law seeks to redress has ancient roots. One of the most familiar Shakespearean verses is Othello's lament that "Who steals my purse steals trash. . . . but he that filches from me my good name robs me of that which not enriches him, and makes me poor indeed." Justice Potter Stewart once wrote that the individual's right to protect a good name through the law "reflects no more than our basic concept of the essential dignity and worth of every human being—a concept at the root of any decent system of ordered liberty." Moreover, the high Court reminded us not long ago that "there is no constitutional value in false statements of fact."

Libel law has ancient roots in Anglo-American jurisprudence. As prominent Washington attorney Bruce W. Sanford notes on the first page of his leading treatise on this subject: "English legal systems have provided a remedy to defamed persons since pre-Norman times." The focus of libel law has always been on potential injury to reputation—as Sanford notes in a later chapter, "words or pictures that may diminish a person's good name."

So powerful has been the historic commitment to deter or redress such harm that, until very recently, libel suits constituted one of the rare claims against newspapers, book and magazine publishers, and broadcasters that were seen as posing no threat to freedom of expression. That was the view even where judgments might entail large money damage awards that could cripple a publisher and would, at the very least, inhibit future risk-taking in the gathering and dissemination of news. Yet the Courts consistently viewed libelous speech as unprotected. In the first comprehensive treatise on the law of free expression, *Free Speech in the United States*, Harvard Law School professor

Zechariah Chafee recognized in 1940 the latent conflict between libel and liberty of the press. "Here," he noted uneasily, "we have a possible deterrent on speech by heavy damages which might be very serious if abused." But Chafee dismissed the problem in a single paragraph (the only mention of civil liability as a free-speech concern in nearly 600 pages.) It was enough for him that "the issues are decided by a jury which represents community opinion on what is defamatory" and that "there is a check by the appellate court." Moreover, "expressions by a writer of his opinions on public matters . . . are protected, and truth is a defense if proved—sometimes a difficult task even if it actually exists." Finally, Chafee observed that British juries "are more ready to give substantial damages than in this country"—reflecting that in England there was "a greater sensitiveness to the value of reputation [which] may be the indication of a more civilized community." This brief treatment would hardly have caused Chafee's readers to sense any deep anxiety about the latent tension between libel and liberty.

Within a year of the publication of Chafee's treatise, a unanimous Supreme Court would confirm the basis for his apparent comfort. In 1942, the Court sustained the conviction of a Jehovah's Witness proselytizer named Chaplinsky for having publicly insulted and affronted a New Hampshire police officer. In rejecting Chaplinsky's First Amendment defense—several other Jehovah's Witnesses had recently prevailed against local sanctions on free-speech grounds—the Court cited "certain well-defined and narrowly limited classes of speech, the prevention and punishment of which have never been thought to raise any Constitutional problems." Along with "the lewd and obscene, the profane. . . .and the insulting or 'fighting' words" must be included "the libelous." The explanation for such denial of constitutional protection? Nothing less than the summary dismissal of such concern by one of the Court's most conscientious civil libertarians, Justice Frank Murphy, who wrote that "such utterances are no essential part of any exposition of ideas, and are of such slight social value as a step to truth that any benefit that may be derived from them is clearly outweighed by the social interest in order and morality."

The Supreme Court did not leave the issue there. A decade later, the justices upheld an Illinois law that made criminal the sale or distribution of publications which "portray depravity, criminality, unchastity, or lack of virtue of a class of citizens, of any race, color, creed or religion [or which] exposes the citizens of any race, color, creed, or religion to contempt, derision or obloquy, or which is productive of breach of the peace or riots." The law had been applied to punish one Beauharnais, the leader of a white-supremacist group called the White Circle League which took an active role in the Chicago area during a time of intense racial conflict. In *Beauharnais v. Illinois*, the Court relied heavily on what it had said earlier in *Chaplinsky v. New Hampshire* about "fighting words" and other disfavored categories of speech. The justices treated the Illinois statute (which had counterparts in virtually every state) as a "group libel law" and upheld it partly on breach-of-the-peace grounds and partly because they found helpful an analogy to the law of defamation. The rejection of Beauharnais's First Amendment claim recalled the disparaging view of libel that had been central to the earlier case: "Libelous utterances not being within the area of constitutionally protected speech, it is unnecessary, either for us or for the State courts, to consider the issues behind the phrase 'clear and present danger.' Certainly no one would contend that obscene speech, for example, may be punished only upon a showing of such circumstances. Libel, as we have seen, is in the same class."

That was about the last word from the Court until the *New York Times* privilege case, to which we shall give attention a bit later. For now, what we know is that as recently as a half-century ago the justices placed libel near the bottom of the expressive hierarchy. We also know they deemed it closely analogous, at least in its lack of First Amendment protection, to obscenity and fighting words. What we do not understand, and probably never will, is why defamation remained so long and so confidently an outcast from the community of protected expression. Even the dissenters in *Beauharnais v. Illinois*—the judgment was 5-4—had nothing good to say about libel. Rather, they insisted such a sanction must be measured by "clear and present danger" standards, which the Illinois law and the particular conviction would clearly have failed. Just what was so bad about libel—in contrast to other more protected forms of speech—we never quite learned.

The early cases may, however, provide a few possible clues. As the Chaplinsky Court's enumeration of disfavored speech categories strongly implied, one reason libel was consistently denied First Amendment protection may have been the Court's belief that it was a "well defined and narrowly limited class of speech." As the cases with which we began this chapter demonstrate, many types of false and harmful words that laypersons would assume amount to libel in fact do not, for a variety of reasons of which we should quickly take note before turning to the constitutional limits that constitute our major focus.

For one, a statement must be "published" in order to be actionable as libel or slander. If one person falsely accuses another by private letter, by phone, or in a face-to-face conversation, some legal remedy may exist, but it is not defamatory unless a third party hears or reads the accusation; without such "publication," there cannot be the requisite harm to reputation, only hurt feelings. Even where someone else does hear or read the words, as Dean Yeagle learned to her dismay, much offending language does not amount to libel even though it may well harm one's reputation. A great deal of name-calling falls into this category. Few of us would welcome publicly being called an "idiot" or "incompetent" or "crazy," but we realize that such epithets and many like them seldom generate successful libel suits. Even such seemingly specific charges as "fixer of parking tickets" or one who "completely loses his cool" have been placed by courts on the non-defamatory side of the line.

Such judgments are never easy, as the sharp division in *Yeagle v. Collegiate Times* exemplified; for two members of the court, a negligent suggestion or accusation that a reputable administrator is a "director of butt licking" deserved to go to the jury.

Another basic element played a prominent role in the Texas cattlemen–Oprah Winfrey case. A statement must clearly be "of and concerning" the plaintiff before recovery is possible. In dismissing one of the libel counts, the federal judge in Amarillo noted that not only were none of the Texas producers individually named on the Winfrey broadcast, but there was not even any specific reference to the state of Texas. Plaintiff Paul Engler candidly acknowledged on the witness stand that there were "about a million" cattlemen across the country and that producers in Kansas and Colorado had used feeding practices comparable to those in Texas. Thus the case fell far short of the mark, however harmful the broadcast may have been. Even a somewhat more focused statement—for example, that "prominent Texas cattlemen" engaged in suspect feeding practices—would almost certainly have failed the "of and concerning" test. It is not essential that one be identified by name, but if that is not the case, the group must at least be small and discrete enough that a reader or listener would readily make the connection.

Most basically, a statement must be false in order to constitute libel; factually accurate charges may gravely harm one's reputation—indeed, they may do far greater harm precisely because they are correct—but telling the truth is almost always protected. Although there are rare situations in which a technically truthful claim is presented in so misleading or pejorative a manner that it puts the subject in a "false light" and may become actionable for that reason, proof of truth is almost always a complete defense to a libel charge. Moreover, the Supreme Court has made clear that the burden of alleging and proving falsehood falls on the libel plaintiff rather than forcing a defendant to establish the truth. Otherwise, truthful disclosures may be the subject of legal redress only under the most exceptional conditions where, for example, they reveal a legally protected trade secret, disclose legal proceedings that have been sealed, or violate a valid national security protective order or classification. Elsewhere, as the biblical command notes, "the truth shall set you free."

One further issue deserves brief mention here. The advent of broadcasting potentially altered the status of libel law, though in the end the variation of medium mattered less than one might have expected. In 1937, singer Al Jolson was being interviewed on a national radio show. The host mentioned a hotel in the Delaware Water Gap region of Pennsylvania. Jolson, without warning, exclaimed, "That's a rotten hotel." Two things happened in fairly short order. The Summit Hotel brought suit against the station and the network, and broadcasters developed a means (eventually the one- or two-second delay) that would enable them to keep off the air spontaneous and potentially libelous statements such as Al Jolson's interjection.

In the actual case, the broadcaster prevailed since the hotel could not show the degree of fault which Pennsylvania law required to hold any medium liable for the defamatory statements of others. This ruling broke with an early line of precedent, which had treated broadcasters like publishers and thus strictly liable for any harmful statements regardless of fault or negligence. The law began to mitigate strict liability in two ways. As broadcasters developed political clout, a number of states enacted laws to relieve or reduce the potential liability of stations for carrying otherwise actionable messages.

Moreover, the courts began to look more closely at the relative responsibilities of the parties and increasingly absolved broadcasters where (as in the Jolson case) fault could not fairly be found. That was the situation, for example, where a local station was sued on the basis of material created by the network and carried live without any opportunity to edit or revise—a situation wholly unlike that of newspapers who relied heavily on wire-service copy but had ample opportunity to review and revise stories and to delete potentially harmful or even locally inappropriate material before going to press. In one special situation—political broadcasts that federal communications law force stations to carry with no legal right to edit or delete content—liability for defamation would be unconscionable and would thwart the congressional "equal-time" policy for political broadcasts. Elsewhere, the combination of increased reliance on fault as the key to liability and more sophisticated self-protection methods mitigated the broadcaster's peril.

Several other issues unique to radio and television reached the courts. At first, it was unclear whether broadcast defamation should be viewed as libel or slander, since it was, after all, oral and not written. Although by this time the distinction made relatively little difference anyway, most courts eventually treated such material as libel, not slander, leaving the latter term to cover only direct oral communications. Finally, perhaps the most distinctive feature of broadcasting as a medium is the pervasive regulation by the Federal Communications Commission (FCC). Though libel seldom attracts the FCC's attention, one broadcaster's license was revoked in the 1930s chiefly because it repeatedly aired defamatory material. And in the 1960s, the FCC warned ABC to avoid serious distortion of history which could mislead viewers—in this case certain episodes of the series *The Untouchables* that dealt with Al Capone's conviction and incarceration—especially "where the result is to damage the reputations of identifiable individuals or groups" (specifically, prison guards at Alcatraz during Mr. Capone's residence at that facility). Unusual though it was, that admonition reminded broadcasters that the Commission may and occasionally does take defamation into account as part of its oversight of the broadcaster's duty to serve "the public interest."

Thus, it is conceivable that an especially active FCC could seek to regulate or even preempt some part of the state law of defamation in order to ensure uniformity in the regulation of licensed broadcasting. Nothing that drastic has ever happened, and today it seems quite unlikely that it will. Thus we conclude this brief foray as we began: For most purposes, broadcast defamation has been treated substantially the same as print libel, with the few variations and exceptions we have noted here. While life is vastly different on the Internet, as we shall see in Chapter 3, other electronic media seem to operate more or less within libel standards framed for print publications.

Though much more could be said about the refinements and peculiarities of common-law libel, one other general precept may suffice. As Professor Chafee noted long ago, courts have always recognized a clear difference between statements of fact and statements of opinion. To some degree, the "name-calling" doctrine reflects the reality that most epithets are closer to opinion than to fact. Indeed, many courts simply rejected claims against anything that could be deemed opinion; for example, almost anything contained in a newspaper editorial was automatically not actionable as libel. In 1990, the Supreme Court reaffirmed but also slightly narrowed that distinction, dispelling the notion that there was a "wholesale exception for anything that might be labeled 'opinion'" while keeping the basic distinction intact.

There is one closely related and intriguing issue, that of fiction and libel. Occasionally a supposedly fictitious character in a novel or movie so closely resembles a real person that the universal disclaimer about "any resemblance" being "purely coincidental" may not protect the publisher, producer, or author. If a plaintiff can prove that the characterization, although it is nominally fictional, meets the "of and concerning" test and is so negative as to harm his or her reputation, the format or context does not categorically preclude recovery of libel damages.

Until the early 1960s, libel suits were treated largely the same regardless of the status of the plaintiff. Thus, a governor or mayor or judge, if defamed, could recover damages as readily as an ordinary citizen. Since such a person's reputation was likely to be worth substantially more than that of the ordinary libel victim, the resulting damages might be substantially greater. All this was about to change in a most dramatic way that has reshaped the course of libel law. During a series of demonstrations by African-American college students in Alabama, a group of national civil rights leaders paid for and placed in the *New York Times* an advertisement headed "Heed Their Rising Voices." The text of the ad indicted official policies and repressive measures on the part of Montgomery, Alabama, officials and police, not only toward the students but also toward leaders such as Dr. Martin Luther King, Jr.

Soon after the ad appeared in the *Times*, Montgomery City Commissioner L. B. Sullivan filed a libel suit against the newspaper. A state court jury awarded him substantial damages, and the Alabama Supreme Court affirmed. Though Sullivan was never named in the ad, he insisted that the repeated references to "police" and to other Montgomery agencies for which he bore official responsibility left readers no doubt that he was the culpable party. He also noted in his complaint that the ad contained certain factual inaccuracies, which could easily have been corrected by consulting the news files of the *Times*. For example, the dining room at Alabama State College had never been "padlocked" as the ad charged, and no students were denied meals during the demonstration. Dr. King had not been arrested seven times, as the ad claimed, only four. There was also much dispute about an assault upon him, which the ad claimed had occurred after one of the arrests.

Though the *Times* eventually published a retraction at the governor's request, that did not satisfy Commissioner Sullivan or the Alabama courts. The trial judge deemed the pejorative statements in the ad to be "libelous per se," which meant they would support substantial damages without proof of any specific harm to the plaintiff's reputation. Thus, the trial court ruled, and the state supreme court concurred, "punitive damages may be awarded by the jury even though the amount of actual damages is neither found nor shown." While a half-million-dollar judgment obviously would not bring the *New York Times* to its knees, the potential impact of such awards could cripple small newspapers and other media in the south at the height of the civil rights era. Thus, an appeal to the U.S. Supreme Court seemed appropriate, even though the high Court had not qualified or even questioned its view of the unprotected status of libel over the previous quarter-century.

The justices proved more than ready for such a case. In the spring of 1964, they ruled unanimously that, whatever state law might provide, the First Amendment required a privilege of fair comment on the official conduct of those who held public office. Several factors supported that conclusion. Those who enter public life assume certain risks—the notion best expressed by President Harry Truman as "stay out of the kitchen if you don't like the heat." Moreover, as the Court later noted, "public officials . . . usually enjoy substantially greater access to the channels of effective communication and hence have a more realistic opportunity to counteract false statements than private individuals normally enjoy." In short, if you are a prominent person and call a press conference, they will come. The Court had also just expanded legal protection for federal officials who made inaccurate statements about private citizens, so there seem a certain symmetry or reciprocity in expanding the privilege on the other side.

Most basic, however, was the court's belief, eloquently expressed by Justice William J. Brennan, Jr., that "debate on public issues should be uninhibited, robust, and wide-open, and that it may well include vehement, caustic and sometimes unpleasantly sharp attacks on government and public officials." That concept did not automatically encompass libel, as Justice Brennan recognized. That step was yet to come. "Erroneous statement is inevitable in free debate, and . . . it must be protected if the freedoms of expression are to have the 'breathing space' that they need to survive," Brennan wrote.

The Court had already held this principle in other settings and was now ready to apply it to the nation's news media.

What the justices created was not, however, an absolute privilege but, even for high-ranking public officials, a qualified one: "The constitutional guarantees require, we think, a federal rule that prohibits a public official from recovering damages for a defamatory falsehood relating to his official conduct unless he proves that the statement was made with 'actual malice' — that is, with knowledge that it was false or with reckless disregard of whether it was false or not." Actually, New York Times Co. v. Sullivan turned out to be a remarkably easy one in which no further proceedings could occur, for two reasons. First, the Court found that the statements cited in the ad could not have been "of and concerning" Commissioner Sullivan — thus serving notice that this vital element of libel law would henceforth be judged by federal constitutional standards as well.

Second, also as a matter of First Amendment principle, the allegations that formed the basis of Sullivan's libel suit could not meet the test of "actual malice," even though the Times had conceded there were factual discrepancies between things said in the ad and news stories in their own files. Such variances could not, as a matter of First Amendment law, amount to the requisite "actual malice," nor did the undoubted delay in publishing a retraction help to meet that stringent test. The actual disposition of New York Times Co. v. Sullivan thus turned out to be substantially easier than if, for example, there had been greater doubt either about the "of and concerning" issue or about the editorial conduct at the Times.

While this monumental judgment answered many questions, it also raised a host of others that would perplex the courts and commentators in the years that followed. First, could such a privilege be confined to "official conduct," as Justice Brennan's original formula implied it would? It very soon became apparent that all facets of a high-ranking public official's life were fair game — "anything which might touch on an official's fitness for office." It soon became clear that candidates for public office were within the scope of the privilege, because campaign coverage needed as much "breathing space" as coverage of incumbents.

But who is a "public official"? Arguably there is value in permitting fair comment about any person who serves on the public payroll. Curiously, the high Court has never done much to clarify that seemingly basic issue, though it has suggested that a line might be drawn somewhere down the roster that would exempt most low-level and maybe some mid-level public servants, or at least limit the privilege to false claims about their "official conduct." How far back in time should the privilege reach — to former office-holders as well as incumbents? A few years after New York Times Co. v. Sullivan, the justices predictably extended the privilege to all such persons, ruling that a onetime county board member who had falsely been called a "small time bootlegger" had to demonstrate actual malice in order to prevail.

The hardest questions were yet to come. Should the privilege stop with those who hold public office, when coverage of some persons in the private sector posed strikingly similar issues? With virtually no explanation, the Court a few years later ruled that "those who by reason of the notoriety of their achievements or the vigor and success with which they seek the public's attention are properly classed as public figures" are also within the privilege since they "stand in a similar position" to public officials. Obviously defining "public figure" is even harder than classifying "public officials."

Perhaps the most difficult issues are those presented by people who have not generally sought the spotlight but nonetheless find themselves in it and are the subject of false and damaging publicity. Some years ago the Supreme Court recognized a potential problem but insisted that "the instances of truly involuntary public figures must be exceedingly rare." Yet, as the case of Richard Jewell reminds us, such a view may have proved to be overly sanguine. And even if the case of the person thrust unwillingly or unwittingly to the fore is rare, that does not make its resolution any easier. There is, however, at least one helpful accommodating principle. Since the early cases, a fairly clear distinction has emerged between "general" and "limited," or "special-purpose," public figures. For some notorious or highly celebrated people, almost any facet of life is fair game for the media—subject, of course, to proof of actual malice. For others, such as Richard Jewell, comment is fair and privileged only on that part of the subject's life which has occasioned the notoriety or has become "public." Thus, although this issue never reached the courts, one assumes that any false stories about how Jewell treated his dog, or about his relationship with his family, would not be privileged and would be treated as though Jewell had never reported the bomb or agreed to be interviewed about it. Even so, the process of delineating the scope of the public-figure doctrine is interminable.

There is one other important issue of scope. Beyond public officials and public figures, Justice Brennan always believed that the New York Times privilege should encompass "media reports of private individuals in events of public or general interest." Though he expressed that view in a plurality opinion, it never claimed a majority. Indeed, by the 1970s, his fellow justices had begun to retreat from the broader implications of the doctrine set out in New York Times Co. v. Sullivan. In 1974, in a case brought by Chicago lawyer Elmer Gertz, the Court insisted that whatever the context, a private individual was not fair game for media comment and that "the extension of the New York Times test proposed [by Justice Brennan] would abridge this legitimate state interest [in protecting private plaintiff's reputations] to a degree that we find unacceptable."

The majority did, however, retain the "actual malice" standard for punitive damages in such cases and insisted that even actual damages could not be imposed without a finding of some fault on the part of the publisher or broadcaster. A decade later, the Justices sounded a further retreat from the broad privilege. In a suit brought by a private company against Dun & Bradstreet, a credit-rating firm, the majority completed the circle. The *Gertz* judgment and its retention of "actual malice" for punitive damages was limited to situations of public concern or interest. Where a completely private person who is outside the spotlight has been defamed and sues for redress, recovery of both actual and punitive damages may be had on the basis of fault alone. Under this ruling, actual malice no longer entered the equation.

Several factors undoubtedly caused the Court to retreat to a degree that seemed quite surprising, given the unanimity of the ruling in *New York Times Co. v. Sullivan*. Basically, some of the justices now felt the creation of such a privilege had done more harm than good to public service and public discourse through largely unintended consequences that no member of the Court had anticipated in 1964. Writing in the *Dun & Bradstreet* case in 1985, Justice Byron White voiced the most pointed criticism. The *New York Times* standard, he warned, "countenances two evils: first, the stream of information about public officials and public affairs is polluted and often remains polluted by false information; and second, the reputation and professional life of the defeated plaintiff may be destroyed by falsehoods that might have been avoided with a reasonable effort to investigate the facts."

Balancing "First Amendment and reputational interests at stake," White concluded that "these seem grossly perverse results." As though to confirm such forebodings for many skeptics, it was not too long before the cabinet nomination of Texas Senator John Tower foundered over not fully substantiated, but deeply damaging, rumors of a cloudy personal life. Many, even those who were normally quite supportive of the *New York Times* privilege, have wondered with Justice White whether the cost of creating such a shield may not have been too high in its impact upon the nation's public service.

Though the Supreme Court has not addressed these issues in over a decade, the controversy persists. In his eulogy at Justice Brennan's funeral in the summer of 1997, President Bill Clinton celebrated steps in the great justice's legacy. Thanks to Brennan opinions, recalled the president, "every citizen's vote counts equally. . . . No person may have property taken without due process. . . . Prisoners may challenge the validity of their convictions." Then, near the end of the list, "the media are free to comment critically about public officials." At that moment, Clinton smiled and gazed down at the funeral bier. "Mr. Justice," he continued, "that's a decision you can appreciate some of us in public life may not be quite as enthusiastic about as some of your others." After a pause, the president added, "and that's probably why you were right." Such ambivalence, even within the First Amendment community, reflects a realistic view of a precedent that has had profound implications for the press and the public sector. How much for good and how much for bad, and whether the good outweighs the bad, are questions that will continue to be debated well into the new century.

Perhaps we have thus far been asking the wrong question about the *New York Times* decision. Our central focus has been on wondering "Why did the Court go so far?" rather than posing a quite different issue—"Why did the Court not go further?" That is the question posed by Yale law professor Thomas I. Emerson in one of the few major treatises on the law of free speech and press. Writing in his 1970 treatise, *The System of Freedom of Expression*, barely a half decade after the New York Times ruling, Emerson recognized that the decision "represent[ed] a significant advance in the treatment of First Amendment issues." Yet he also noted three ways in which the Court's treatment of libel fell short of the degree of protection it gave most other forms of speech and press.

First, Professor Emerson observed, "the Court fails to accept the fundamental premise of the First Amendment that other social interests cannot be advanced through abridging freedom of expression." It was not enough, even for the *New York Times* Court, "that the punishment of intentionally false statements through the medium of libel laws will substantially interfere with the operation of an effective system of freedom of expression." Rather, he continued, "the Court decided that at some point this injury to the system is to be disregarded in favor of the government's interest in not being subject to attack by the citizen-critic." The result of that view—actually more an assumption than a decision on the 'part of the justices—"takes the Court back to the balancing test" which had prevailed in an earlier and far less protective time.

Emerson's two others observations seem equally telling. The *New York Times* ruling left open the possibility that a public official who proved "actual malice" could still recover. The issue for the Court at this point was whether "calculated falsehood" deserved First Amendment protection, which the "actual malice" standard effectively denies it. Justice Brennan's answer was that such material "is no essential part of any exposition of ideas"—which, as Emerson pointedly noted, marks a "relapse" to the long-discarded views of the 1940s. Such an explanation, he continued, "fails to take into account that false statements, whether intentional or not, perform a significant function in a system of freedom of expression by forcing citizens to defend, justify and rethink their positions." Moreover, such a rationale for keeping "calculated falsehood" within the reach of civil liability "disregards another tenet of First Amendment theory—that it is no part of the government's business to decide for the citizen-critic what is of social value in communication and what is not." Thus, Emerson concluded with obvious disappointment, "at a key place in the doctrinal analysis the Court loses its way."

The third flaw that Professor Emerson found in the *New York Times* doctrine was one which later cases have partially remedied—that the Court "made no real effort to work out rules that were susceptible of effective administration." The apparatus which the Court would fashion to make the test workable has in some ways created more problems than it has solved. For a time, it looked as though proof of "actual malice" would be virtually impossible. What publisher or editor, after all, would volunteer that he or she acted with knowledge of falsehood or with reckless disregard for the truth? And how else would a plaintiff be able to establish the elements necessary to meet the actual malice test? Predictably, the Court would answer in 1979 in a way that created profound anxiety among the news media: Libel plaintiffs who are public officials and public figures may put an editor or publisher on the stand at trial and may probe his or her "state of mind" to get at the "malice" issue. This powerful plaintiff's tool seemed for a time to tip the scale dangerously out of balance, though in practice it has been less damaging than initial media reaction suggested it would be.

To restate briefly Professor Emerson's central point before placing it in context: "The majority of the Court," he wrote in his 1970 treatise, "fails to appreciate how inconsistent are the concepts underlying libel law with those underlying a system of freedom of expression." Despite the strong rhetoric about how public discourse needed to be "uninhibited, robust and wide open," when the dust settled, there were still situations in which free speech and press could be subordinated to "individual interests in economic ventures, standing in the community, or general good feelings." In short, despite some laudable movement away from traditional libel law, the New York Times ruling may have broken less new ground than its proponents initially claimed and may have retained more discredited precedent than one would have wished.

The basic question for us, three decades later, is whether the resulting balance is a healthy one for free speech and free press. We have Justice White and others on and off the Court saying "too far." And we have Professor Emerson and others who share his disappointment saying "not far enough." How an objective observer should resolve the dilemma depends on our view of two sub-issues: How powerful is the rationale for doing what libel law does? and How far does it reach into the realm of civil liability?

The "underlying interests" inquiry has received remarkably little attention. It has never been fully addressed by the courts, which generally assume that injury to reputation is different from—and deserves a higher level of deference than—a host of other interests that might seem to warrant restricting speech but have not been allowed to do so under the First Amendment. Sensitivity to the feelings of racial and ethnic and religious minorities, women, and gay and lesbian persons affords a startling contrast.

Here the courts (including the Supreme Court) have been remarkably consistent in banning all legal remedies directed at "hate speech" and the like. The judgment has been uniform and confident that the First Amendment simply does not permit civil or criminal sanctions to be invoked, even against the most scurrilous and worthless of slurs and epithets, however much we might wish to protect vulnerable groups from such vilification. Yet we continue to tolerate libel and slander suits against false statements that injure reputation without even posing the questions that prove fatal when it comes to speech codes and hate-speech laws.

A partial answer may be that injury to reputation by falsehood has always been assumed to be an interest the law must redress. Moreover, as it is between the person who utters or publishes libel and the victim, it is quite clear which of the two is the more blameworthy and which is innocent. Then too, there is the potential permanence of such harm; despite retraction and apology, a reputation once falsely tarnished may well never fully regain its luster. Finally, the awarding of money damages (at least those which measure actual loss, leaving aside punitive damages) is probably the only effective means by which to redress the injury that has been wrongfully inflicted. Any attempt to enjoin a future libel would be routinely rejected by the courts as an impermissible prior restraint, largely on the ground that post-publication damages afford an "adequate remedy" consistent with a free press.

Perhaps a more satisfying answer lies in the degree to which libel law is circumscribed. Long before the New York Times ruling created a federal constitutional privilege of fair comment, courts recognized various situations in which a false and damaging statement might be immune from legal recourse. Indeed, the very privilege established in the New York Times case had long existed as part of the common law in several states. It was partially recognized even in Alabama, and the precise language which Justice Brennan invoked in framing his Times test came from a 1910 Kansas Supreme Court judgment which recognized the importance of press comment on public officials and their conduct. Though the privilege of fair comment is the only one that has been federalized, the existence of other privileges embedded within the common law has been a stable premise of the balance between liability and liberty in this area.

The high Court's steady extension of the constitutional privilege well beyond the facts of the case of New York Times Co. v. Sullivan also shapes the balance. Much more than the "official conduct" of public officials soon turned out to be fair game for media comment. Candidates for public office and those who had once held but had long since left office were also covered by the privilege. Not only those who are clearly recognized as "public officials" and "public figures" but also much less prominent people such as Richard Jewell are now covered by the privilege and may recover damages only if they prove "actual malice." In practice, meeting that test has turned out to be a rather daunting task that has thwarted many a lawsuit in which lay observers would have said the publisher had acted "maliciously" but a court ruled that much more must be established to meet the legal standard. Indeed, in the *New York Times* case itself, while the justices did not define this key term, they gave clear guidance that the bar must be set quite high, by ruling that the admitted failure of the *New York Times* to verify the contents of the advertisement could not, as a First Amendment matter, amount to "actual malice."

Many other dimensions of libel law serve at least to mitigate the risk that civil suits can be used to stifle free expression and communication. The emphasis on "reputation" as the source of injury implies, for example, that merely hurt feelings or wounded pride will never form the basis for a libel suit. Nor, as we have noted, can there ever be a defamation suit unless someone other than the victim had read or heard the false accusation. As the Texas cattle producers found to their dismay, false statements that may indeed cause them great harm will not be deemed libelous unless they are clearly "of and concerning" the plaintiffs. Expression of "opinion," however misleading and damaging it may be to another's reputation, is broadly exempt from libel actions.

A host of accusations and charges that would probably seem libelous to most lay observers—such as calling Dean Yeagle "Director of Butt Licking" before her university community—turn out to be not actionable, either because they are no more than hyperbole or because in other respects they lack the indispensable quality of being factual. In these and other ways, the scope of libel law turns out to be somewhat narrower than one might suppose, and the actual reach of the *New York Times* privilege turns out to be more protective than it appeared to Professor Emerson in the years immediately after the ruling.

One other Supreme Court decision adds an important dimension to this protection. *Hustler* magazine publisher Larry Flynt had a penchant for parody and caricature of both people he thought overly pious or pompous and advertisers whose boasts caught his fancy. The November 1983 issue of his magazine featured an especially biting parody. The format was that of a well-known liquor advertising campaign which had recently featured celebrities recalling their first encounter with Campari, the sponsor. This one, however, was entitled "Jerry Falwell talks about his first time" and featured a photo of the evangelical preacher and a purported interview with him describing a "first time" that involved a drunken incestuous rendezvous with his own mother and a goat in an outhouse.

Falwell was outraged by the parody and sued Flynt and *Hustler*, claiming they had not only defamed him but had also invaded his privacy and intentionally inflicted emotional distress. The privacy claim was quickly dismissed by a federal district judge. The jury found in Flynt's favor on the libel count, deciding that the parody "could not reasonably be understood as describing actual facts about [Falwell] or actual events in which he participated." But on the emotional distress count, the jury did award substantial damages. The court of appeals affirmed that judgment against *Hustler,* ruling that the *New York Times* standard did not apply to emotional distress claims and that First Amendment interests were adequately protected by the state law requirement of intent.

At this stage of the litigation, the Supreme Court agreed to review what it recognized as a "novel" First Amendment issue. To the surprise of most observers, the Court not only applied the *New York Times* privilege to the tasteless *Hustler* parody, but it did so unanimously. Chief Justice Rehnquist wrote an uncharacteristically strong affirmation of freedom of the press (he had previously been one of the skeptics on the Court about the *New York Times* privilege). Recalling the legacy and "sometimes caustic nature" of political cartoons and the historic role that parody, satire, and caricature have played in enlivening public discourse, the Court ruled that a public figure (which Falwell surely was) could not recover damages for emotional distress without proving actual malice.

The Court went one important step further, just as it had in the original *New York Times* case. It ruled that Flynt's conduct could not, as a matter of First Amendment law, amount to "actual malice." That conclusion seems remarkable in light of Flynt's concessions at the trial, which the Court reproduced. At one point during cross-examination, Flynt was asked, "And wasn't one of your objectives to destroy [Falwell's] integrity, or harm it, if you could?" The publisher candidly replied, "To assassinate it." If such a goal did not constitute actual malice as a matter of law, the standard is very high indeed. In fact, the net result seems to be that a public official or public figure could never recover damages on such a theory, since a stronger case of actual malice than Rev. Falwell's case against *Hustler* and Larry Flynt would be hard to imagine.

The implication of *Falwell v. Flynt* is even broader. What the Court seemed to be saying through so decisive and unanimous a ruling is that when the front door of defamation is barred, as it was here by the non-factual nature of the statements, back or side doors such as intentional infliction of emotional distress are if anything less accessible on First Amendment grounds. There have been virtually no efforts to test alternative paths of recovery since the saga of *Falwell v. Flynt,* and for understandable reasons. In short, it seems likely that libel offers the most accessible route—perhaps the only route—to recovery of damages for any statements of a roughly comparable sort.

We still have not fully answered Professor Emerson, though we have substantially narrowed the range of potential concern. He was quite correct in reminding us that, although libel actions were sharply limited by the *New York Times* decision, a serious First Amendment anomaly persists. We do not strike such a balance in other areas. An angry political speaker who works up a crowd to fever pitch and is charged with incitement or breaching the peace does not avoid conviction merely by showing that there was no "actual malice" in his remarks. The appropriate constitutional inquiry, to the contrary, is whether the charged words amounted to a "direct incitement to imminent lawless action," malicious or not. One who utters racist, sexist, or homophobic epithets may not be sent to jail or fined on proof that his words reflected "actual malice"—as they would almost certainly do in such a situation. Even where we deal with presumptively unprotected expression such as obscenity, the distributor's state of mind—whether malicious or not—does not enter an equation that looks at other factors instead.

Thus libel remains, as it has always been, a unique area of First Amendment law, in which civil liability may be imposed on one who falsely injures the reputation of another. If certain forms of libel are more protected today than they were a half-century ago—when the Supreme Court gave defamation no more credence than obscenity and fighting words—that protection is still partial and circumscribed. The net effect of the Supreme Court cases that followed *New York Times v. Sullivan* is that—as far as the First Amendment goes—a private person, who is not involved in a public issue, need prove only fault on the speaker's or publisher's part to be home free.

Ironically, the common law of a good many states actually provides broader protection than does the national Constitution, demanding something beyond mere negligence as a basis for exemplary or punitive damages. Yet as far as the First Amendment is concerned, those who publish or broadcast false and injurious words are at least better off today than they were fifty or even forty years ago. Things are not likely to get much better for libel defendants in the next half-century—but neither are they likely to become worse. Perhaps that is the best that can be expected in this inescapably murky corner of the law.

3.

Libel on the Internet

On his first day as a White House assistant in August 1997, Sidney Blumenthal was startled to learn that his personal life was featured in the *Drudge Report,* an Internet gossip column which had broken the Monica Lewinsky story months earlier. Editor and author Matt Drudge reported that Blumenthal was rumored to have "a spousal abuse past that has been effectively covered up." The source? Unnamed "GOP operatives." When taken to task by a happily married Blumenthal, Drudge at once retracted the story, publicly apologized, and removed the offending paragraph from his digital journal. Drudge later admitted to *Washington Post* media critic Howard Kurtz that this was "a case of using me to broadcast dirty laundry," adding "I think I've been had." The implication was that one of Drudge's partisan sources had tricked him into floating a rumor that its creator had dared not disseminate.

The apology and retraction were too little and too late to mollify the Blumenthals. They promptly filed in federal district court a 30-million-dollar libel suit against Drudge and America Online (AOL). The Internet service provider (ISP) was named as a defendant because AOL furnished the Internet vehicle by which readers could access the *Drudge Report.* In fact, just weeks before the Blumenthal story appeared, AOL had proclaimed to its subscribers the imminent availability on its service of "the nation's hottest Internet gossip columnist." The defendants both moved for dismissal of the case, on a variety of grounds. Not among those grounds were the merits of the claim of libel which, given Drudge's concession and retraction, would have been difficult to dispel.

In Drudge's defense, the principal plea was that a court in Washington, D.C., lacked jurisdiction to proceed against a California citizen (Drudge) solely because residents of the District had electronically received his offending statements. For AOL, the defense was quite different; Congress had recently adopted (as part of the Communications Decency Act) a sweeping immunity provision which absolved Internet service providers of liability for any statements posted by persons other than their own employees.

Several months later, U.S. District Judge Paul Friedman issued a preliminary ruling. He held that Drudge was subject to the jurisdiction of a Washington, D.C., court, despite his California residence and his tenuous ties to the District, since he had done more than simply post a Web site that could be accessed in the nation's capital. At the same time, the judge dismissed AOL from the case on the basis of the broad congressional immunity, which he felt literally applied to such a claim. This ruling was a reluctant one: "If it were writing on a clean slate," added Judge Friedman, a court such as his would keep the Internet service provider in the case as a possibly liable defendant and a more-than-casual participant in the harm of which the Blumenthals had complained in their lawsuit. But the slate was far from clean; the will of Congress to free Internet service providers from such risks seemed unmistakable, and the result was therefore unavoidable. Although the Blumenthals eventually settled the case for a modest sum in early May 2001, the daunting and novel legal issues it posed will surely return to the courts in another libel suit before long.

A year or so later, early in 1999, a quite different sort of digital libel case began to take shape. An Internet Web site called *Grant Street 1999* featured tidbits about politics in and around Pittsburgh. One of its first postings charged that Court of Common Pleas judge Joan Orie Melvin had lobbied Pennsylvania governor Tom Ridge to advance the judicial appointment prospects of a friend. Such intervention would have been a violation of the code of judicial ethics. Judge Melvin promptly filed a libel suit against America Online, the digital host of the offending Web site—naming no responsible author because both the site and the particular story were anonymous. The case was initially filed in a Virginia court—the home of AOL—but was dismissed because a state judge ruled (with the strong support of the American Civil Liberties Union) that the contacts with the Old Dominion and its courts were insufficient to warrant litigation there.

The focus of the case then shifted back to Pittsburgh, where Judge Melvin then sought to compel AOL to reveal the identity of the author of *Grant Street 1999*. In the intervening months, several other courts had acceded to such pleas and had unmasked anonymous posters, mainly in cases involving baseless claims posted on Internet message boards and chat rooms that could have devastating effects on the fortunes of a company or on the value of its stock. Though *Melvin v. Doe* may have lacked such urgency, a fellow judge of the Court of Common Pleas ruled in November 2000 that unmasking an anonymous critic was no less warranted in Judge Melvin's case. The order was, however, quite limited in scope. It guaranteed that only Judge Melvin's lawyer would learn the identity of *Grant Street*'s publisher. The order has been appealed to the Pennsylvania Supreme Court, where an intriguing array of adversaries will address the unmasking issue. America Online has again joined the American Civil Liberties Union, as it did during an earlier phase of this case, in urging protection for the anonymous critic. AOL argues that its commitment to "the continued growth and development of the Internet and other online fora" argues for anonymity among its users, giving Internet service providers a major stake in such litigation.

A third and very different case deserves inclusion in our survey of this rapidly changing legal landscape. Kenneth Zeran was a successful Seattle realtor until one day in April 1995, when his phone began ringing incessantly. It took Zeran a few hours to learn why so many angry people whom he had never met were calling to accuse him of capitalizing shamelessly on the previous week's bombing of the federal building in Oklahoma City. Someone, it turned out, had anonymously posted in an Internet chat room a bogus ad for "Naughty Oklahoma T-Shirts," listing Zeran's phone number and urging interested (or concerned) persons to "Call Ken." The messages on the putative T-shirts were highly inflammatory; one fairly representative message read "At last, a day care center that really keeps kids quiet—Oklahoma City, April 19, 1995." Others were similarly outrageous, as Zeran discovered when he finally got to read the message that had brought such unwelcome traffic to his phone and in the process had effectively shut down his telephone-based real estate business.

Zeran at first demanded that America Online—through which the posting had appeared—remove the message, which the provider did. The very next day, however, another equally inflammatory (and equally contrived) T-shirt ad was posted, also without attribution. Plagued not only by calls which the Internet message had directly generated but also by indirect messages brought about through an Oklahoma City radio talk show on the same subject, Zeran retained an attorney and filed a libel suit against AOL in Virginia federal court.

Zeran and his lawyer knew that a libel claim against an Internet service provider would face heavy odds because of the broad immunity which Congress had conferred on such companies. They sought to avoid the effect of that law in several ways—pointing to AOL's unresponsiveness to Zeran's further pleas for help and noting that an admitted gap or lapse in AOL records made it impossible to identify the author of the T-shirt messages. Zeran thus argued that the basis of liability was not only defamation but also negligence, stemming from a provider's failure to take reasonable care to protect the reputation and the livelihood of a totally innocent victim of an outrageous scam.

The federal courts were not impressed, and Zeran's claims were dismissed at both the trial and appellate levels. All the judges ruled that however the case might be characterized—as libel or negligence or by any other theory —an Internet service provider enjoyed the full benefit of congressional solicitude for an emerging digital industry which had wielded political leverage at the moment of optimal impact. The net effect of such a ruling was to leave a wholly innocent person totally without recourse against Internet postings even though, had such inflammatory messages been allowed to remain on a physical kiosk or notice or message board, an employer or proprietor would face potential liability if negligence or libel could be proved. If any doubt lingers that some legal issues come out differently on the Internet, *Zeran v. America Online* provides the most graphic evidence of at least one such contrast.

In fact, closer review of these three cases reveals several crucial variations. The general principles of libel law, which we noted in Chapter 2, apply to the Internet just as they do to print material. A statement must have been false and must harm the reputation of another person, must have been "published" in the hearing or reading of a third party, and must be factual in nature rather than simply an expression of opinion. There are, however, several intriguing inter-media differences. In fact, it is not only the legal standards that may vary as we move from traditional to electronic format. Some Internet publishers in these early stages of transition seem to view their roles somewhat differently. Matt Drudge, perhaps the most visible of such new media exemplars, has argued that Web publishing should be governed by a more lenient standard. In support of this more relaxed view, he notes that he and others like him have no battery of lawyers and editors to review and correct their drafts; that deadlines occur not daily but hourly, or even more frequently, as news breaks and must be posted; and that an erroneous or misleading statement that is posted one minute can be corrected and effectively deleted the very next minute.

Drudge may take an extreme view of such contrasts, which is reflected in his assertion that he need be "right only eighty percent of the time," but he is hardly alone. One might recall transgressions by more reputable digital media—for example, the *Dallas Morning News*'s Web edition posting of a purported (but totally fabricated) confession by Oklahoma City bomber Timothy McVeigh or a rumor which appeared only in the on-line edition of the *Wall Street Journal* that a White House guard told a grand jury he had observed a tryst between President Clinton and a staff member other than Monica Lewinsky (for which even Matt Drudge never produced documentation). Upon learning that this rumor had reached the Web via the *Journal,* a presidential spokesman remarked that "the normal rules of checking or getting a response to a story seem to have given way to the technology of the Internet."

Several factors may account for this different culture. The editorial staffs of print and Web editions for the same publication are often quite separate. The review process for digital publication is concededly much faster, and scrutiny of the sort that newspapers have long imposed on printed stories is much harder to achieve. The competition for primacy is surely more intense on the Internet, although radio and television have long faced minute-to-minute deadlines and have never sought a more lenient standard of accuracy and responsibility. Such factors are present and have been pressed by Matt

Drudge and others in partial extenuation, at least in the public mind. It remains to be seen to what extent they may find favor with the courts, which have yet to reach the central issue of substantive defamation law and liability in any of the early Internet lawsuits.

However, the courts have already probed these issues in preliminary rulings, and have at least hinted at their views on deeper legal questions. Let us return to the threshold question in the Blumenthals' suit against Matt Drudge —whether a California resident can be sued in the courts of the District of Columbia on the basis of offending material posted on a Web site. Such issues, even in federal courts, are decided on the basis of state "long-arm" statutes. These laws set jurisdictional standards, which are subject to constitutional due process limits which prevent states from hauling into their courts people or businesses having less than "minimum contacts" with the state. Normally a person such as Matt Drudge would not be found to have such contacts if, for example, he published a newspaper or magazine in California which a Washington resident had bought in Los Angeles and had brought back to the District, where he discovered its libelous content. But Judge Friedman thought Drudge's situation was legally different, and on that basis he made one of the most important early rulings on jurisdiction on the Internet.

By this time several other federal district courts had ruled on similar issues in cases that involved claims other than libel but were clearly analogous on the issue of jurisdiction. The emerging standard differentiated between "passive posting" of material that could be accessed by an Internet user in any state, including the one where the suit had been filed—a presence that would not likely create the "minimum contacts" to support jurisdiction—and engaging in any more active pursuits within, or accessible from, the forum state. Sending a single e-mail message to a person in that state might be enough. Creating an interactive Web page and using that page to communicate with residents of the state (especially for commercial purposes) would almost certainly suffice. Though the actual results vary considerably from state to state because of differences among their "long-arm" statutes, it seems increasingly clear that any presence beyond "passive posting" may make a person subject to the courts of any state in which his words are accessed and cause harm.

Judge Friedman saw Matt Drudge's presence in the District in terms that would keep the Internet gossip columnist before his court. There was much more to the case than "passive posting." The *Drudge Report* was an interactive Web site, and D.C. residents had used its two-way potential quite extensively. Drudge also spent considerable time and energy gathering news in the capital, both in person and by other means, generating what Judge Friedman termed "a number of non-Internet related contacts with the District." Much of the focus of the *Drudge Report*, including its epochal Monica Lewinsky revelations, fell inside the Beltway. And in the very case that was before the court, the harm done by a concededly false accusation was to the Blumenthals, who were D.C. residents.

One factor might have led this court the other way, but in the end it did not. District of Columbia law contains an exemption for "news-gathering," which permits a journalist to pursue stories without automatically risking being sued in Washington courts. Drudge argued that he should, as a "newsgatherer," be exempt from suit in the Capital. But Judge Friedman, revealing what may have been his predisposition about the defendant, rejected this claim in a footnote: "Drudge is not a reporter, a journalist, or a news gatherer. He is, as he himself admits, simply a purveyor of gossip. His argument that he should benefit from [the news-gathering exemption] merits no serious consideration." On reading this slight, Drudge remarked somewhat irreverently: "OK, so I'm not a journalist. I'm a kangaroo. I'll see you in court." Thus ended, at least for the first round, the issue of jurisdiction over Matt Drudge and his California-based Web site. Whether courts in the District have power to try claims against Drudge is a close and difficult issue, though Judge Friedman's resolution of it accords fairly well with the way other courts have ruled on jurisdiction over out-of-state Internet communicators.

The role of America Online as a defendant in the *Blumenthal* case raised profoundly difficult and quite different issues. Here AOL was no merely passive conduit for material that had been created and posted entirely by a separate entity, as it had been in both the Zeran and Melvin cases. The network paid Drudge a monthly stipend for his column, which had become his sole consistent source of income. Shortly before the Blumenthal story appeared, AOL had widely promoted the imminent arrival of the *Drudge Report* as an added inducement for prospective subscribers. A press release entitled "AOL Hires Runaway Gossip Success Matt Drudge" proclaimed that "maverick gossip columnist Matt Drudge has teamed up with America Online," and stressed the prospective appeal to "an audience ripe for Drudge's brand of reporting."

Perhaps conscious of possible legal risk, AOL reserved in its contract "the right to remove, or direct [Drudge] to remove, any content which, as reasonably determined by AOL, violates AOL's then-standard Terms of Service," and could require "reasonable changes" in submitted copy, if proposed material would adversely affect operations of the AOL network." Despite that clause, and despite his own sense that a server would be a proper party to such a suit under any other conditions, Judge Friedman dismissed AOL from this case because of what seemed to him the inescapable design of Congress, reflected in section 230, the immunity provision, of the Communications Decency Act.

That provision had been added, late in the legislative process, to reverse a New York State case that had found Prodigy to be the "publisher" of defamatory material posted in a chat room which it made available to its subscribers. An earlier federal case had reached a very different conclusion in a libel suit against CompuServe, ruling that the Internet service provider was roughly the equivalent of a newsdealer or a bookstore when it came to material posted by someone else and thus could not be held as a publisher. In the later Prodigy case, the circumstances were quite different. Discussions in the particular chat room were closely monitored by a Prodigy employee, who had the legal and electronic capacity to remove possibly libelous or otherwise harmful material. Moreover, Prodigy held itself out to subscribers as a "family friendly" provider that was concerned about unacceptable content and willing and able to filter out such material.

Thus the New York court found the analogy to a publisher more appropriate than the bookstore/newsdealer analogy which had seemed apposite in the CompuServe case. On that basis, liability might be imposed—and with that prospect, there followed intense anxiety and alarm within the digital provider community. Resort to Congress was both urgent and effective, resulting in an unprecedented grant of immunity in section 230. In contrast, in several other situations where Congress has heeded the pleas of a vulnerable industry (manufacturers of swine flu vaccine and nuclear reactors, most notably) the result had been not a blanket immunity from civil liability, but rather a cap or ceiling on damages.

In 1996, however, the Internet service providers convinced the Congressional leadership that nothing less than full immunity would adequately protect the fledgling industry from the prospect of more suits like the one against Prodigy in the New York State courts. The federal courts have uniformly assumed that a broad reading was mandated by the urgency and the depth of congressional concern. No exceptions have been recognized despite ingenious arguments to the contrary; Kenneth Zeran was by no means the only plaintiff to try a creative end run around the high barrier section 230 imposes. No matter what one labels the cause of action—even in one recent case calling the providers "Web site hosts" who had negligently fulfilled their mission—the perceived legislative design to immunize the provider seems invariably to trump any plaintiff's claim.

Even so, the Blumenthals' suit was not exactly the one Congress had in mind. Yet Judge Friedman felt compelled to bring this case within the ambit of section 230's protection. As long as AOL had no role in the actual production of the offending copy—which no one claimed it had—that seemed to be the end of the matter. When the Blumenthal case eventually reaches a higher court, this issue will doubtless be revisited. Surely the view that Congress did not mean the immunity to reach quite so far is credible, given the extensive and mutually beneficial relationship between Drudge and AOL. The desire to protect a fledgling technology from liability for acts that are clearly not its own could stop well short of immunizing such a symbiosis as that between gossip columnist and Internet service provider.

The case never did come to judgment on the merits. For two years after the initial ruling, the parties were mired in contentious discovery proceedings. Judge Friedman, in a second opinion, chided both sides for their "rudeness, childish bickering, name calling, personal attacks, petty arguments and allegations of stonewalling and badgering of witnesses," which he termed "the kind of conduct that rightly gives the legal profession a bad name."

Suddenly and unexpectedly, in the first week of May 2001, the parties announced that they had settled the case. The Blumenthals agreed to withdraw their libel claims, and even offered to pay Drudge's court-related travel costs of $2,500. Sidney Blumenthal insisted to the end that filing the suit had been warranted—"the only way to make absolutely clear the story was a malicious and reckless lie." But he explained that continuing the quest now seemed pointless; the case had already cost his family dearly, while Drudge appeared to have inexhaustible support from "political supporters who use a tax-exempt foundation." Moreover, Drudge seemed to face no downside risk; "bad publicity for him is good for his kind of business."

The settlement between Messrs Blumenthal and Drudge left unanswered a host of what *Washington Post* media columnist Howard Kurtz called "potentially groundbreaking issues about electronic journalism"—especially the status of America Online as a possible defendant. Drudge managed to claim victory as he left the battlefield. "My name became synonymous with the lawsuit," he noted, adding that "the First Amendment protects mistakes. The great thing about this medium I'm working in is that you can fix things fast"—even though the lawsuit had been in the courts for almost four years, and had settled nothing.

Before we leave the curious role of the Internet service provider as defendant, it may be useful to note a few issues that section 230 does not resolve. The immunity is very broad indeed, not only covering liability for material someone else posted but also permitting the service provider—with complete legal impunity—to remove material it deems objectionable or in violation of its policies. Even though the provider may not be held liable either for leaving up or taking down content posted by another person for whom it bears no responsibility—that much is clear from *Blumenthal v. Drudge*—this exemption does not render the ISP irrelevant to all such lawsuits.

Central to both *Melvin v. Doe* and *Zeran v. America Online* cases is the role of the provider as a pathway to or means to the identity of the poster or author of the offending material. Actually, there was a specific and important difference between these two cases. In *Melvin*, the identity of the author was known to the provider and could be disclosed if a court so ordered, as it eventually did. In *Zeran*, however, AOL had somehow lost whatever information it once had about the author's identity—a fact which Zeran cited as evidence of negligence, but which the appeals court dismissed, remarking in a footnote that "the issue of AOL's record keeping practices . . . is not presented by this appeal."

The status of anonymous posters, and how and when they may be identified at a plaintiff's behest, has reached the courts with growing frequency. The issue has, almost without exception, been resolved in the plaintiff's favor, usually in emotionally appealing cases where an anonymous author has impaired the fortunes of a business, or the value of its stock, by posting allegedly false and libelous statements. Thus, when the Pittsburgh trial court ruled that Judge Melvin was entitled to unmask her anonymous detractor—at least to the extent of enabling her attorney to know who published *Grant Street 1999*—that ruling was entirely consistent with what other courts have done in this area.

In the weeks that followed the *Melvin* ruling, however, two events altered the landscape substantially. Both rulings created new precedent, indicating the speed with which the law is evolving here. At the end of November 2000, a New Jersey state judge indicated for the first time that anonymous posters on a Yahoo! message board might be allowed to resist disclosure in a classic corporate libel suit. The ruling stopped short of recognizing an absolute right of secrecy, but it substantially raised the level of proof that a corporate plaintiff must meet in order to unmask its critics—and that was where this court blazed a new path. To some degree, this novel judgment may have been a way of rewarding cooperation with the judicial system. Two defendants who had retained an attorney, and who had formally asked that their identity not be revealed, received the benefit of the higher standard. The other two, who had essentially ignored and disrespected the court, were unmasked as readily as others were in similar cases. Civil libertarians hailed the ruling. They found in it the first clear recognition of a First Amendment–based interest in Internet anonymity that matches an interest that has long been recognized and extensively protected in print and other traditional media.

No sooner had the celebration abated then another ruling raised questions about the potential use to which such disclosure or unmasking orders may be put by creative plaintiffs. In what appears to be the first case actually awarding money damages to a libel plaintiff against an anonymous Internet posting, a former Emory University Medical School professor recovered $675,000 from a person who had accused him of egregious wrongdoing on a Yahoo! message board. The charges, which were manifestly false, had caused a relocation and a drastic change in the defamed physician's career. The plaintiff had sought the aid of a court to unmask the anonymous author, identified only as "fbiinformant." Eventually this inquiry led to a company and its owner as the source of the scurrilous message. The physician filed suit against the now-revealed company and its founder. The federal judge who presided over the trial called the anonymous Internet postings "about as despicable as any course of conduct that one could engage in."

The plaintiffs' lawyers insisted this is the first recorded judgment against an anonymous Internet posting, and those who follow such litigation closely seem to agree. Previous cases in which either the identity of the poster is no secret (*Blumenthal v. Drudge*, for example) or in which that identity comes to light through an unmasking order have either not progressed to the judgment stage or have sought remedies other than damages—typically a court order to remove the message, retract, or apologize in ways that will diminish the potential harm to a company's reputation or that of its chief executive officer. Undoubtedly there will be many more cases in which damages are sought and recovered, but for now the beleaguered Emory physician appears to be the trailblazer.

The new year brought more good news for Internet critics. In late February 2001, a federal judge in Los Angeles dismissed a libel suit brought by Global Telemedia against two investors who had posted disparaging comments about the company on a financial bulletin board. The ruling was based on a California law which seeks to protect public interest groups from harassing and costly litigation, or so-called SLAPP suits (Strategic Litigation Against Public Participation.) The judge not only dismissed Global Telemedia's suit, but also ordered it to pay the defendants' legal costs.

Two months later, near the end of April, a federal judge in Seattle struck a major blow for anonymity on the Internet. In rejecting claims of a corporate plaintiff, the court refused to compel disclosure of the identity of 23 anonymous Internet critics who had posted on a bulletin board views critical of a business referral service that was in legal difficulty. Although the judge conceded that some of the postings were "downright nasty" and accused corporate officers of clearly criminal conduct, the right to continued anonymity seemed paramount as a means of free expression. The successful Internet critics had active support from the Electronic Frontier Foundation and the local ACLU chapter, both of which saw the ruling as a strong protector of digital communication.

One further footnote on Internet service provider liability seems in order. While the provider may, with complete impunity, permit offending material to remain on its system or remove that material, section 230 seems to leave open one important and difficult issue. When an Ohio consulting firm complained about unflattering postings they read on a Yahoo! message board, and subpoenaed Yahoo! in a lawsuit for the information, they received it promptly. The previously (and confidently) anonymous poster first learned of Yahoo!'s action when he was summarily fired and was denied both a cash bonus which he had believed he would soon receive and a large block of stock over which he was about to have complete control. The unmasked author then filed his own suit against Yahoo!, claiming the provider had abridged his privacy rights by disclosing his identity to his employer without notifying him or giving him a chance to contest the action. Though Yahoo! insists that its policy has always been to notify such posters if they are about to be unmasked, it also maintains that the law requires no such notice. This novel suit will surely test that question, and the extent to which the immunity that providers and networks enjoy in other areas extends to this action as well.

Before leaving the realm of "publishing" on the Internet, two other questions deserve our attention. Libel law requires that a message must have been "published" before it can generate liability. Thus if A orally and falsely accuses B when no others are within hearing or sends B a sealed letter that no one else intercepts, there may be a cause of action for intentional infliction of mental or emotional distress, but not for libel or slander. That conclusion follows because, as we saw in Chapter 2, harm to reputation is the key to defamation, and if no one else heard or read the statement, there could be no injury to reputation. The issue has seldom arisen in traditional media; an allegedly defamatory message is either public or not, and seldom does a court have occasion to inquire further.

In cyberspace, there are more complex variations that courts have not yet addressed but eventually will encounter. For example, an e-mail reply that was meant only for the sender but has carelessly been sent to the entire original address list has almost certainly been "published," even though the speaker clearly intended that it should reach only a single person. More difficult is the status of the practice of "backing up," by which some portion of all e-mail is routinely stored in large servers for at least a brief period. Since a system administrator could theoretically read such stored messages (though would almost never do so) there is at least the potential for third-party access, and thus "publication"—although probably to no greater degree than the prospect that a private phone call could be intercepted or overheard on an extension or that a private letter could be opened and read by an interceptor in the mail room. Suffice it to say that at some point in the development of Internet libel law the courts may need to address this issue, among others, to reconcile what is happening in cyberspace with familiar rules of libel in print.

The other "publication" issue has already been to court several times. If a damaging story appears on a given day on a newspaper's or magazine's Web site and the next day appears in its print edition, the precise time of first publication may become relevant. States typically set rather short time periods within which a libel suit can be filed; if the filing is untimely, even by a day, it must be dismissed. Thus a libel victim might claim that filing a lawsuit one year or two years (depending on the limitations period) from the *print* publication would be timely. A creative New York libel plaintiff, who had filed late, argued that Internet publication was basically different; those who posted defamatory digital material, he suggested, "make a conscious decision every minute of every day not to remove it" and thus keep a cause of action alive as long as the message exists in cyberspace.

This claim, not surprisingly, fared poorly in the courts. A state judge and a federal district judge in New York both recently ruled that the "single publication" rule governs here. That rule has long been settled in other media —for example, between a first press run and a later edition or between a newspaper and a magazine or between a radio and a television broadcast. It transcends any differences between media and thus bars any attempt to extend the filing time beyond the first publication, in whatever form it occurs. Once seemingly settled by this early pair of cases, this issue is not likely to be re-opened, though hope among otherwise time-barred plaintiffs could eventually spawn further ingenuity.

The question of who may be held liable for Internet postings deserves closer scrutiny. Return for a moment to Kenneth Zeran's case. The federal courts did not for a moment suggest that Zeran had not been wronged, for surely he had, nor did they suggest that, of the several parties (including AOL), it was he who was a truly innocent victim of a wretched scheme whose perpetrator remains, to this day, unidentified. All the courts said was that, given section 230 of the Communications Decency Act, an Internet service provider could not be held liable—even if it had carelessly lost the record which would have enabled Zeran to locate his tormentor. Such cases may be rare, but the issue of potential liability on the part of others than ISPs is certain to expand in importance as the impact of section 230's immunity becomes broader and more evident.

The question then becomes Who else? The only obvious answer seems to be the browser or search engine. There has been abstract discussion about browser liability and at least one threatened lawsuit—by a corporate director who claimed that damaging personal information would never have come to light but for the capacity of a Yahoo! browser to track it down on the Web. Such a claim seems contrived and fanciful; while the browser does not enjoy the same section 230 immunity as the Internet service provider, it would be outlandish to hold a search engine liable simply for leading curious Web surfers to material that someone else had created—the metatags for which, moreover, had been fashioned by the creator and simply located by the browser. Yet in an environment where the browser's or search engine's pockets may be about the only ones of any depth, the creativity of plaintiffs and their lawyers in fashioning such remedies seems likely.

Implausible or not in this country, such a prospect has now become real halfway around the globe. In December 2000, a court in India allowed criminal charges to proceed against six directors of a search engine company, Rediff Communications Ltd., for allowing its system to be used as a means of accessing Web sites that contained pornographic material. The order resulted from a complaint filed by a law student who was outraged by the range of material one could access through Rediff's browser; the student came forward as a public prosecutor. The lawyers for Rediff argued, without success on the first round, that all the objectionable Web sites were based in the United States anyway and that current technology gave them no capacity to block access for Indian subscribers. The prospect of any liability under these conditions—let alone criminal liability—is more than enough to get the attention of any browser or search engine and to suggest that much more will likely happen soon in this arena.

A closely related issue—the prospect of liability based on hyperlinks—is also more than hypothetical. A New Zealand computer magazine was successfully sued because it featured among commended sites a link which led users to defamatory material. Such a prospect seems remote in this country. The mere fact of citing, or even creating, a link which may facilitate access to related digital material hardly seems to implicate those who merely guide research or inquiry in the defamation that one may discover at the end of the journey. The link creator or citer should no more be legally accountable for someone else's libelous statements than should an author who simply includes in a print article a footnote reference to what turns out to be defamatory material. The one possible exception might be the creation of a deep link, which would carry the reader directly and immediately to actionable statements and would in the process bypass contextual or explanatory material that might mitigate the impact or even deter casual visitors from probing further. Even such a case would seem to present a doubtful basis for liability, though it is at least worth noting in the interests of caution and completeness.

Now that we have disposed of a host of procedural matters, it is time to address the central substantive issues about libel on the Internet. There are those who argue, as Matt Drudge has done, that postings in cyberspace should somehow be freer and less accountable than speech in more traditional media. Thus, the argument runs, the threshold of liability and the reach of libel and other laws that hold speakers and writers liable for injury to others should be substantially lower than it is for print and broadcast media. This claim for clemency does have a certain superficial appeal. After all, we know that many normally restrained and reserved people seem to lose their inhibitions when they go on-line. Especially when they believe they are speaking anonymously, some users somehow feel they may accuse or castigate with virtual impunity. Moreover, there is Matt Drudge's special claim on behalf of the electronic publisher—that because the on-line journal lacks the battery of editors, lawyers, and proofreaders who protect the print publisher and is under nanosecond deadlines, those who communicate exclusively on the Internet ought to be held to a lower and more lenient standard of liability.

Legal experts more seasoned than Matt Drudge have advanced similar views. Professor Lyrissa Barnett Lidsky of the University of Florida has recently posed a strikingly similar thesis in a 100-page law review article. Her concern is the rapidly rising tide of suits brought by corporate entities and their officers against a wide range of Internet critics—suits in which, as we have noted, courts have been uniformly willing to unmask anonymous critics. She posits that many such cases are filed not so much to vindicate unfairly tarnished reputations or to obtain tangible redress, but for the far less laudable goal of silencing critics. Such use of libel law, she fears, creates a serious risk of unduly inhibiting Internet discourse and of silencing whistle-blowers and others whose voices need to be heard. The dilemma, as Professor Lidsky appreciates, is how, on one hand, to provide redress for those whose have suffered genuine harm at the hands of irresponsible authors—the central and historic mission of libel law—while on the other hand sustaining "robust, uninhibited and wide open" discourse in cyberspace.

Some such critical commentary by whistle-blowers may, of course, be legally privileged and thus not easily subject to damages. An employee typically enjoys broader latitude in speaking critically about the company and its policies, as well as its senior executives, than does an outsider. There are various other relationships within which a speaker may stray from the absolute truth without incurring liability. Yet the common law of libel and slander offers but modest shelter for such critics. In any event, most of the Internet commentators about whom we should be concerned these days probably do not fall within any such privileged relationship.

The Constitution offers two further potential safeguards for the cyber-critic. Basic to the law of libel, as we learned in Chapter 2, is the *New York Times* privilege of fair comment. That privilege extends beyond the coverage of public officials, to whom it was initially confined, and now protects media comment on people who are "public figures" even though they hold no public office. When such a person sues for defamation, he or she must demonstrate more than mere negligence to overcome the privilege. The *Times* case and its progeny require proof of "actual malice"—either actual knowledge that the story was false or "reckless disregard" of its veracity. When faced with such a burden, many libel plaintiffs are unable to recover damages for even false and damaging statements on the basis of which a purely private individual could obtain substantial damages.

The issue of how fully the *New York Times* privilege applies to Internet libel raises several intriguing issues. An initial question is whether this privilege of fair comment is somehow limited to "publishers" of the traditional newspaper and magazine type. There is more than superficial basis for such a narrow application. When Justice Brennan, speaking for the Court in *New York Times v. Sullivan*, wrote eloquently of the need for "debate on public issues [that is] uninhibited, robust, and wide open" he clearly had in mind the nation's major news media, including, but not limited to, the *New York Times*. Most of the ensuing cases involved newspapers, magazines, radio and television broadcasters, and the like. Thus, when the precise issue of the scope of the privilege reached the Vermont Supreme Court in the early 1980s, that court's refusal to extend the *New York Times* privilege to a credit-rating agency (Dun & Bradstreet) seemed quite plausible. The Vermont justices observed that credit-rating firms were not the "type of media worthy of First Amendment protection" under the *New York Times* doctrine.

That the U.S. Supreme Court rejected so stinting a view was not surprising. What was puzzling was how little guidance the justices, who were split three ways in a confusing judgment, gave. The plurality simply disagreed with the Vermont ruling and reached the same result on different grounds without really explaining why the lower court's view of the privilege was wrong, much less how far it should extend. Only Justice Brennan, writing for himself and three others, really addressed the issue. Their concurrence began by conceding that credit reporting was "a type of speech at some remove from that which first gave rise to explicit First Amendment restrictions on state defamation law" in the *New York Times* case. Even so, they would extend the privilege to such communications, though without suggesting that any line ought to be drawn between eligible and ineligible speakers. When the dust had settled on the case of *Dun & Bradstreet v. Greenmoss Builders,* all that was clear was the error of the Vermont court in confining the privilege to newspapers and magazines, not precisely why that view was wrong, much less how far the privilege should reach beyond a credit-rating company whose reports circulate internationally and are heavily relied upon for all sorts of major financial judgments.

The specific issue of privilege for Internet libel has not yet reached any court, but commentators have already speculated at considerable length. There seems to be a consensus that any Internet poster should be able to claim the *New York Times* privilege when speaking of a public official or public figure. Several theories support that view. Long before digital communication became a legal issue, some observers argued that the privilege of fair comment could not logically be confined to the major news media. After all, the Supreme Court's ruling equally protected the individual co-defendants in the *New York Times* case, among them four individual Alabama African-American clergy. There would be something illogical about shielding a potentially libelous statement only if the defendant were a newspaper or magazine publisher but not if that same speaker held a less exalted role in society. This view seems to be rather widely shared, with little reputable authority to the contrary.

More recently, and with specific focus on cyberspace, the Supreme Court observed in *Reno v. ACLU,* the decision striking down the "indecency" ban on Internet material, that "any person or organization with a computer and access to the Internet can 'publish' information." Thus, unless and until some court reaches a different conclusion and limits the privilege to traditional publishers, we should assume that any defamatory statement posted on the Internet about a public official or public figure falls within the privilege. The only possible exception would be person-to-person e-mail—though the absence of the requisite "publication" would presumably thwart any possible libel suit long before a court reached the issue of fair comment. So let us assume the privilege applies to any message posted on the Internet which could conceivably generate a defamation suit.

The next, and in some ways the most intriguing, issue is what the scope of the *New York Times* privilege in cyberspace should be. In print, it applies to all plaintiffs who are "public officials" and "public figures." Neither term has been defined with perfect clarity, though the general contours of both groups have emerged from several decades of litigation. To take a recent and related case, we know that Atlanta security guard Richard Jewell became a public figure for libel purposes, mainly because he welcomed media attention right after he had reported the bomb that exploded in Centennial Park during the 1996 Summer Olympics. From these and a host of other cases, courts have a feel for the difference between people who, like Jewell, are at least "limited public figures" and the rest of us who remain private individuals beyond the reach of the *New York Times* privilege. Public figures (and of course public officials) must prove "actual malice" in order to recover more than nominal damages in libel suits.

Should the definition of "public figure" be different in cyberspace? This very question would eventually have arisen in the *Blumenthal v. Drudge* case, had it not been settled before the court reached the merits. Sidney Blumenthal is clearly both a prominent public official and a public figure; his case would need to meet the "actual malice" standard regardless of the medium in which the injurious statements appeared. His wife Jacqueline is, however, in a quite different position. At the time of Drudge's aspersions about their marital relations, she held a relatively invisible White House post, which would hardly qualify her as either a "public official" or a "public figure" under the prevailing standard. Had it not been for the *Drudge Report*, she would have escaped notice even from most Washington insiders. If such an accusation had appeared in a newspaper or magazine and she had filed suit, she would almost certainly have been treated as a private person, and would therefore have needed to prove only the falsity of the statement and some lack of care on Drudge's part; she would have had no duty to establish the actual malice a public figure must show.

The issue is whether the line ought to fall elsewhere on the Internet. One close observer of cyber-law argues that the standard should be different—that in cyberspace, every libel plaintiff should be treated as a "public figure" and thus be required to prove actual malice in order to prevail. The reason? One of the factors which led the Supreme Court to create the privilege in the first place was the reality that people who are highly visible have far better recourse to the media for their own defense than do ordinary citizens. As Justice Goldberg noted in his *New York Times* concurrence, "The public official certainly has equal if not greater access than most private citizens to the media of communication." Some years later, Justice Powell added his concurrent view that public figures have "significantly greater access to the channels of effective communication and hence have a more realistic opportunity to counteract false statements than private individuals."

The situation arguably is different in cyberspace. Justice Stevens stated in *Reno v. ACLU*, the indecency-on-the-Internet case, that "any person or organization with a computer connected to the Internet can 'publish' information." Thus, runs the argument, any libel victim, whether celebrated or obscure, may post at once "a nearly universal and instantaneous response." That being the case, the argument concludes, every Internet libel plaintiff should be treated as a public figure.

This argument relies heavily on the seminal reasoning of Michael Godwin, founder of the Electronic Frontier Foundation. In his view, "Now we live in a world [in] which, thanks to the Internet, all sorts of people have access to mass media." Moreover, Godwin adds, the retraction that Matt Drudge quickly posted when the Blumenthals took him to task was far likelier to reach readers of the defamatory story than would a typical print retraction. Thus, he concludes, "the balances that underlie libel law have shifted" to the extent that "Drudge is going to win the case"—at least the case brought by Sidney Blumenthal, if not Jacqueline's suit as well. The end result of such reasoning would be to blur, if not to obliterate entirely, the distinction in cyberspace between public and private plaintiffs that is crucial in print. Thus, in the case of *Blumenthal v. Drudge*, both spouses would need to prove actual malice even though in print the higher standard would apply only to Sidney and not to Jacqueline.

This is a startling notion indeed, and it risks making the Internet a sort of haven or refuge for irresponsible critics and mudslingers. It rests, moreover, on rather tenuous legal principles. For one, the greater ability of public officials to reply to libel was never a central premise of the *New York Times* decision. It was mainly Justice Goldberg who stressed the "if you call a press conference, they will come" point, and even he did so more as a makeweight than as a core of the privilege. The focus of the seminal ruling, and of later cases that defined the fair comment privilege, was much more on the First Amendment value of "robust and uninhibited debate." Moreover, the two justices who stressed this factor were talking about libel plaintiffs who were indisputably public officials or public figures. Thus, the "everyone a public figure in cyberspace" theory stands the privilege of fair comment on its head, invoking as its central premise a factor that was at most peripheral to the Court's reasoning in *New York Times Co. v. Sullivan*.

This novel argument reflects another and even more basic flaw. It simply does not match the technology of cyberspace. As Michael Hadley observes in a law review article devoted solely to this issue, the "everyone-a-public-figure" notion "ignores the realities of the Internet." It is true that a remark posted in a chat room may invite fairly prompt refutation, at least if the target or victim of a digital accusation (or a protective friend or colleague) is a current participant in the chat room or soon becomes aware of the charge. But that is the only context in which the "everyone a public figure" notion fits at all well. Elsewhere, as Hadley notes, "the ability to reply in cyberspace, just like in the real world, depends not just on one's access to the Internet, but also on the ability and willingness of others to access one's reply."

The hurdles for anyone seeking instant redemption are substantial. Consider once again the very real case of Jacqueline Blumenthal. We would first need to assume she had her own personal Web page at the time the *Drudge Report* marked her a victim of "spousal abuse." Even if that were the case, the likelihood that most readers of the initial accusation would seek out that page in search of the truth seems conjectural at best. Few personal Web pages receive that sort of attention, even at times of special interest in the proprietor. Save for the remote possibility that Drudge had agreed not only to apologize and issue a retraction but also to post hyperlinks to the Blumenthals' personal Web pages, the claim that any libel victim can "call a press conference in cyberspace" seems highly tenuous. The only remaining option is one that has always existed with respect to the print media—the right to send a corrective or mitigating letter to the editor, which the medium may or may not choose to publish and which it of course may not be legally compelled to run. Since neither a retraction nor a letters-to-the-editor invitation has ever served in print to transform a private person into a public figure following a libelous publication, there seems to be little reason to treat the Internet differently for this purpose. Accordingly, the case of Jacqueline Blumenthal (the one relevant case that has actually been to court) should be treated no differently in cyberspace from the way courts would treat a baseless charge of spousal abuse that had appeared in print editions of the *Globe* or *The National Inquirer.*

This conclusion seems legally inexorable, but it does not quite close the circle. Recall Professor Lidsky's deep concern about the potentially chilling effect of libel suits on outspoken Internet critics—especially given the strong inclination of courts to order disclosure of the identities of anonymous posters in chat rooms and newsgroups. She argues that cyber-libel is and should for some legal purposes be treated differently—not by classifying every plaintiff as a public figure, but in subtler and more thoughtful ways. Her concern stems, in fact, from the same reality that triggered the less credible theory—that every speaker on the Internet can become a libel defendant, often under conditions that would seldom if ever give rise to a libel suit in traditional media.

Professor Lidsky outlines the following scenario: If a disgruntled employee grouses about company policy in the cafeteria line, writes an angry letter to the union newspaper, or posts a flier on a kiosk in the plant, even a thin-skinned management is likely to overlook or disregard such criticism. Such a response is less predictable on the Internet, however. There is little likelihood that an angry charge posted on a physical bulletin board will cause stock values to plunge overnight. But put the same statement on that company's Yahoo! chat room, or even in a less visible digital medium, and the potential risks magnify greatly, even though there should be no greater reason to credit the dyspeptic views of an anonymous employee—let's call him "packer29"—than if the same views were placed visibly on a kiosk outside the main gate of the company. Comments which in print would heretofore have been "beneath notice," observes Lidsky, now become potential targets; those who engage in the digital equivalent of "water-cooler gossip" may now become likely libel defendants.

That prospect is hardly remote, as recent experience attests. A stock price may be substantially impaired by a wholly false chat-room charge about a CEO, a new product line, a potential buyout, a possible strike, and so on. If and when that happens, the same management which for decades laughed off rumors posted on the kiosk and letters in the union weekly may now feel a duty to seek redress. The path for doing so is now clearly marked. A suit against the Internet service provider or host—most often against Yahoo!, which maintains the bulk of the message boards where such postings occur—would promptly yield the identity of "packer29" (who had naively assumed his cover could never be blown.) He or she would then become the real defendant, whether or not there was any serious prospect of recovery. And, fears Professor Lidsky, one such suit may effectively chill criticism within and far beyond the plant where the unmasked critic worked. Word of such legal action travels fast among corporate critics; others would be unlikely to incur a comparable risk once the risks are known.

The solution is not as simple as the beguiling but ultimately untenable notion of treating every libel plaintiff in cyberspace as a public figure. One other possibly mitigating element of defamation may be helpful here. There has always been a fairly clear line between statements of fact and statements of opinion; the former are actionable, while the latter are not. Thus if A writes or posts that B is a "deadbeat" or a "tax evader," that sounds libelous. But if the charge is that B is "immoral" or "cruel" or "heartless," such a claim might well impair B's reputation but would in this country be treated as opinion and thus not legally actionable. Professor Lidsky's salutary solution relies on this longstanding distinction. She urges that we develop a broader concept of "opinion" for claims of libel against Internet critics that will maintain the basic responsibility and accountability of those who abuse the right freely to post on the Internet almost anything about anyone but will protect the Thomas Paines and Benjamin Franklins of cyberspace. This suggestion is intriguing and may well offer a sounder balance than anything previously ventured, which is surely more satisfying than the "everyone a public figure in cyberspace" notion.

We might return, finally, to Matt Drudge's own curious view of the legal burdens he and others like him should bear. His is the perspective of a gift-shop proprietor turned online publisher, hardly the perspective of a media lawyer or even of a seasoned editor or publisher. Lest we be overly pious, we should recall that soon after his startling revelations in the Clinton-Lewinsky scandal, Drudge was invited to address the National Press Club and drew a standing-room-only crowd. His audience included many traditional journalists who regularly decried Drudge's activities and standards and would undoubtedly have shared Judge Friedman's view that he could not claim the "news-gathering" exemption. It was that ruling which caused Drudge to exclaim, "So I'm not a journalist. . . . I'm a kangaroo."

Drudge's central thesis in his argument for a more relaxed standard is that on-line publications such as his lack access to the battery of editors, lawyers, proofreaders, and other guardians of accuracy and propriety upon whom mainstream print publications usually rely. He also argues that the frantic speed of Internet news may provide an excuse. In the end, such claims miss the mark and fail to justify a more lenient standard of care for digital publishers. Libel law has never set different standards for small media and large ones, for those that are profitable (and thus better able to afford expert counsel) and those that are not, or for those that publish only "news that's fit to print" and those that will use any story potentially appealing to the salacious interests of prurient readers. Nor have the pressures of deadlines or the pace of fast-breaking news ever provided extenuation. Indeed, the traditional news media, especially broadcasters, have for decades been required to make instantaneous judgments that carry potentially grave legal consequences. Thus the case for letting the *Drudge Report* and its on-line peers off the hook seems tenuous at best. A single standard should apply to all who disseminate potentially defamatory material, regardless of the medium or its exigency.

If Matt Drudge is misguided in this regard, he deserves greater deference on another point. To their discredit, established journalistic gatekeepers at first denied press credentials for the House and Senate galleries to reporters from exclusively on-line publications. The first such access was eventually granted, though only after the applicant submitted a sheaf of print newspaper clippings and thus established his credentials as a traditional newspaper reporter. Later the gatekeepers relented still further and did admit a small number of on-line journal representatives. One result of this process has been internecine struggle among the electronic media. Merrill Brown, then editor-in-chief of the on-line news service MSNBC, cautioned that digital publishers "must not let the behemoths of the news media judge us by the gadflies of the Internet. We are not Matt Drudge any more than Liz Smith is the mainstream media."

Fair enough, one might add. The problem with Matt Drudge, in the end, is not the medium but the message. His limitation is surely not the novelty of the digital outlet he has used so skillfully—and occasionally, by targeting innocent people such as the Blumenthals, so harmfully. The problem, rather, is the belief that when you post your dispatches on the Internet you need only get it right 80 percent of the time. Such a lenient standard has never been acceptable in print or on the air. Giving it greater credence on the Internet would do irreparable damage to an exciting and immensely promising source of news and information.

4.

Threats and Incitement on the Internet

In the fall of 1997, 10-year-old Jeffrey Curley was kidnapped and brutally murdered in Cambridge, Massachusetts. The attack, his family soon learned, was the work of two young men in the neighborhood. They had attempted to lure Jeffery into a sexual relationship, having offering him a new bicycle before abducting him and eventually taking his life. The assailants, Charles Jaynes and Salvatore Sicari, were soon charged and convicted for the murder and are serving life sentences in state prison. The Curley family sued Jaynes and Sicari for wrongful death and recovered substantial damages—though the prospect for collecting any part of that judgment from longtime prison inmates is quite remote.

The Curleys then discovered a potentially more promising avenue of legal recourse. Jaynes, it turned out, had visited the Boston Public Library the day before the attack. Through one of the library's public computer terminals, he had accessed the Internet Web page of the North American Man-Boy Love Association, or NAMBLA. This organization openly advocates a more relaxed view of relations between men and boys. Its publications and its Web site condone—indeed encourage—such relationships. With this information, the Curleys retained Cambridge attorney Lawrence Frisoli, who filed a civil damage lawsuit against NAMBLA, claiming that material in its print publications and on its Internet Web site had incited Jaynes to molest and eventually to kill Jeffrey Curley.

Defending NAMBLA in court proved a particularly unwelcome task, even for lawyers ready and willing to handle unsavory clients in civil liberties cases. Several months after the suit was filed, the local branch of the American Civil Liberties Union (ACLU) stepped forward and offered its services. Conceding that "this is not a real popular cause," Massachusetts ACLU executive director John Roberts insisted that "the First Amendment issues are clear." A more formal statement issued by the ACLU expressed the group's sympathy for the Curleys and for other crime victims, but explained its commitment in this way: "Regardless of whether people agree with NAMBLA's views, holding the organization responsible for crimes committed by others who read their material would gravely endanger our important First Amendment freedoms."

The ACLU's role in this case had an ironic twist. Only months earlier, the very same civil liberties group had gone to the aid of Robert Curley, Jeffrey's father, in a workplace dispute. The senior Curley, a longtime Cambridge fireman, was politically conservative and a deeply religious person. He had objected, on grounds of conscience, to a mandated diversity training session for all city employees. Describing the program as "feel-good crap," he asked to be excused. When the city refused to exempt him from the diversity training, ACLU volunteer lawyer Harvey Silverglate interceded. He wrote to the city, citing a solid line of Supreme Court cases in which comparable concerns based on conscience or principle had provided a First Amendment basis for exemption. Eventually the city relented. Robert Curley, thanks to the ACLU, thus became the only one of 2,000 Cambridge city workers excused from the diversity training program.

When he learned, months later, that the same group which had rescued him would be defending the organization he and his wife sought to hold legally liable for Jeffrey's death, his reaction was remarkably temperate. "They are very consistent in who they defend," Curley observed of the ACLU. "It takes a lot of nerve to defend the groups they have over the years. They have a lot of courage."

Taking on the cause of NAMBLA in the Curley case would test that courage. Many other observers were far less understanding of this commitment. When the Curleys' lawyer charged that the ACLU had been "hiding behind the First Amendment for a long time," the *New York Post* concurred editorially, adding its view that "it's a sad commentary that the ACLU can't recognize a deceitful use of free-speech rights when it sees one." Many longtime ACLU members and supporters saw this cause as far less sympathetic than such despised clients as the Ku Klux Klan, the American Nazi Party, and others that the organization had defended over the years. Advocacy of consensual relations between men and boys, which could uncritically be equated with pedophilia, crossed the line for many good and thoughtful civil libertarians.

For the ACLU, however, the issue seemed no less clear or vital than many other unpopular causes it had championed. The Bay State chapter's executive director, John Roberts, explained to the *Boston Globe:* "For us it is a fundamental First Amendment case. It has to do with communication on a Web site and material that did not promote any kind of criminal behavior whatsoever." Roberts went on to acknowledge that "those who commit illegal acts can be punished for their wrongful conduct." He might well have added another point that undoubtedly played a major part in the ACLU's thinking— that the Curley case promised to be the very first court test of how far, and under what conditions, material posted on an Internet Web site could form the basis of a civil-liability judgment for inciting criminal behavior. ACLU lead attorney Harvey Silverglate later observed that "this might be a test case," adding: "Every time there is a new technology, somebody is claiming the First Amendment protection is not as strong as for the old technologies." The Curleys' suit would centrally implicate that claim as applied to the Internet.

There is no shortage of constitutional law bearing upon the issues of advocacy and incitement in old-fashioned media. The problem is to what degree, if at all, such precedent controls communication on the Internet. The doctrine began with Justice Oliver Wendell Holmes's famous statement in 1919 about shouting fire in a theater. (Though we often misquote his maxim, Holmes in fact confined his concern to one who "falsely" shouted fire, and never used the word "crowded," a gratuitous addendum of later scholars and jurists.) A half-century later, after the dust had settled on the post–Cold War and McCarthy periods, the Supreme Court would articulate in the case of *Brandenburg v. Ohio* a standard which has proved remarkably durable. It remains to this day the guiding principle for judging all criminal charges of the clear-and-present-danger type: Government, declared a unanimous Court, may not "forbid or proscribe advocacy of the use of force or of law violation except where such advocacy is directed to inciting or producing imminent lawless action and is likely to produce such action."

Several years later, the justices added an important corollary in the case of a student radical named Hess: Where a speaker had been charged with incitement for delivering an inflammatory speech to a volatile crowd, the Brandenburg ruling controlled; because his words were "not directed to any person or group of persons, it cannot be said that he was advocating, in the normal sense, any action." With a few minor variants, the Brandenburg-Hess principle has resolved all later cases in which free-speech claims arise against charges of incitement or breach of the peace.

Although the early cases involved criminal charges, the same precepts soon became equally applicable to claims of civil liability. In 1964, when the Supreme Court first recognized a media privilege of fair comment on the actions of public officials in *New York Times Co. v. Sullivan*, there was some doubt whether First Amendment protection applied at all outside the realm of criminal sanctions. Justice Brennan, writing for a unanimous Court, put all such doubts to rest when he declared: "What a State may not bring about by means of a criminal statute is likewise beyond the reach of its civil law of libel." At least when the basis for seeking civil damages is libel or slander, that declaration settles the question once and for all. The high Court has never qualified its commitment to the basic doctrine of the privilege of fair comment.

What is less clear is the degree to which other sorts of civil damage claims are tempered by the protections that speakers and publishers enjoy in the criminal courts. In the early 1980s, the Supreme Court agreed to review a large judgment that Mississippi courts had imposed on the NAACP for having organized and led a successful boycott of retail stores that persistently refused to hire African Americans. The goals of the protest included pressuring those retailers to seek changes in government policy with regard to civil rights and equal opportunity. It was quite likely that an effective boycott would have a devastating economic effect on local merchants. The stores did lose much of their business as a direct result of the boycott. When they brought suit against the NAACP and its local officers to recover some of those losses, the state courts found a clear basis in Mississippi tort law for imposing damages on the organizers of the protest.

The Supreme Court saw the issues of this case very differently. In *NAACP v. Claiborne Hardware Co.*, the justices ruled unanimously for the NAACP, calling the group's advocacy "essential political speech lying at the core of the First Amendment." The Court explained further: "While the State legitimately may impose damages for the consequences of violent conduct, it may not award compensation for the consequences of nonviolent, protected activity. Only those losses proximately caused by unlawful conduct may be recovered." The high Court also insisted that the *organization* could not be held liable in damages for even unlawful actions of certain of its *members*; to recover damages from the organization, it would be essential to prove "that the group itself possessed unlawful goals." Thus, the Court recognized in the *Claiborne Hardware* case a vital symmetry between civil and criminal liability—that civil damages could not be imposed on the basis of advocacy which the Brandenburg-Hess standard would protect from criminal sanctions.

While it may seem a long way from civil rights boycotts in Mississippi in the 1970s to NAMBLA's Web site in Massachusetts in the late 1990s, the same principles should guide any determination of potential liability for actions based upon an organization's message. To the extent that NAMBLA's publications, and its Internet web site, may have advocated changing the laws that constrain relations between men and boys—even to the extent of totally exempting or legalizing sexual relations between men and boys—such advocacy is clearly and fully protected. However abhorrent prevailing national sentiment may find that message, the courts have made quite clear that seeking a change in the law is well within a person's or an organization's First Amendment right. Indeed, we often forget that, in addition to ensuring "the freedom of speech and of the press," the First Amendment expressly protects "the right of the people peaceably to assemble, and to petition the Government for a redress of grievances"—a right that classically includes efforts to change the law or even the constitution itself. Thus, the Massachusetts ACLU was quite correct in stating that "there are no illegal ideas" and that "the expression of even offensive ideas is protected by our constitution."

The rub with the Curley case comes, however, in two other respects. One has to do with the message and the other with the medium. In their lawsuit, the Curleys claim that when Charles Jaynes accessed the NAMBLA Web site at the Boston Public Library and read NAMBLA magazines that police found in his possession after the murder, he had been aroused or inspired by advocacy of criminal sex between men and boys. The group has openly condoned such relationships and has in various ways made them seem attractive and alluring. The *Boston Globe*, in one of several unsympathetic media comments about the case, suggested editorially that "NAMBLA encourages sex with children." The Curleys have charged that "NAMBLA facilitates, for its members, sex with boys," and that NAMBLA members "teach each other how to do it—how to abduct them, what to look for in children, who are easiest to abduct, how to impede law enforcement. . . . Jaynes used techniques shared by NAMBLA to lure [Jeffrey] away." Lawrence Frisoli, the Curleys' lawyer, calls NAMBLA "the mafia of child pornography," and insists that the group's Web site promotes the rape of boys because it allegedly helps adults select their victims and avoid arrest. A former Boston social worker and FBI agent has claimed that "NAMBLA . . . is helping members prey on children by trading names of vulnerable boys."

Some months later, in April 2001, Frisoli would augment the original complaint by filing with the court what he viewed—and proclaimed to the media—as even more damaging evidence. The addenda were affidavits by former NAMBLA members or infiltrators which attributed to the organization a more aggressive role in training members to have sex with children, especially young boys. NAMBLA again vigorously denied such an inference, insisting that it did not openly condone or advocate such behavior.

Had such views been presented at a NAMBLA meeting which Jaynes attended, there would be at least a possibility that the speaker might be charged with incitement, assuming that the evidence met the very stringent Brandenburg-Hess test of direct advocacy of imminent lawless action. Even so, there would be no basis on which to impose similar guilt upon the organization, or to hold it liable in damages, unless it could be shown that the group specifically advocated unlawful ends. Thus, as far as the message is concerned, even the view of the case that is most favorable to the Curleys' position seems a stretch at best.

Now the medium becomes crucial. Where the message is conveyed in ways other than a face-to-face conversation or a person-to-person phone call or e-mail, the basis for liability is attenuated. The courts have yet to rule on what would seem a fairly obvious issue—whether words that are disseminated in print or on the movie or television screen or, for that matter, on an Internet Web site can ever form the basis for civil liability. Among other obstacles, the Supreme Court's basic Brandenburg-Hess standard would be extremely difficult to meet. That principle demands that the person or group uttering inflammatory words have been directly advocating imminent lawless action under conditions likely to produce such a result.

If the words have been available in print or have circulated in some other medium for some time, can there ever be the requisite "imminence?" And if the words have been uttered to the world at large, as is invariably the case with such media, can there ever be the "directness" which the Supreme Court's test presupposes? Finally, as courts have consistently noted in analogous cases, it is nearly impossible for plaintiffs who are seeking recovery against a publisher or broadcaster to establish the vital causal connection between the words and the unlawful conduct. Tort law requires, as a basis for awarding damages, proof of a clear link between cause and effect. Such a nexus is at best elusive in situations such as this.

Let us return to the precise issue of the NAMBLA Web page. The Curleys' case is clearly one of first impression. If potential liability of other mass media is as uncertain as it is under the current state of the law, the status of Web messages available to any computer owner with Internet access seems even more problematic. Consider several situations, however, in which a digital communication might warrant liability under traditional First Amendment standards. If one NAMBLA member were to send an e-mail to another member, or to a group of members, specifically urging an attack upon or illegal relations with a named boy, or with a group of boys, such a message would almost certainly come within the Brandenburg-Hess principles.

If the same sort of message were posted in a news group or chat room that was known to be frequented by actual or potential pedophiles, criminal and civil sanctions might also follow. Or if NAMBLA maintained on its Web site a "contact us" type of interactive link, through which members could seek specific instructions in luring or enticing a vulnerable boy and thus get help in breaking the laws against pedophilia, sanctions might well follow if the evidence of intent and probable effect met the incitement standard.

The actual situation of the Curley case, however, seems rather remote from any of these culpable situations. NAMBLA insists that its Web site contained "merely philosophical statements and information about contacting NAMBLA as an organization seeking changes in public attitudes and laws." Even if some of the posted material, to which Jaynes apparently had access shortly before Jeffrey's abduction, were more sharply focused and gave an attractive or alluring cast to man-boy relationships, that would seem to form no basis for awarding civil damages to the family of a victim. Here, as in traditional-media cases, a plaintiff would face two daunting challenges — proving the required nexus between the Web material and the criminal act and refuting the presumptively protected nature of the material. To the extent that the Internet Web site may have been a vehicle for NAMBLA's views on how the law should treat man-boy sex, its message may have struck most readers or viewers as hateful and despicable, but it was not necessarily unlawful or actionable.

While the Curleys' case is indeed one of first impression on the particular issue it poses, this is not the first liability claim against an Internet Web site for allegedly harmful content. Several years earlier, Planned Parenthood filed suit in an Oregon federal court against the American Coalition of Life Activists (ACLA), a militant anti-abortion group in the Pacific Northwest. ACLA members had created and displayed posters that declared certain physicians who performed abortions to be "wanted" as criminals. They also targeted some of the doctors on a "Deadly Dozen List" which appeared in several formats. That list declared that the named physicians were "guilty of crimes against humanity" and provided substantial information about the accused persons. Such data as home addresses and unlisted home phone numbers, physical characteristics, type of automobile, and known habits would easily enable an anti-abortion activist to locate and harass the targeted physician.

ACLA also created a document known as the Nuremberg Files. It appeared first in print form. In January 1997, it was posted on the Internet Web site maintained by a sympathizer named Neal Horsley. The Nuremberg Files not only targeted doctors and clinic staff who performed abortions; they also celebrated the tragically frequent occasions on which the lives of doctors and other clinic staff members were taken by militant anti-abortionists. Specifically, the death of a "wanted" physician would be graphically noted by having a disembodied hand drawing a line through his or her name. The very day that Dr. Barnett Slepian was murdered at his home in Buffalo, his name was crossed out by such a moving hand on the Nuremberg Files Web site. The Internet version of the Files also (as the federal judge described it) "bears drawings of what appear to be lines of dripping blood."

In the national context of mounting violence toward abortion clinic staff, a group of doctors and nurses brought suit against ACLA and several of its officers. For reasons that have never been clear, the Web site proprietor (Neal Horsley) was not included among the named defendants. This lawsuit sought damages in an amount well over $100 million for violation of several laws—chiefly the Federal Access to Clinic Entrances Act, which Congress had passed several years earlier to supplant existing and more general laws that seemed increasingly inadequate to protect abortion clinics and their staff from attacks by militant protestors. The suit also alleged violations of the federal Racketeer Influenced and Corrupt Organization Act and an Oregon anti-coercion statute. After several preliminary hearings and three rulings by the district judge, the case was finally submitted to a jury which, in the spring of 1999, found in the plaintiffs' favor on all the issues and awarded them damages of $109 million. The case has been argued before the federal appeals court in San Francisco.

The basis of Planned Parenthood's suit against the anti-abortion group is not, as in the case of *Curley v. NAMBLA*, allegations of incitement or advocacy. Instead, the focus in the Oregon case is on threatening language and images, which the plaintiffs claim have so intimidated them and so imperiled their lives and their professional practice, that legal liability is warranted. The suit recognizes that not all threats are legally actionable, since much threatening or menacing language has been found to be protected speech despite its ominous tone. But the Planned Parenthood plaintiffs argue that threats of the kind that were posted on the Nuremberg Files Web site fall outside the First Amendment. The district judge, following case law on threats within his federal circuit, agreed with the plaintiffs and rejected the free-speech claims that had been advanced by the ACLA defendants. The judge reached that conclusion despite his recognition that "no statement [on the posters or on the Nuremberg Files Web site] is expressly threatening, in the sense that there are no 'quotable quotes' calling for violence against the targeted providers."

Such menacing but unfocused statements would almost certainly be viewed as protected speech in other federal circuits and many state supreme courts. Curiously, the Supreme Court ruled only on the status of threats, and that ruling was in the highly specialized context of threats against the life of the president of the United States, which is specifically forbidden by an act of Congress. For threats against anyone of lesser stature, lower courts have made clear that there must be substantial and reasonable apprehension on the part of a person claiming to have been threatened before a legal claim, civil or criminal, can be recognized. Since the lower courts have been left largely on their own in this area, the standard for what constitutes a "true threat," to which First Amendment protection is denied, varies greatly across the country.

The Oregon branch of the American Civil Liberties Union filed a brief supporting the position of the ACLA defendants—not because ACLU condones militant anti-abortion advocacy, but because (very much as with the suit of the Curleys against NAMBLA) it feared that an emotionally appealing case could set an extremely dangerous precedent. The ACLU brief argued that only those threats could be actionable which "a reasonable person would perceive as a threat" and which the speaker "intend[ed] . . . be taken as a threat to inflict or cause serious harm to the listener, thereby intending to place the listener in fear for his or her safety." The statements in this case, however ominous and hostile they must have seemed to abortion clinic staff members, probably would not meet so rigorous a test. Thus, whether nor not such threats are fully protected by the First Amendment, the Oregon ACLU has argued that they ought not to support an award of damages—else civil liability might also be imposed on those who make menacing statements on behalf of labor unions, civil rights or consumer groups, and others given to strong words in publicly debated causes. This issue will receive major attention as the Planned Parenthood case goes forward.

The immediate focus for us is, once again, the novelty of the medium. No previous cases address the scope of liability for statements posted on an Internet Web site. One might argue that threats on the Internet should be treated just like threats in any other medium. That was essentially the view the district judge took in *Planned Parenthood v. American Coalition of Life*

Activists. At first he found no need to differentiate between the posters or the print version of the Nuremberg Files, on the one hand, and the Nuremberg material as it appeared on Horsley's Web site in 1997, on the other. Yet even Judge Jones, when it came to entering his final order, was not quite comfortable treating print and digital statements identically. He was initially disposed to order the removal of the Nuremberg Files from the Internet, but then realized that the Web-site proprietor, Neal Horsley, was not a defendant in the case and was therefore not subject to such an order. The judge then did the next best (and only) thing he could do; he enjoined the ACLA officers who were within his jurisdiction from providing any further material about the targeted physicians "to the Nuremberg Files or any mirror web site that may be created." An accompanying footnote defined a "mirror web site" as "a web site that takes the content from a web site created by an independent party and reproduces it on his or her own computer ('the web server') and locates it at a different Internet address"—a fairly candid recognition on the judge's part of the probable futility of such an effort to prevent proliferation of the proscribed material.

This order in turn triggered a fascinating collateral proceeding. Neal Horsley, who had never been sued as a defendant and thus was not subject to Judge Jones's order, felt no immediate need to remove or relocate the Nuremberg Files. But his Internet service provider, MindSpring, proved substantially less comfortable with the continued availability of the Web material that had given rise to such a huge damage award. The day after the jury returned the $109 million judgment against the ACLA offices, MindSpring removed the Nuremberg Files. This action surprised many observers, since by this time Congress had expressly conferred on all Internet service providers immunity from liability for the content of offending material posted by a user. On that basis, a federal judge in Washington, D.C., relieved America Online of any liability for defamatory statements posted by Internet gossip columnist Matt Drudge, whose column it had actively recruited and touted as a valuable service for its subscribers. The risk that MindSpring could ever be held liable to abortion clinic staff seemed extremely remote. The basis for MindSpring's action was not publicized.

Mr. Horsley would not, however, go quietly into digital obscurity. He promptly filed a lawsuit of his own, seeking $218 million for what he claimed was MindSpring's abridgment of his free expression as a subscriber. Such a claim seems most unlikely to succeed, if only because section 230 of the Communications Decency Act—which, as we have seen, absolves Internet Service Providers of liability for harm resulting from material posted by others, also relieves ISPs of most potential liability for removing offending material. That, MindSpring claims, is precisely what it did to Mr. Horsley's site, and did so only after the jury had rendered its heavy damage award against ACLA.

Meanwhile, the central issues of the case had reached the federal court of appeals for the Ninth Circuit, based in San Francisco. Many organizations had filed briefs supporting the Planned Parenthood Plaintiffs. Even the Oregon ACLU, which had expressed concern in the trial court, now urged that the jury's award be affirmed. They were joined by the attorneys general of twelve states and a host of organizations committed to reproductive rights and women's health, as well as the American Jewish Congress. Only the Thomas Jefferson Center for the Protection of Free Expression filed on the other side —and took pains to argue not that ACLA's message was necessarily protected speech, but only that such rhetoric could not be punished under the standard which the trial judge had applied to determine when statements were "threats."

To the amazement of most observers, the appeals court in late March 2001 reversed the judgment on quite broad First Amendment grounds. Reviewing the facts, the court noted that "neither the posters nor the website contained any explicit threats against the doctors" even though they occurred in a national context of repeated violence against abortion clinics. Moreover, none of the statements that gave rise to the suit "mention violence at all." While the posted material may have "put the doctors in harm's way," they did not directly authorize or threaten such harm. In short, the record did not contain the kinds of "true threats" that would subject the person making them to liability. Noting that "the First Amendment protects ACLA's statements no less than statements of the NAACP," the appeals court expressed its concern that if this damage award could stand, it would then be difficult if not impossible to distinguish a similar judgment against a civil rights or consumer or labor group which had engaged in highly charged rhetoric.

"Political speech," the opinion continued, "may not be punished just because it makes it more likely that someone will be harmed at some unknown time in the future by an unrelated party." That was precisely what the Supreme Court's Brandenburg and Hess decisions had said government could not do. Here there was little doubt that posting addresses and other vital information on the Nuremberg website "made it easier for any would-be terrorists to carry out their gruesome mission," but that was not enough to satisfy the First Amendment.

Toward the close of this unanimous ruling, the appeals court cautioned that, to the extent a jury might find that the charged statements were "infused with a violent meaning," that was largely because of "the actions of others." If the speaker could be held liable on that basis, "it could have a highly chilling effect on public debate on any cause where somebody, somewhere, has committed a violent act in connection with that cause." Such an attribution or inference, the Supreme Court had made clear on several occasions, would not permit the suppression of speech by criminal or civil sanctions.

It was unlikely that so controversial a ruling would go unchallenged.

Senator Barbara Boxer immediately called the decision "an outrage" and "an offense, a direct attack on women's rights and the doctors that help to realize those rights." The plaintiffs at once asked the full court of appeals to rehear the case and reinstate the trial court judgment. In so doing, they had the support of an extraordinary amicus curiae brief filed by 12 U.S. Senators and 31 Representatives. These members of Congress shared the plaintiff's view that the Ninth Circuit had misapplied the Freedom of Access to Clinic Entrances Act by refusing to allow a jury to base a damage award on the protective provisions of the Law (which lower federal courts had consistently upheld.)

The full court of appeals may well agree to rehear the case en banc. Of the federal circuits, the Ninth has been readier than some others to question the judgment of one of its panels. On the other hand, the author of the opinion, Judge Alex Kozinski, is generally viewed as conservative on many issues, including some facets of free speech and press. Whether or not the full appeals court does rehear the case, and whatever the outcome, Supreme Court review would likely also be sought by the losing party. Final resolution of the case is likely to take some time.

However one feels about the merits of the Ninth Circuit's ruling, the absence of special attention to Internet threat issues was striking. Whatever else it does, this case should remind us how different life and law may be in cyberspace. District Court Judge Jones, contemplating the potential proliferation of "mirror sites," and feeling the need to add an appropriate restraint to his decree, certainly recognized at least one such difference. Many other possible differences are imperfectly understood at this early stage in litigation about Internet threats and the like. They cannot, however, be ignored or disregarded by simply assimilating print posters and Internet postings, as some courts have done. A few relevant factors may be noted in the context of the Planned Parenthood case, since it is the most relevant medium we have for analysis.

When courts in the past have determined whether words that are claimed to be "true threats" should be denied First Amendment protection for that reason, they are usually aided by evidence both of the speaker's purpose and of the probable state of mind of the person being threatened—a video or sound recording, testimony of observers, impact on other listeners, and so on. Digital material yields no such analysis. Words on a Web site or in an e-mail are accompanied by no evidence whatever of affect. No tone or intensity of the speaker's voice affords any insight into the speaker's purpose or into the probable perception of the listener. The point was well made in recent congressional testimony by Thomas Fuentes, chief of the FBI's Organized Crime Division. He was explaining to the committee how much more problematic his agents had found surveillance of Internet communication: "The difficulty with e-mail is that you really don't hear the tone of voice. You can't tell if the person is screaming. . . . Are they saying this tongue-in-cheek, or do they really mean it?" In this sense, there seems to be a much clearer case for a wholly objective measure of both intent and impact. Perhaps it is partly for this reason, in assessing the potential of the threats posted on the Nuremberg Files, that Judge Jones relied so heavily on the larger national context in which militant anti-clinic attacks have occurred.

In seeking to define the nature of, and assess liability for, threats on the Internet, two different elements seem to argue at cross purposes. The very anonymity and affectless quality of Internet communication may actually make its messages more ominous to many who communicate electronically. Even when an address appears on the message, the precise source of a disturbing communication may be unknown; the person who sent it could be in the next room or halfway around the world. There is also a tendency among Internet speakers to lose many of those inhibitions that ensure civility in person and in print when they are on-line. Although we may in time become inured to a level of "flaming" that we never expect in more traditional settings, that prospect makes it no easier to receive with equanimity a message that pushes the outer limits of discourse. While it is not yet clear what bearing, if any, this factor may have on courts' view of liability for Internet threats, it nonetheless marks an important respect in which cyberspace is different.

The other difference is more dramatic and bears directly on the *Planned Parenthood* case. Because of its graphic qualities, the Nuremberg Files Web site was potentially more ominous and frightening than similar messages in other anti-abortion media. Not only was there the moving hand which drew a line through the name of Dr. Barnett Slepian and other physicians, literally as they were dying from the assassin's bullet; there were also the red streams of dripping blood, which were apparently designed to draw the site visitor's attention (and disgust) to an image which purported to be that of a recently aborted fetus. These are emotions one simply cannot evoke in print or other traditional media. Movies and television can and do provide graphic images, indeed often at the urging of sponsors who seek to exploit the baser instincts of viewers, but such images are not summoned on demand as on a Web site and do not assault or shock the viewer in the same way.

To describe such differences does not, of course, provide a legal standard by which to judge threatening material on the Internet. At this early stage, it may suffice to note that such differences exist and to recognize that they may well reshape in cyberspace the standards which courts have invoked for judging threats in traditional media. In some respects, threats on the Internet may be less menacing—and thus less readily actionable in a case such as *Planned Parenthood v. American Coalition of Life Activists*—than the same material in spoken or printed form. Yet in other ways digital messages can be more threatening than those with which we are more familiar: The hand that strikes a deceased physician's name as an apprehensive colleague watches and the dripping blood that dramatizes the aborted fetus have a capacity to shock and terrify that no other medium affords. We will need more cases than this one to provide appropriate standards and guidelines. For the moment, it is clear that we have embarked on a completely new course.

No discussion of digital threats would be complete without mention of the extraordinary case of Jake Baker. As a University of Michigan undergraduate in the mid-1990s, Baker was to become an Internet pioneer. Two types of messages got him into trouble both with the university and with federal law-enforcement officials. Soon after enrolling at the University of Michigan at Ann Arbor, he began an active e-mail correspondence with a Canadian Internet user known only as Arthur Gonda. In fact, Gonda's identify never was confirmed. As a federal judge would later observe: "'He' could be a ten-year old girl, an eighty year old man, or a committee in a retirement community playing the role of Gonda gathered around a computer."

Jake Baker exchanged a rich array of fantasies with this remote correspondent. The two shared at length and in great detail elaborate plans for their sexual gratification at the expense of many young women—residents of Baker's dormitory, other female students at the University of Michigan, and high school students in the Ann Arbor area. None of the putative victims, of course, ever learned of these fantasies—nor, given the person-to-person nature of the correspondence, were they likely to; the text of these sexual fantasies reached federal law-enforcement officials, in fact, only because Baker surrendered his hard drive after his arrest. The events leading to that arrest involved a very different use of the Internet.

Jake Baker had also contrived a lurid tale of sexual exploits, which he posted on the Internet in an alt.sex newsgroup. The story, captioned "Pamela's Ordeal," used the actual name of one of Baker's female dormitory neighbors. Rape, torture, and eventually murder pervaded the story, most graphically through a prolonged account of torture inflicted through the medium of a red-hot curling iron. As though to caution potential readers, Baker posted his own warning note beside the story—"pretty sick stuff." The story at first went unnoticed, not only in Ann Arbor, but across the country. One night a Michigan alumnus in Moscow, surfing the Web, came upon Baker's grim tale. Disturbed by the implications for the image of his alma mater, the alumnus called the president's office and demanded that appropriate action be taken.

The university, it turned out, already knew a good deal about Baker and his fantasies; he had already had extensive psychological counseling and was being observed, though the student mental health center thought him relatively harmless. When the university alerted federal law-enforcement agents in Detroit, the agents were far less tolerant. Baker was arrested at once on federal charges of interstate transmission of threatening material. After a night in jail, he sought release on bail. A federal magistrate refused, however, to set him free; he explained that he feared for the safety of his own 13-year-old daughter so long as Jake and his keyboard were at large. For the next thirty days Baker remained behind bars and off the Internet—a period of incarceration which the federal district judge later termed "inexplicable." The government's rationale—to prevent "Jake Baker and other like-minded individuals from acting on their violent impulses and desires"—struck the judge as "farfetched."

Eventually Baker's case went to trial—curiously, not on the basis of "Pamela's Ordeal," but solely on the basis of the e-mail correspondence. Incredibly, "Gonda" was named as a co-defendant, despite the obvious impossibility of even serving any such person with formal charges, much less bringing him/ her to court. There was no easy explanation for the omission of the story from the criminal charges. Pamela, the dormitory neighbor whose named had been used in the "pretty sick" story, first learned of her notoriety when a Detroit reporter called her, immediately after Jake's arrest, to get her reaction—and found her completely oblivious to her presence on the Internet. Officially, government lawyers explained in court that they dropped the story because "it did not constitute a threat." The judge later observed, in dismissing the case, that "the government's enthusiastic beginning petered out to a salvage effort once it was recognized that the communication which so much alarmed the University of Michigan officials was only a rather savage and tasteless piece of fiction."

That left only the Baker-Gonda e-mails, which both the district judge and the federal appeals panel found to fall far short of the standard Congress and the courts had established for "threatening communications." To meet that test, the message would need to be "so unequivocal, unconditional, immediate and specific as to the person threatened, as to convey a gravity of purpose and imminent prospect of execution." Certainly none of the e-mails that were in evidence here could be possibly be so judged as applied to Gonda, whom Baker treated always as a partner rather than a putative victim. Only the young women who were the subject of the shared fantasies could have been apprehensive about Baker's messages. None of them did, or for that matter ever could, see the messages, contained as they were in person-to-person e-mails.

However devious and dangerous the writer's designs may have been, the absence of a communication channel likely to bring such designs to their attention seemed dispositive of the government's case against Jake Baker. Thus Judge Avern Cohn explained the basis for his dismissal of these charges:

> Baker is being prosecuted . . . for his use of words, implicating fundamental First Amendment concerns. Baker's words were transmitted by means of the Internet, a relatively new communications medium [which makes it] possible with unprecedented ease to achieve world-wide distribution of material, like Baker's story, posted to its public areas. . . . But Baker's e-mail messages, on which the indictment is based, were not publicly published but

privately sent to Gonda. . . . The case would have been better handled as a disciplinary matter [by the University of Michigan].

Though Judge Cohn's conclusion seemed clear and easy, the appeals court was not unanimous in affirming his ruling. One judge felt the case should go to trial, since a jury might have found a conspiracy to intimidate young women in and around Ann Arbor—overlooking the exquisite difficulty that "Gonda's" anonymity would pose to any such prosecutorial tactic. Judge Krupansky, the dissenter, felt he should publish for the whole world to read the entire Baker-Gonda e-mail exchange and—though it was never in the record of the case—the graphic text of "Pamela's Ordeal."

While the actual case against Jake Baker turned out to have little merit— indeed it embarrassed both the university and the United States Attorney's office—one can readily imagine situations not dramatically different from Baker's that might give rise to criminal charges and civil recourse. First, let us consider the Baker-Gonda e-mails. In the actual case, there was no possibility whatever that these ominous messages could have reached anyone whom they would have made apprehensive. If, however, such threatening fantasies had been posted in an Internet chat room or news group where potential targets or intended victims might have read them—even if such people were unlikely or infrequent visitors—that would present a very different situation. Whether the statutory standard for "threatening communication" could be met would still be uncertain, though at least such a case might well have been sent to a jury rather than being dismissed outright, as the actual Baker case was dismissed. And if the same messages had been posted on an e-mail discussion group or other message channel that included any of the potential victims— even if many or most recipients were non-victims—that would also be a very different case.

Finally, the case would be wholly different if such ominous messages had actually been electronically addressed to people who would find them threatening. Now, in fact, the situation is no longer hypothetical. A very real case arose some months after Jake Baker's case ran its course. By this time there was a specific statute on the books, addressing the use of the Internet to convey threats. Richard Machado became the first person charged and convicted under the new law. While he was a student at the University of California-Irvine, he sent messages to sixty individually named Asian students which unambiguously threatened their safety. In repetitious e-mailed phrases, Machado declared his intent: "I will find and kill every one of you personally." The criminal case against Machado was an easy one; had he raised a First Amendment defense (which he did not) any federal judge would surely have analogized this case to familiar charges based on personally directed and threatening telephone messages, letters, and other menacing uses of traditional media.

Soon after Machado had been sentenced, similar charges reached another federal court in Southern California—this time, ironically, in the reverse situation of an Asian student who had e-mailed threats to Hispanics. Kingman Quon was a marketing major at California Polytechnic-Pomona when he unleashed a digital tirade against forty-two faculty members at California State University, Los Angeles and twenty-five students at the Massachusetts Institute of Technology. Quon's messages charged that Hispanics had unfairly received the benefits of affirmative action programs and contained death threats as well as profane and vulgar epithets. When Quon was charged under the same federal law that had first been invoked against Machado, he was contrite and apologetic, pleading that he had "snapped" under intense academic pressure. Despite his plea, he was sentenced to two years in federal prison. In a novel use of sentencing power, the judge also ordered that Quon not be allowed to use a computer or access the Internet without a probation officer's permission for an additional year after his release.

There have been other early skirmishes in the courts. Pennsylvania's attorney general, Mike Fisher, filed a complaint in state court charging a group identified as ALPHA HQ with having used its Web site to intimidate two named state Human Relations Commission officials and with posting ethnic intimidation, terroristic threats, and harassing messages on the Internet. When the group failed to appear in court to answer the charges, the Commonwealth won a default judgment—hardly a ruling on the merits, though at least a portent of possible future intervention.

In fact, this case reflects mounting concern about "hate sites" and the like which seem to appear with ever greater frequency—and virulence—on the Internet. Several organizations regularly monitor such sites. HateWatch is one such group with a concern for what they deem abuses and misuses of cyberspace. The Anti-Defamation League of B'nai B'rith (ADL), for another, has an active monitoring program, which identifies and reports such activity; in extreme cases, it may recommend or initiate action to combat such uses of the Internet. A recent ADL report, "Poisoning the Web: Hatred Online," covered a variety of such messages and sites—from bomb-making manuals to racism in various forms to homophobic Web sites. The Gay and Lesbian Alliance Against Defamation (GLAAD) also conducts a thorough review of homophobic Web sites. GLAAD recently made special efforts to remove a Web game in which an animated skateboarder—identified in the caption as gay—turns out to be the shooting target for those who play the game.

Internet service providers are conscious of the degree to which their systems make possible such postings. Although federal law immunizes service providers from civil or criminal liability for material posted by others, however harmful or offensive it may be, each provider establishes policies for subscribers and occasionally invokes such policies—as MindSpring did to remove Neal Horsley's anti-abortion Web site the day after the Planned Parenthood judgment. On the day in the summer of 2000 when Vice President Al Gore announced his selection of an Orthodox Jewish running mate, a predictable flurry of anti-Semitic postings appeared on the Internet. America Online, at least, took immediate steps to curb such comments, though within a few hours they seemed to have subsided on their own.

The major Internet service providers clearly possess such authority by agreement with their subscribers, although any monitoring extensive enough to ensure its uniform and consistent application would be unimaginable. Then there is the fascinating question raised by Neal Horsley's suit against MindSpring—whether a large and powerful provider could face legal liability for taking such action on the basis of (and thus designed to suppress) a message that has offensive or abhorrent content. A government entity clearly could not act to remove or suppress a particular message in digital form any more than it could in print form. For a publicly operated network—a state university, for example—to remove a Web site because it found the content objectionable or offensive, but not unlawful, would be a clear and blatant act of censorship.

It is not yet clear whether any comparable constraints will apply to private providers. There are certain large and powerful private entities (utilities which enjoy a legal monopoly, for example) to which the doctrine of "state action" applies in ways that sharply limit the right to control speech. In some states, even large shopping centers and malls have been required to treat the speech of picketers and protestors as though the First Amendment applied. Will the time come when courts will view the largest and most powerful of the Internet service providers in much the same way? The case for protecting a subscriber's freedom of expression against a large Internet service provider is at least plausible and awaits a proper test case.

Meanwhile, private action in other forms would incur no comparable risk. The Anti-Defamation League, a leader in the field of monitoring hate sites, has placed on the market a filter which blocks access to a number of Web sites which ADL researchers have identified as hate-bearing. The filter also contains links to sources of information about such anti-Semitic groups as the Ku Klux Klan. Though the ADL does not release information about the number of sites which the filter blocks—much less a detailed list of those sites—the roster is substantial and constantly expanding. The evanescent quality of hate sites—many leave the Web as new ones join—greatly complicates the task of those who monitor such material and design filters by which users may be spared the worst forms of digital animus.

A final question becomes inescapable in this context: What remedies, if any, exist for the person who claims to have been a victim of hateful material posted on the Internet—either to recover damages or to have the offending Web site shut down by government intervention? For example, concerned educators and parents have often asked whether families of victims of the

Columbine High School tragedy could not somehow recover damages for the gravely threatening messages that Eric Harris and Dylan Klebold had exchanged by e-mail, and even posted on their respective Web pages, just before they slaughtered fellow students.

The two cases with which we began this chapter offer the best insight we can provide. The Curley family's suit against NAMBLA alleges that material posted on the group's Web site incited a person who had recently viewed that site to commit a brutal murder. Proving such a claim will prove extremely difficult—at least assuming that the federal court where the suit was filed would apply the same First Amendment standards that govern words in any other medium alleged to have incited a listener or reader to kill. The case would become easier for the Curleys only if the courts were to view the Internet as so different a communication channel that new and different legal standards should apply, so that "incitement" would mean one thing in personal communication or in print but something very different in cyberspace. That prospect seems remote indeed, and for good reason, given the analogous qualities of the relevant media. Even so, it is too early to rule out such a possibility.

When we shift from incitement to threats—the focus of *Planned Parenthood v. American Coalition of Life Activists*—the analysis becomes even more problematic. The district judge and the jury found the printed words on the posters and the postings on the Nuremberg Web site threatening enough to warrant very substantial damages against those who uttered them, apparently without regard to the medium. The court of appeals reversed, equally disinclined to differentiate between media.

The constitutional standard for defining and protecting free expression should be the same across quite disparate media. What is or is not a "true threat" in print probably would or would not be a "true threat" on the Internet, despite the greater potential of digital postings to evoke fear and apprehension by images of a hand crossing out a doctor's name, or blood dripping from an aborted fetus. Thus the need is not for different results or outcomes, and certainly not for different First Amendment standards, but rather for recognition of the important factual differences that the age of the Internet now makes possible.

5.

Privacy: Paparazzi and Other Intruders

On a summer afternoon in 1990, Ruth Shulman and her son Wayne were passengers in a car that careened off a California freeway and turned over in a drainage ditch. Both were pinned in the car and had to be removed by the Hurst Jaws of Life emergency device. A rescue helicopter was soon dispatched to the scene. Along with the flight nurse, a videocamera crew was also on board the helicopter. Joel Cooke, the photographer employed by Group W Video, was filming emergency rescue operations for a television segment, which aired a few months later. The broadcast contained extensive footage of Ruth Shulman, in obvious pain and confusion right after the accident. At one point, she says on camera, "I just want to die." At other times, she asks questions which reveal a severe degree of disorientation. At no time was she aware that the rescue was being filmed, and her consent was not sought or obtained.

The accident left Ruth Shulman a paraplegic. After she watched the Group W broadcast from her hospital room, she and her husband retained an attorney and filed suit against Group W and others involved in the filming and broadcast of the accident segment. Ruth observed that "the whole scene was pretty private," adding that "I certainly did not look my best, and I don't feel it's for the public to see." The Shulmans claimed that the filming and broadcast of this segment had invaded their privacy and entitled them to compensation. The California trial judge dismissed the suit, noting that the accident and the rescue were matters of public interest and had considerable news value. To hold a broadcaster liable for filming such an event could, said the trial judge, seriously chill freedom of the press.

Eight years after the accident, California's Supreme Court took a very different view of the case. The high court agreed with the trial judge that the material in issue was newsworthy and that its filming could not create liability for invasion of privacy. But the supreme court felt differently about the Shulmans' claim of "intrusion." They sent the case back for a trial on such issues as whether the camera crew had acted wrongfully by accompanying the accident victims in the rescue helicopter and by taping communications between Ruth Shulman and the nurse without the patient's consent. The high court also ruled that the news media had no constitutional right to "intrude on plaintiffs' seclusion and private communications."

A few years later, a similar set of events unfolded across the country. Richard and Nancy Wolfson were senior executives of U.S. Healthcare, a corporation of which her father was the chief executive officer. The company had suddenly become the subject of considerable media interest and scrutiny. After the Wolfsons had denied requests for interviews, they found themselves and their family the focus of persistent and aggressive media surveillance. Their single-family house in a wealthy Philadelphia suburb became the target of intense interest from a camera crew developing material for an upcoming segment of *Inside Edition.* The photographers on the scene trailed the Wolfsons everywhere they went from the moment they left their driveway; during the day they used "shotgun" microphones to pick up conversations a considerable distance away. The camera crew stationed a van containing sophisticated equipment for the detection and recording of remote words and images just outside the Wolfsons' home. The Wolfsons scrupulously kept the shades drawn on all their windows throughout the day and made certain that all their doors were closed and locked.

To escape their tormentors, the Wolfsons arranged a hasty vacation visit to Nancy's father's winter home, located well within a gated community facing the Intercoastal Waterway in Jupiter, Florida. There, to their dismay, the Wolfsons found that their pursuers had rented a boat and taken to the water to continue their surveillance, complete with the same equipment that had extended their sound- and image-gathering capacity well beyond the van in Pennsylvania. The family continued their practice of keeping the blinds drawn and the doors closed; they also made certain that their children were never outdoors on the water side of the house, a policy which denied the family any chance to swim or pursue other pleasures they had hoped to find in Florida.

The Wolfsons were at least secure in the knowledge that a "shotgun" microphone cannot penetrate a closed door or window, though it is capable of capturing sounds as far as sixty yards away from speakers standing close to an open door or window. At no time did the surveillance crew physically trespass on the property of their targets. And, though they were not yet aware of this fact, no conversation between the Wolfsons was recorded because the sound technician inadvertently failed to activate the system when the microphone was trained upon them.

Claiming that they had become "prisoners in [their] own home," the Wolfsons brought suit in federal court, back in Philadelphia, against the photographers who had so altered their lives. Mrs. Wolfson declared that "we tried to live a normal life . . . for our kids. Here we take them away and [the surveillance crew] are following us." Despite such valiant efforts, she noted, "We just couldn't hide, we couldn't get away from anything." The family claimed their privacy had been invaded to a degree that warranted recovery of damages as well as an order to cease and desist.

The district judge was very sympathetic to the Wolfson's plight, noting, among other factors, Nancy's pregnancy. Even though no physical invasion of their property had occurred, either in Pennsylvania or in Florida, the judge found support for their claims in the law of both states (which applies to such issues in federal as well as state courts). What turned the case in the plaintiffs' favor was the court's conviction that "the harassing, hounding, frightening and terrorizing conduct [of the surveillance crew] intruded upon Mr. and Mrs. Wolfsons' right to be left alone." Thus, the microphones and cameras, as well as those who operated them, were directed to restore the Wolfsons' sense of privacy. The surveillance ceased, and the judgment was not appealed.

Though the technology may be new and sophisticated, the issue these cases raise has ancient roots. Among the views invoked after the tragic death of Princess Diana in Paris while being pursued by the paparazzi was this seemingly contemporary perspective:

> The press is overstepping in every direction the obvious bounds of propriety and of decency. Gossip is no longer the resource of the idle and of the vicious, but has become a trade, which is pursued with industry as well as effrontery. To satisfy a prurient taste, the details of sexual relations are spread broadcast in the columns of the daily papers.

Many readers naturally assumed this was the latest lament from Princess Diana's eloquent brother, Earl Spencer—who, it later turned out, had reasons of his own to fear media scrutiny. In fact, it was nothing nearly so contemporary. This indictment of excess, in fact, appeared in a *Harvard Law Review* article published in 1890. It was the very first legal commentary on the need for and value of privacy and on the aggressive means by which the news media endangered privacy. The authors of this seminal article were a prominent Boston attorney, Charles Warren, and his extraordinary junior colleague, Louis D. Brandeis, who would later serve many distinguished years on the U.S. Supreme Court.

The occasion for their collaboration was nothing nearly as majestic as the death of a princess. The Warrens had hosted a gala Beacon Hill dinner party, the guest list of which somehow found its way to the pages of a Boston daily. When casual readers could so easily penetrate the facades of hitherto impenetrable Boston mansions, the Warrens and their neighbors were outraged.

Massachusetts law, they soon discovered, gave no recourse for such an invasion of privacy. Nasty letters to the editor were not likely to yield much satisfaction. It was for this reason that Warren enlisted his brilliant young colleague in the cause. In this article, the first to be widely cited in the fledgling *Harvard Law Review*, they proposed the creation of a new legal right—which few nineteenth-century courts recognized—a right to be left alone by the press. They also urged that the news media should be accountable in damages for any breach of that right.

Fortunately for freedom of the press in the United States, Messrs. Warren and Brandeis were only partially successful in their mission. It is true that most states now permit recovery of damages for some types of invasion of personal privacy. Minnesota joined the pack in 1998, leaving North Dakota and Wyoming as the only two states whose courts have never recognized privacy as a cause of action. Yet, given the potentially chilling effect on free expression, courts have been extremely reluctant to grant recovery in damages for the accurate reporting even of highly personal and embarrassing information. Just so deep is our national commitment to the First Amendment as a means of discovering and learning the truth.

The quest for the protection of privacy reached unprecedented levels in the closing months of the twentieth century. As a direct result of the pursuit of Princess Diana by the paparazzi, and even though a French court eventually absolved the photographers of all blame for the accident, lawmakers in this country fashioned a host of new remedies by which to protect personal privacy against the press. Congress, starting in 1998, gave prolonged consideration to a bill which would have sent photographers to jail for "persistently" pursuing a subject to obtain footage or photos for commercial gain. No such bill ever became law, partly because proponents could never quite agree on the preferred approach.

California lawmakers, about the same time, enacted the most stringent of safeguards aimed at photographers who aggressively pursue subjects or intrude upon their privacy to obtain images, even when the cameras and those who control them are stationed in public places. Enacting such a law may have been redundant. Only months earlier, as we noted, the California Supreme Court in *Shulman v. Group W Productions* had already extended existing privacy law to provide recourse against "offensive intrusion" by the media into a private area, even without physical trespass. Similar measures were introduced in several other states during the post-Diana period, though apparently none of them ever passed.

Even a cursory review of our national history suggests that such tensions recur rather regularly. A recently published memoir, *Under a Wing*, by the daughter of Charles and Ann Morrow Lindbergh recalled the intense publicity surrounding this hero of the 1920s and his family. "The [media] assault," notes a reviewer, "started even before the Paris flight, with reporters bursting into the young aviator's hotel room unannounced and grilling his mother about his chances of being killed. Photographers obstructed his landing after one practice flight, and he broke his tail skid avoiding them. The papers implied that he'd caused the accident himself. But all this was nothing compared to what followed success."

Yet the post-Diana period, with its focused quest for substantially more stringent curbs on the news media, has presented a threat of far more ominous proportions. Whatever the reality, the international perspective seems to have been that Americans had elevated the protection of privacy to new levels. Soon after Vladimir Putin assumed office as Russia's new president, his Security Council secretary sought an analogy to justify tighter curbs on media access to the Kremlin and its officials: "If a paparazzi [*sic*] in American crosses the boundary of private property, he is thrown out, usually with signs of physical violence on his face. And this is followed with a lawsuit claiming damages for violation of private property and privacy." The perception is fascinating, however much the current condition of U.S. privacy law may have been altered in translation.

As a prelude to a closer analysis of the tension between privacy and publicity, it may be useful to summarize briefly the contending claims—the case for privacy on one hand, and the case for publicity on the other. Let us begin with a commonsense view of the case for privacy. Given a choice, most people would wish to retain complete control over the pubic release of private information or images. Take the poignant case of the late tennis star Arthur Ashe. He knew for many months that he had acquired AIDS through a blood transfusion administered just before technology made it possible to detect and remove such impurities from donated plasma. He must have known that his secret would become public, if only through his inevitable death. Yet Ashe was hardly prepared for the phone call he received one day from a sportswriter who claimed to have impeccable information about his illness, and gave him, in effect, a day or two to break the news himself or have it broken for him in the national media. Ashe quickly called a press conference at the New York television studio where he had been a frequent sports commentator. The writer's inquiry had forced his hand in a wholly involuntary and unwelcome way.

Though Arthur Ashe, like many prominent people with well-kept secrets, must have known that damaging news would eventually become public, he fervently wished to control the timing and the manner of any announcement in order to protect his family, close friends, and business associations. His concern was not unlike that of the Charles Warrens and their Beacon Hill guest lists, though of far graver personal import. It was far more than mere vanity. Quite simply, his was the natural human desire to control one's life and what others know about one's life in ways that media intrusion may undermine or destroy. Such a wish for dominion over one's image and reputation, even against truthful revelations, seems to deserve some measure of legal protection.

Such protection may in fact be found in our most basic charter of liberty. The U.S. Constitution protects privacy in myriad ways. Most obvious is the Fourth Amendment's guarantee of the sanctity of the home against improper searches, which may these days increasingly be carried out by sophisticated means that do not entail a physical entry or trespass. One may easily forget that this amendment safeguards one's "papers and effects" as well as one's home. The Third Amendment also protects personal privacy, although resisting the quartering of troops in one's home is not a major concern for most of us.

The Fifth Amendment's self-incrimination clause, as the Supreme Court has stressed, "enables the citizen to create a zone of privacy which government may not force him to surrender to his detriment." And, by implication, the Bill of Rights encompasses such personal privacy as the marital relationship, specifically the use of contraceptives. Undoubtedly this interest will in time extend beyond marital unions into the realm of sexual preference and orientation.

Finally, one should not overlook the degree to which the First Amendment itself encompasses privacy, and does so in two distinct ways. For over a half-century, it has protected citizens from being forced to declare or express a belief that is abhorrent to them—whether by being required to salute the nation's flag or to display a state's motto on one's license plate. To that degree, the sanctity of one's innermost thoughts remains beyond government compulsion.

The First Amendment also now protects freedom of association, an expressive liberty nowhere mentioned in the text of the Constitution but since the late 1950s deemed by the Supreme Court no less vital to citizens' rights than the more explicit guarantees of freedom of speech, freedom of the press, freedom of assembly, and the right to petition. Recognition of associational freedom permits citizens to withhold from government not only how they vote but also to what organizations they belong and contribute. This shield has been crucial to the survival of unpopular or regionally suspect groups such as the NAACP, whose efforts in the courts brought recognition of freedom of association. It even thwarts government efforts to find out about how citizens spend their spare time, as a federal judge recognized some years ago in ruling that Baltimore could not refuse to hire a police recruit with outstanding test scores because he spent his weekends in a nudist colony.

Any such litany of the constitutional parameters of privacy seems, however, to imply a negative corollary. Where privacy is not protected against governmental or other invasion, conflicts between privacy-based claims and countervailing precepts (especially freedom of the press) should be (and usually have been) resolved in favor of the non-privacy or publicity interests. Thus the balance should weigh against legal efforts to restrict publicity (or make it the focus of damages) in the interest of protecting privacy, at least when the privacy claim is not rooted in the Constitution. The presumption that such publicity is protected should usually outweigh any contrary legal inclination to protect personal privacy from unwelcome scrutiny.

The Supreme Court's most recent attention to these issues cast a long shadow toward the privacy side of the equation. Following a well-established journalistic practice of "ride-alongs," two *Washington Post* reporters accompanied police officers while they served an arrest warrant on a suburban Maryland suspect. Other residents of the suspect's home sued the police for invasion of privacy on the basis of the reporters' presence and the unwelcome publicity that ensued. The police argued that the presence of journalists would inform the public about law-enforcement activity, would help to keep the police honest, and might incidentally enhance the image of law enforcement.

Such arguments fell on deaf ears at the high Court. Sustaining the privacy claims of the Maryland citizens in the spring of 1999, the justices rejected any mitigating factors related to the ride-along and soundly condemned the practice as inherently invasive. The fact that those who rode along were reputable journalists seemed at best irrelevant and at worst venal. The key to the case was the privacy of the suspect citizens, a constitutional interest "at the core of the Fourth Amendment."

While the First Amendment clearly "protect[s] press freedom from abridgment by government," that guarantee proved to be of no help here—and not only because no journalists were actually among the defendants. None of the interests which the police had advanced deserved more than passing mention. As for the quite plausible claim that inviting reporters on such forays might make the police more accountable, the Court thought this goal could be equally well served by videotaping the entry.

In the unkindest cut of all to the news media, Chief Justice Rehnquist observed that "the *Washington Post* reporters in the [suspects'] home were working on a story for their own purposes. They were not present for the purpose of protecting the officers, much less the [suspects]." While no journalists had been sued, and thus none were parties to this case, the Court's condemnation of a well-established means of news-gathering could not have been more categorical. The Court gave no deference to a journalistic goal of informing readers of the national capital's major daily about crime and law enforcement, at least where that goal entailed crossing the threshold of a private home.

The tone of the opinion—especially the pointedly disparaging comment that the reporters were "working on a story for their own purpose"—suggests that the current Supreme Court may be realigning the balance between privacy and publicity in favor of the privacy interest, though alarm would be premature. And the import of this ruling for journalists soon became clear, since the very next week there appeared on the Supreme Court docket a ride-along case in which journalists had been sued and thus were parties to potential liability, as they had not been in the Maryland case. The justices, without opinion, sent this case back to the lower courts with the clear implication that what they had said the previous week controlled the fate of the reporters as much as that of the police officers who had invited them.

Let us now turn to the other side of the debate—the case for the press and publicity. When privacy and publicity come into direct conflict, the Supreme

Court has provided generally helpful guidance. Through a series of cases, none of them very recent, the justices have recognized the need to accommodate two sets of interests of a very high order. The Court has articulated several guiding principles. First, the Court has found highly suspect any attempt by government to suppress the truth or to deter its widespread distribution. "State action to punish the publication of truthful information," the justices have warned, "seldom can justify constitutional standards." Here, however, the key word is *seldom*; the justices have always stopped short of creating an absolute privilege for publishing the truth.

Perhaps most revealing is the fact that in every one of the relevant cases, legal sanctions were set aside by the Court because three essential conditions had been met—the information before the Court was truthful, it held obvious public interest, and there was no showing that it had been unlawfully obtained. That result has followed even where state law may purport to bar publication of certain highly sensitive information—for example, the identity of a juvenile offender, the name of a sexual assault victim, or an adverse report on the performance of a state court judge—to take three of the actual prohibitions which the Supreme Court has ruled unconstitutional.

In such cases, the justices have not been insensitive to the deep value of the countervailing personal interests which they compel to yield to the interest in publicity. The high Court has expressly recognized a "sphere of collision between claims of privacy and those of the free press" and has consistently stressed the importance of a free press "to our type of government in which the citizenry is the final judge of the proper conduct of public business."

The Supreme Court has recently and substantially buttressed the free press side of the equation. On May 21, 2001, the Justices ruled that a radio talk-show host could not be held liable in damages for broadcasting the contents of an audio tape that had been obtained in clear violation of federal and state wiretapping laws. Even though the person who made the recording risked both civil and criminal consequences for invading the privacy of the parties to the phone call, the broadcaster posed a constitutionally different issue.

Several factors led the Court to overturn the damage award. For one, the subject matter of the intercepted conversation was of utmost public importance and interest–the terms for settlement of a contentious public school teachers' strike. The tape provided an unquestionably accurate recording of the crucial phone call. Moreover, the only illegal conduct was that of the unknown person who taped the conversation; there was no suggestion that the broadcaster had played any role in the interception.

Most important, in the high Court's view, "the enforcement of the [wiretapping] provision in this case . . . implicates the core purposes of the First Amendment because it imposes sanctions on the publication of truthful information of public concern." Thus, concluded Justice Stevens for the six-member majority, "privacy concerns give way when balanced against the interest in publishing matters of public importance." Here, significantly, the Court invoked a seemingly unguarded concession which Warren and Brandeis had offered in their 1890 article, that "the right of privacy does not prohibit any publication of matter which is of public or general interest."

Despite this generally helpful matrix, we lack detailed guidance on two crucial issues. The Supreme Court has never had occasion to rule on whether a *failure* of the news media to meet any of the three conditions would be fatal to the claim of freedom of the press—whether, for example, courts could penalize the release of information which had been unlawfully obtained by someone other than the reporter who published it. The other issue on which the courts have given remarkably little guidance is whether there may be some truthful disclosures which meet all three of the high Court's conditions but might nonetheless be so intrusive or so damaging that the affected or injured person might still be able to recover for invasion of privacy.

The Supreme Court, we must recall, has always been very careful to say "seldom" and not "never" of the nexus between truth and invasion of privacy. It is crucial to ask whether that formulation admits of an "ever" situation in which one might still be able to recover damages for a truthful disclosure about his or her private life. We approach that question in two very different but equally important legal contexts—privacy of information and privacy of images.

I. Privacy of Information

We turn first to information that may invade or imperil privacy. The classic example is that of the poignant case of Arthur Ashe, which we have noted briefly. Normally, information that becomes public despite efforts to conceal it—whether it pertains to Arthur Ashe's health or the Warrens' dinner guest list—is fair game unless it is untruthful, in which case there may be legal recourse for libel. Even then, as we have seen in Chapter 3, not every publication that defames will give rise to a damage claim. Yet when even truthful information is so supremely sensitive and so potentially damaging as the information about Arthur Ashe's illness, it is fair to ask whether special considerations might not apply.

Arthur Ashe's fervent desire to control the timing and manner of any story about his health reflected much more than personal vanity. It went to the very core of his personal life and his relations with family and friends—and of course the potentially devastating effect on professional associations and business prospects. The case for breaking the story seemed at the time, and still does seem, unconscionably weak. Some editors even justified forcing Ashe's hand on public health grounds, though they knew perfectly well that his infection had come from an impurity in transfused blood which, for the past decade, has posed no health risk that could not easily be detected. Yet the news media insisted they had not only the right but to some degree even a duty to share this disclosure with the entire world, whatever might be the impact on the affected person and his family. That was surely one of the darkest hours of modern journalism.

One might view the Ashe disclosure from two quite different perspectives. A responsible student of the mass media would hope that the editor or publisher in sole possession of this news would have found some way not to release it—at least not until Mr. Ashe had time to do so in his own way. Yet from the perspective of that newspaper's attorney or a judge asked to grant some form of legal relief against the disclosure, the case looks very different. One who is committed to a free press must, however reluctantly, defend the right of the media to print, when, where, and how they choose, an accurate story that would cause such anguish to a revered sports hero. It was the truth, after all. It was also highly newsworthy. There was no hint of illegality in the way in which the media obtained the information; it apparently came through a chance disclosure by one of the handful of friends to whom Ashe confided his condition in presumed confidence.

The issue of HIV or AIDS infection poses the sharpest tension between privacy and freedom of the press. The inevitable question is whether disclosure of AIDS infection or HIV status is qualitatively different from other information that people fervently wish not to be made public. There are surely differences of degree—the stigma that such news almost automatically creates, deep fears about a contagious and potentially fatal disease, and the possibly devastating effects on family, professional, personal, and business relationships.

Several early trial court cases involving AIDS disclosure in the workplace stopped short of recognizing an actionable privacy claim. In each instance, however, the reason for not allowing recovery for damages had more to do with the very limited dissemination of the story or with the court's uncertainly about the identity of the subject. All three courts did, nonetheless, recognize that revealing a person's AIDS condition or HIV infection is different, at least in degree, from almost anything else that might truthfully be said about a person's private life.

As we await the first case that will squarely test this issue, it is not too early to ask whether the news media should be concerned about publicizing accurate and newsworthy information on this topic. Or can they continue to rely comfortably on a First Amendment defense for telling the truth, which would presumably provide a solid shield in any other situation? Courts will surely be sympathetic to the AIDS victim whose life has been altered, perhaps ruined, by a disclosure that (as in Arthur Ashe's case) may serve a purpose no nobler than selling more papers or raising Nielsen ratings. Despite the normal presumption in favor of printing or broadcasting the truth, the strength of the media position in such cases may be weakened by sympathy for the embattled or beleaguered subject who is seeking legal protection for his or her privacy.

There are several caveats, even for the boldest and most brazen of publishers. One of the Supreme Court's conditions, we recall, is that the information not have been "unlawfully obtained." Such sensitive data about health and disease does not normally come to light unless someone has had access to legally privileged medical files. Though there have been no cases involving tainted news, it would seem that "unlawfully obtained" should cover more than direct larceny by the reporter writing the story. An invasion of private files or databases need not, in order to defeat the free press claim, have been perpetrated by the editor or on his or her orders. It would probably suffice to show that the media were active, knowing, and willing beneficiaries of someone else's trespass, larceny, or hacking, even if the editor was unaware of the precise means by which the story came to light and failed to inquire.

One might also ask whether an intrusive medium has exceeded the very limited purpose for which an infected person might have revealed his illness. There is a federal court case on that very point. A Delta Airlines ground agent in New York sought the aid of the city's human rights commission to recover the job he lost when the airline learned he was HIV positive. The commission prevailed, and the employee was delighted to be back at work. Flush with victory, the agency issued a press release about the case. Though the Delta employee was not named, he brought suit against the city, arguing in his complaint that details in the press release unmistakably apprised his co-workers and friends of his condition.

The core of the airline agent's case was that he had shared his secret with the agency for a very limited purpose—to recover a job which had been unlawfully terminated—but that the commission had gone far beyond that goal by issuing its rather self-serving press release. While the federal courts stopped short of awarding damages against the city, they recognized this as an unusually appealing privacy claim. They clearly declined to say "never" to potential liability for invading a person's privacy in such a compelling case. The actual case was apparently settled at that stage.

Let us carry the issue one important step further. Suppose a New York newspaper or TV station had based a story on the commission's unfortunate press release, magnifying the humiliation for the Delta employee far beyond the initial announcement. Conventional wisdom would say that the news media may never be penalized for reporting truthfully the official acts of a public agency. Yet there is something different about this case—both in the devastating nature of the information and the way in which a disclosure made for one purpose was used, without permission or even warning, for a different and far riskier purpose.

The Delta-HIV case actually has a fascinating precursor in which recovery was allowed. A sexual assault victim filed a complaint at a Los Angeles police station. She agreed to be photographed for evidentiary purposes. She did not expect, and was startled to learn, that within a few days some graphic photos of her private parts had replaced photos from *Penthouse* and *Hustler* in precinct stations across the city. She sued the department and the culpable officers in federal court and prevailed, partly because the way the intimate photos had been used went so far beyond the purpose for which she had agreed to be photographed and her reasonable expectation at that time. This case, together with plausible variants on the Delta-HIV case, suggest that a categorical "never" may be a bit risky in this extremely sensitive area.

Several other legal remedies ought to trouble an AIDS-insensitive editor or publisher. Beyond libel, which requires proof of falsehood, reputation is protected in some states by the closely related concept of "false-light privacy." Even a truthful disclosure may be reported in such a way as to *imply* or *suggest* something damaging or offensive about a person. In the AIDS context, the false-light risk seems especially severe—an obvious implication, for example, that either sexual promiscuity or drug injection brought about the disease. Only where, as in Arthur Ashe's case, the infection has a clearly benign explanation, should the news media rest comfortably on their First Amendment protection for truthful reporting.

Finally, some thought should be given to the long-recognized tort of intentional infliction of emotional distress. As far as public officials and public figures are concerned, any such claim was put to rest by the Supreme Court's First Amendment rejection of Rev. Jerry Falwell's claims against *Hustler* magazine and its publisher, Larry Flynt. Such recourse may, however, survive for less notorious plaintiffs. A California appellate court recently sustained just such a claim against a Sacramento television station. Its camera crew had interviewed several unsupervised children about the murders of two of their playmates—a tragedy about which the subjects first learned from the reporter, on camera. In allowing recovery of damages for emotional distress, the appeals court had little sympathy for a reporter who, in its view, was "bent upon *making* news, not gathering it" and thus should be liable to the family.

We might now summarize the status of private information before turning to images. Revealing that someone has AIDS or is HIV positive presents an exceptionally compelling case in which to recognize a claim for invasion of privacy against disclosure of truth. We can only speculate what courts will do with the "pure" privacy situation. The short answer, which is possibly sufficient, is that such a case may well be emotionally more appealing but is legally indistinguishable. The longer answer, which is consistent though more cautious, is that many courts will probably seek means, consistent with the First Amendment, of granting some relief to victims of such disclosures. Those courts may treat such revelations as inherently stigmatizing, which could invoke the false-light doctrine. Other courts may presume that such sensitive information would never come to light unless there were some sort of illegality—breach of a legally protected privilege, for example—or unless reasonable expectations for very limited use of the information had been violated or exceeded, as in the Delta employee case. There will almost certainly be a third group of judges, no less sympathetic to privacy plaintiffs, who will balance the equities differently and deny relief. They will remind us that the truth is often painful, and sometimes devastating, but that it is no less the truth when it inflicts such harm.

II. Privacy of Photographic Images

Now we turn to the paparazzi and the currently precarious condition of those who aggressively or surreptitiously gather photographic images. Here, of course, the basis for a claim of constitutional protection is rather different. We are now concerned less about what the media may *publish* than about how they may *gather* material to publish or broadcast. The media have been less successful in claiming constitutional status for getting news than for disseminating it. Reporters may not, for example, withhold the identity of confidential sources from a grand jury. And if a source is promised confidentiality but that promise is later broken by the media through disclosure of his or her name, the source may recover damages from the duplicitous medium even though its conduct consists of publishing truthful information with obvious public interest that was not unlawfully obtained.

The press can seldom make a special claim of access to places where news is being made. Even the well-established right of reporters to attend and report on criminal trials is really a right of the general public, which the media alone clearly could not be denied. Once in the courtroom, a reporter's access guarantees no more than use of pen or pencil and paper. Cameras are admitted by grace rather than by right; tape-recorders, laptops, and sketchpads are usually allowed, but by judicial option rather than by First Amendment fiat.

It is in this rather different context that courts have addressed the growing tension between the hounded or embattled subject and the aggressive or intrusive paparazzo. The issue is not one of access; rather, it is about whether the taking or the use of an image or picture may be restrained, or redressed in other ways, by the subject because of the way in which, or the place from which, it was taken. Here too there is a simple rule which seems nearly sufficient. The conventional wisdom is that one has no legal recourse against being photographed in a public place—no matter how embarrassing the image may be or however much the subject might wish he or she had not been there, had dressed or behaved differently, or had been in the company of a different person. Simply venturing out onto the street makes one fair game for cameras, whether those cameras are obvious and visible to the subject or concealed in places from which one would never expect to be observed, much less photographed. The rationale, reflected in the treatise of Dean William Prosser, the nation's preeminent scholar of tort law, and later embodied in the American Law Institute's Restatement of the Law of Torts (which both codifies and seeks to shape legal principles), is that taking a person's photograph in a public place "amounts to nothing more than making a record, not differing essentially from a full written description, of a public sight which any person would be free to see."

The clarity of the view of this issue in the United States is matched by its novelty. In the spring of 1998, the Supreme Court of Canada reached a strikingly different conclusion. The case involved a woman who, as a teenager in Montreal a decade earlier, had been photographed from a nearby sidewalk relaxing on the steps of an apartment building. The picture appeared in a magazine article about urban living conditions in two Canadian cities. The subject claimed that the publication of her in an unflattering posture a decade earlier had now exposed her to ridicule among her classmates. On that basis she sought substantial damages from the photographer.

Canada's Supreme Court, invoking an unusually protective Quebec law, upheld a damage award in the subject's favor. The court noted that the unconsented use of the old picture was "an infringement of the person's right to his or her image," a right available as much to the ordinary citizen as to the celebrity. Although not all provincial courts would extend the right of privacy that far, the Supreme Court's ruling leaves Canadian judges free to grant damages against the publisher of an accurate (if unflattering) picture taken in a wholly public place. Only where the subject appears in a large crowd, as at an athletic event or a rally or demonstration, would Canadian law deem the image so "public" that damages could not be recovered for its dissemination.

Conversely, our legal system makes certain exceptions to the seemingly clear principle of *non-privacy*. Pictures, like words, may of course be defamatory. Images may also create so inaccurate and injurious an impression as to trigger the false-light doctrine. Most important, celebrities have legal power to prevent the unauthorized use for commercial purposes of their likeness, voice, and even name. There are many questions and variations—whether such a right survives the demise of the subject, how far it may apply beyond directly commercial uses, and the like.

Moreover, one relevant Supreme Court case from the late 1970s is occasionally cited as authority for a broad-based privacy claim. Hugo Zacchini made his living being shot out of canons at county and state fairs. One evening his entire act, which had been filmed earlier that day by a TV news camera crew without his consent, was featured on a Cleveland television broadcast. Zacchini sued, and the damages he won at trial survived in a sharply divided Supreme Court. The majority viewed his claim not as one for invasion of privacy—after all, he performed in very public places—but rather as the uncompensated appropriation of very valuable property, resulting in potential dilution of his livelihood. Because it protects property rather than privacy, the decision in *Zacchini v. Scripps-Howard Broadcasting* provides an explanatory footnote rather than an exception.

We thus return to the pure privacy claim. The hard cases concern ordinary people under relatively ordinary conditions. There is surprisingly little certainty about how far legal protection against unwanted images intrudes upon First Amendment freedoms of those who gather and publicize photographic images. Perhaps the most appealing case—rather like the plight of the Wolfson family, with which we began—involves a subject so harried or hounded as to be effectively unable to enter or leave home, take children to or from school, shop, worship, or engage in the myriad essential tasks of life. Long before the federal judge in Philadelphia granted relief to the Wolfsons, Jacqueline Kennedy Onassis and her children had been pursued to the point of paralysis until a federal judge ordered a photographer to remain a certain distance at bay and refrain from other practices that had effectively immobilized this famous family.

Recently, a California judge provided similar relief to Arnold Schwarzenegger and Maria Shriver after a paparazzo grazed their car and nearly prevented delivery of their child to school. Such victims as these probably need no special privacy laws, whether the person who makes life miserable is a photographer or an extortionist. The familiar existing sanctions against harassment, assault, stalking, and the like should suffice where genuine physical or even emotional harm results from invasive or trespassory image-gathering, unless these remedies become a subterfuge for relief the First Amendment properly denies to people who wish simply to avoid the limelight. Invoking such extreme intrusions in support of drastic new curbs on the paparazzi confuses and misrepresents an already complex picture. Such premises also intensify the risk of suppressing protected expressive and creative activity.

Invasion of physical property also poses difficult questions. The sanctity of one's home is, after all, at the core of the Fourth Amendment. If a photographer were to physically break into a house or place of business to obtain a picture, no claim of "newsworthiness" would avail. Trespassing on the lawn or driveway to obtain an image would also invite some remedy. Less clear is how courts should treat the rapidly emerging challenge of virtual or technological trespass, which (like the surveillance to which the Wolfsons were subjected both by land and by sea) may gather images and words from private places without a physical entry or intrusion. One of the bills that Congress considered in 1998 and 1999, but ultimately did not enact, would have banned the use of "visual or auditory enhancement" devices to obtain words or pictures. The California anti-paparazzi law, which took effect at the start of 1999, did just that, by creating for the very first time the actionable offense of "virtual trespass"—allowing recovery of damages against photographers who aggressively pursue subjects or intrude upon their privacy, even by nonphysical means and from public places, to capture unconsented images or words.

It may be useful to get the flavor of the California climate which inspired such novel and far-reaching legislation. The central premise of, and impetus for, the new law was the availability of long-focus lenses and parabolic, or "shotgun," microphones which for the first time made it possible to transcend long distances and penetrate once-impenetrable barriers to capture images and words heretofore assumed to be absolutely private. Richard Masur, president of the Screen Actors Guild, warned a legislative committee that technology had advanced so rapidly, and had enabled such higher levels of intrusion into actors' privacy, that new legal safeguards were imperative:

> We feel that the people of this country are really, really nervous about their privacy. That it's being undermined in a variety of ways—the Internet, surveillance in every store, every bank, even driving down the street. There's real concern about abuse by the press or anyone else of that kind of technology. There are infrared cameras that can not only get a usable photo right through a window with a sheer curtain but tremendously detailed photos through Venetian blinds.

Masur added, with an ominous sense of where technology was headed, "Soon they'll be able to shoot right through a wall." As though to confirm Masur's worst fears, Michael Moore recently announced on *Larry King Live* that he had just made available to viewers of his television program *The Awful Truth* a new Web site that offered, among other tantalizing images, around-the-clock surveillance of a Manhattan apartment owned by Monica Lewinsky's confidant and literary agent, Lucianne Goldberg.

Even without laws like the ones that California adopted and Congress considered, courts have in extreme cases been willing to grant relief against extreme though non-physically invasive image-gathering. The ruling of the federal district judge in the *Wolfson v. Lewis* case is a rare but significant example of such sensitivity. Given the paucity of legal claims of this type, it is too early to tell how far other courts may be disposed to extend traditional trespass concepts to such electronic intrusions. If new technologies penetrate the walls of a house, the case for some relief seems appealing, even though no trespass claim would otherwise exist.

Even images that have been gathered entirely in public places may be problematic. As we noted at the start of this chapter, the California Supreme Court in *Shulman v. Group W Productions* held that an accident victim who was on a public highway and in an emergency helicopter could recover for what amounted to invasion of privacy for the unconsented use of words and images obtained as she was en route to the hospital. That recent ruling reminds us that legal protection of privacy may extend beyond the physical confines of one's home. The critical question, which courts have barely begun to address, is where and to what extent reasonable expectations of privacy beyond the home warrant some relief against unwelcome photographic invasions or intrusions.

Two cases at opposite ends of the spectrum seem fairly clear. On one hand, if a camera or tape-recorder is surreptitiously placed in an article of clothing or a purse or briefcase or wallet, that would seem as clearly invasive of the subject's privacy as breaking into the home. On the other hand, concealing a camera on a street, in a park, in a store, or in some other public place may yield images that are deeply offensive and intrusive but would not amount to a legally actionable invasion of privacy.

The hard cases lie between these two situations. For example, what about a camera concealed in the stall of a washroom, a dressing room, or a locker room? These are places outside the home or the office where some level of privacy is reasonably expected, whatever the form of intrusion. For the California Supreme Court, a rescue helicopter on its way to the hospital is apparently such a place, at least for a dazed and gravely injured patient. If a person spies through a hole in the wall or the ceiling, we consider such conduct an unconscionable (and sometimes unlawful) invasion of privacy. Even though such places do not enjoy the same constitutional presumption of privacy as would the home or office itself, they are not places where one's mere presence should make one fair game for being stigmatized by the lens or the microphone.

Finally, whatever qualifications may be recognized with respect to special situations or extremely intrusive surveillance or information or images that may have an exceptionally damaging quality, the underlying principle should remain firm: The law should not provide recourse for images obtained in a public place in the absence of a clear expectation of privacy for all purposes. This result may not have been the one Messrs. Warren and Brandeis would have wished. It is surely not one that courts in most other countries observe.

Yet the basic constitutional precept remains clear and firm: Embarrassment or distress does not warrant abridging First Amendment freedom to obtain or to disseminate truthful information or images that hold public interest and have not been obtained unlawfully. The pressure to find new avenues of relief for the victim of media intrusion has been markedly intensified both by events of recent years, not only by the tragic death of Princess Diana, and by the rapid development of technology that blurs the line between what is "private" and what is "public"—devices that make the "castle" less insular than it has even been before. In some other legal systems, including those as close and as congenial as that of Canada, such pressure has in fact found legal recognition. In this country, there needs to be clearer understanding, especially by lawmakers bent on redressing perceived sins of the media, of the high level of tolerance the framers demanded for unwelcome, even damaging (though truthful) disclosures. We are sometimes asked to, and do, pay a very high price for our First Amendment freedoms. In few areas are that price and its ultimate value clearer than they are here. It is not only, or even primarily, the interests of the paparazzi and the gossipmongers which are at risk. Indeed, pressures of the type that now threaten information-gathering affect, and could undermine, the full range of basic First Amendment values and interests.

6.

The Perils of News-Gathering

One afternoon in September 1993, the news desk at a Sacramento, California, television station learned that a suburban woman had killed her two small children and had then taken her own life. A camera crew was dispatched to the scene. Their first stop was the house of a neighbor, where three children were playing, quite unaware of the tragedy that had just befallen their young friends. The camera crew questioned the children about the stricken family and about their own relationship with the two young victims. When the children seemed puzzled by the inquiry, the reporter explained, "Well, the mom has killed the two little kids and herself." One of the subjects immediately exclaimed "Oh my God." The crew then recorded for the evening news the children's manifest grief upon learning of the nearby calamity. Although this dramatic segment never aired, the parents of Amanda Mehrkens and Jennifer and Amanda Whittle, the young people who had been interviewed, vowed to seek redress against the station.

The Mehrkens and Whittle families filed a suit in California state court that claimed that the KOVR-TV camera crew knew, or should have known, that the children were friends and playmates of the victims and would thus be shocked to learn of the tragedy. Consequently, the families claimed, the act of filming the children's predictable reaction to this devastating news amounted to intentional infliction of emotional distress, a wrong for which the law had long provided recourse. Though the circumstances of the case were novel, the underlying legal claim had ancient roots.

The California court was highly sympathetic to the two Amandas and Jennifer, who had been interviewed and filmed in their home without warning or preparation. The issue at this early stage was whether such a legal claim could go forward—whether, in short, the families had set forth in their complaint a strong enough case to bring about a damage award if it went to trial and whether they could prove what they had alleged. In giving an affirmative answer to that question, the court stressed what seemed most troubling about the case—a clear conviction that the camera crew and the station were "bent upon making news, not gathering it."

In order to recover damages, a plaintiff would need to prove the camera crew had acted with "a malicious or evil purpose." That standard, the court ruled at this early stage, could be met here by showing that the camera crew "devoted little or no thought to the probable consequences of [their] conduct." Although this case clearly differed markedly from earlier situations in which news media had fabricated or staged vehicle accidents or explosions, the California court felt the Sacramento station had been no less culpable in its dealings with the unsuspecting children who were its subjects.

Almost as an afterthought, the court briefly addressed the station's First Amendment claims. Noting that reporters enjoy no special immunity from the general laws, in gathering news or otherwise, the California judges revealed a clear lack of sympathy for the defendants' conduct: "If indeed [the camera crew] sought to elicit an emotional reaction from the minors for the voyeuristic titillation of KOVR's viewing audience, this is shameless exploitation of defenseless children, pure and simple, not the gathering of news which the public has a right to know. A free press is not threatened by requiring its agents to operate within the bounds of decency." The case ended there and was apparently settled soon after this ruling.

The very next month, at the opposite corner of the country, a quite different tragedy was to spawn another troubling challenge to the gathering of news. Four Maine teenagers were killed when their car was struck by a sleepy long-haul truck driver, who later pleaded guilty to falsely recording his driving hours in the truck's logbook. The tragedy soon led to the formation of Parents Against Tired Truckers (PATT), a group that sought to bring about stricter enforcement of rules about maximum driving times and other regulations. NBC's *Dateline* learned about PATT and thought its mission would make a timely and interesting story. Fred Francis, veteran NBC reporter, was assigned to cover the story. Arrangements were made to interview a Maine trucking company owner named Raymond Veilleux and for Francis to accompany one of his drivers across the country.

The prospective subjects expressed early concern that the coverage might be negative. They were especially uneasy about the role that PATT might play in such a segment. *Dateline's* producer sought to reassure them in two respects. First, as Veilleux later testified, the producer explained that "he'd like to do . . . a little thing to put us in a positive light, instead of all the negative publicity we've had." Second, and more precisely, the NBC representative assured the truckers that PATT had already garnered enough attention for its side of the story, so there would be no occasion to restate its case. The subjects now made clear they "did not want to be involved in the show if PATT had anything to do with it." The producer seemed to concur. He gave no hint to the trusting truckers that PATT's founders had already been interviewed at length by a *Dateline* crew. The subjects gave their assent, and specific plans were developed to film interviews in Maine and to cover a trucker's trip across the country.

When the *Dateline* segment actually aired in April 1995, the Maine truckers and owners felt they had been betrayed. Far from being "positive," the story contained several quite damaging allegations about the record-keeping and driving practices of the long-haul truckers. Moreover, PATT's founders received substantial time to restate the anti-trucker side of the case. That seemed wholly contrary to expectations and assurances. It was not only that NBC had initially promised a "positive" portrayal. After an agreement had been reached, the producer asked if he could film the driver in the process of posting false time records and falsifying time records. Veilleux protested and threatened to withdraw until the producer dropped the request, assuring Veilleux they would "do it [his] way."

Veilleux and his wife, and one of the individual truckers, eventually filed suit against NBC in federal court, seeking damages for various wrongs, including libel, invasion of privacy, infliction of emotional distress, and fraudulent misrepresentation. A jury awarded them damages for several of these claims. NBC then took the case to the First Circuit Court of Appeals, which rendered a rather complex judgment in March 2000. For various reasons, the libel and emotional distress allegations did not seem viable, and the appeals court ruled that they should have been dismissed. The surviving element of the case, however, was the misrepresentation claims. Here the circuit court essentially split the difference. Since federal courts are bound on substantive issues by the law of the state in which the events occurred that gave rise to the lawsuit, the question was how a Maine court would treat the breach of a broadcaster's promise to provide "positive coverage." It seemed clear that Maine judges would not award damages for such a breach, since the promise was not "sufficiently factual" to yield a workable legal standard. Moreover, the federal appeals judges warned that there could be serious First Amendment problems in "using so vague a yardstick in a misrepresentation action founded on speech relating to matters of public concern."

The promise not to include PATT in the *Dateline* segment was, however, substantially more troubling to the appeals court and led to a different legal conclusion. Here the promise had been much more specific. Allowing recovery of damages for the breach of such a commitment would not risk the vagueness of imposing liability on the basis of failing to deliver a "positive" story. The detrimental reliance of Veilleux and the drivers on the producer's assurances was beyond dispute. The plaintiffs had made quite clear their wish not to be involved in a broadcast that gave time or attention to a public interest group which had become their nemesis. Moreover, the producer provided them the desired assurances, with full knowledge that PATT's founders had already been interviewed at some length for the very segment in issue and that their statements would likely end up on the air. Finally, Veilleux had shown that a substantial loss of business could be traced directly to the *Dateline* segment and to the inclusion in the broadcast of PATT's highly emotional message.

The court of appeals thus found this to be the rare case in which a broadcaster's promise had been made, had been relied upon by a reluctant subject, and had then been breached, with serious business losses directly attributable to that breach. Although the subject matter—highway safety and the accurate recording of long-haul truckers' hours—was clearly one of great public interest, neither that fact nor the nature of news-gathering itself would preclude a federal court from awarding damages against the network for such conduct.

A third case should now be mentioned, one that is much more familiar than either of the two that preceded it. ABC Television's *PrimeTime Live* set out in 1992 to verify a report of certain unsanitary practices in Food Lion stores. An undercover investigation seemed the best (indeed, probably the only) means of obtaining the information essential to such an exposé. Two ABC reporters, with the approval of their superiors, applied for jobs at a North Carolina Food Lion store. Their applications not only contained false information about prior employment but also notably omitted any mention of the applicants' day jobs with the network. When they were hired at the supermarket, both reporters took with them and used extensively in the store tiny cameras and microphones. What they found, and filmed, turned out to be deeply embarrassing for Food Lion—outdated chicken that had been "revived" with barbecue sauce and artificial coloring and then moved to the gourmet section, expired beef that was reground and repackaged with fresh beef, fish that was repackaged and kept for sale after its expiration date, and cheese with rodent teethmarks that were removed before the cheese was repackaged and reshelved.

The impact of the *PrimeTime Live* broadcast was devastating for Food Lion—not only in terms of retail sales, which slumped for a time, but also on its stock price, employee morale, and other facets of the business. Food Lion soon filed a lawsuit against ABC in federal court on several grounds; at first they even included libel, although that count soon turned out to be illusory since it was the very accuracy of the broadcast footage that caused Food Lion's problems. The focus of the suit soon became different legal claims—fraudulent methods of news-gathering, breach of an employee's duty of loyalty, trespass, and unfair trade practices. A jury that seemed highly sympathetic to Food Lion (and quite possibly also hostile to a national TV network) awarded roughly $5.5 million in damages for what it saw not merely as highly reprehensible journalistic practices but also as an unlawful way to obtain information.

The trial judge later substantially reduced the damage award. Both parties appealed the case to the federal Fourth Circuit Court, which in October 1999 rendered a judgment that could not have fully satisfied either side. Applying North Carolina law, the appeals court rejected Food Lion's unfair competition claim because the parties could in no sense be deemed competitors. The court also found that Food Lion's effort to recover damages for injury to its reputation was not legally tenable, since it amounted to a back-door libel suit of a kind the U.S. Supreme Court had recently made clear could not be maintained if the material it targeted was not defamatory.

However, the appeals court did resolve the balance of the case in Food Lion's favor. Specifically, the panel ruled that such a retailer could recover damages from the network and its camera crew for breach of a duty of loyalty that was owed under state law to employers. The court also sided with Food Lion on its trespass count, ruling that even in a retail store where the general public is welcome the camera crew substantially exceeded the "implied license" with which they had entered. The appeals court specifically ruled that Food Lion's "consent for [the camera crew] to be on its property was nullified when they tortiously breached their duty of loyalty." Thus, the issues were split in the end, albeit in ways that heavily favored Food Lion's position.

It was also clear, and of greatest concern to First Amendment lawyers and the national news media, that damages had been granted on the basis of a truthful broadcast of highly informative material relating to consumer health and welfare, solely because of the manner in which that information had been obtained. Many of the media groups that supported ABC's legal position in court also took pains to distance themselves from the deceptive and clandestine news-gathering methods that triggered the lawsuit, even to the extent of condemning ABC's unusual if not unique use of hidden cameras and microphones.

Yet on the ultimate legal issues, the media community uniformly laments the precedent which *Food Lion v. ABC* has now established and the ominous portent it creates for future litigation and news-gathering liability. Fairly typical is the comment of former Reporters Committee for Freedom of the Press head Jane Kirtley. She noted with alarm the growing threat in such recent cases to the journalist's premise that exposing corruption, protecting consumer health and safety, and other "important ends justify the use of any means to achieve them." But, she adds ominously, "the judiciary isn't buying that. The essential watchdog role that the press should play in a democracy is lost on many of them."

There was a time, not so long ago, when investigative reporting—and the more aggressive the better—earned praise rather than scorn and liability. The legacy of muckrakers such as Upton Sinclair pervaded popular perceptions of news-gathering through much of the twentieth century and spawned emulation as well as admiration. After Bob Woodward and Carl Bernstein brought down the Nixon administration over Watergate, those two quintessential investigators became role models for a generation of budding journalists. Yet the journalistic community should not have been totally surprised by the apparent change of heart which such recent adverse judgments may reflect. There was at least one ominous portent, long before the case of the Maine truckers or the North Carolina food-handlers. In 1971, the federal appeals court in California decided a case against *Life* magazine that first raised legal doubts about the use of questionable news-gathering methods.

Two *Life* reporters had set out to compile information about a disabled veteran named Dietemann who practiced "healings" through the use of clay, minerals, and herbs. The reporters used false identification to gain entry to Dietemann's house, one bringing a hidden camera and the other a concealed microphone. Their very revealing conversations with Dietemann were transmitted to a third *Life* staff member, as well as to law-enforcement officers, and provided the basis for a highly damaging account of Dietemann's activity in an exposé of medical quackery. The substance of the story, and of *Life*'s suspicions which had spawned the story, were clearly sound; Dietemann eventually pleaded no contest to criminal charges for practicing medicine without a license.

Dietemann brought suit against *Life* and recovered damages for invasion of the home, invasion of privacy, and intentional infliction of emotional distress. The appeals court proved quite sympathetic to all three claims and ruled that each of them would sustain an award of damages. The higher court also rejected *Life*'s attempt to invoke freedom of the press in its defense, noting that "the First Amendment is not a license to trespass, to steal, or to intrude by electronic means into the precincts of another's home or office." *Life*'s attempt to invoke media privileges which the Supreme Court had recognized fell on deaf judicial ears; despite the conferral of such protection upon legitimate news-gathering activity, added the appeals panel, the high Court cases "strongly indicate that there is no First Amendment interest in protecting the news media from [liability for their] calculated misdeeds."

Curiously, this decision—an ominous early warning shot across the investigative bow—was virtually ignored by media lawyers and other close observers at the time. It did not attract scholarly attention until nearly three decades later, when the issue of liability for news-gathering returned to the courts. A more perceptive media community might have appreciated more clearly such storm signals. Whether such prescience would have deterred increasingly aggressive news-gathering practices is, of course, quite another matter.

It is now time to ask how far from precedent—apart from *Dietemann*—recent cases such as *Food Lion v. ABC, Veilleux v. NBC*, and *KOVR-TV v. Superior Court of Sacramento County* (the Mehrkens-Whittle case) depart from previously settled First Amendment precedent. That turns out to be a quite difficult issue in the absence of definitive Supreme Court rulings on the status of questionable news-gathering practices—indeed, on virtually any aspects of news-gathering. But one may find ample support in analogous rulings for both a pessimistic and an optimistic view of the current quandary. The precedents that do offer some insight are at least marginally helpful, and they now need to be invoked in connection with the three recent and troubling cases we have examined. Let us look first at several points on the darker side of the equation.

First, it has long been clear that the news media enjoy no immunity, under the First Amendment or any other provision of the Constitution, from the general laws that apply to all businesses. The fact that some dimensions of publishing and broadcasting are free from government control does not serve to insulate a broad range of business activities, which are as fully regulable as those of any other commercial enterprise. Thus, newspapers and radio and television stations must pay taxes, must offer their employees the lawful minimum wage, must withhold income taxes, must provide a safe working environment, and must avoid discrimination on grounds of race, religion, age, and gender (and in some states on grounds of sexual orientation as well). This is basic law, wholly consistent with the historic and special status of the news media under the First Amendment.

Even within these general legal obligations, however, we should note several significant qualifications. When it comes to taxes, for example, the Supreme Court has been vigilant in striking down taxes that discriminate against the news media. The justices have also voided taxes that differentially treated various elements within the media—laws that, for example, tax newspapers more heavily than magazines—unless such variation can be justified in ways that would not be required elsewhere.

Moreover, while the news media may of course be barred from discriminating in employment on the basis of race, gender, nationality, age, and religion, certain remedies might be treated differently in the journalistic context. Thus, if a press operator or a driver or a custodian is fired for racial or religious reasons, it is irrelevant to a claim for reinstatement that the employer is a newspaper or a broadcaster. If, however, the person who has been wrongfully discharged is a columnist or a news anchor, a court or agency would not quite so readily compel the reinstatement of the plaintiff, since ordering a media employer to take such action could raise novel First Amendment issues. In the few instances where such a dilemma has occurred—for example, a wrongly discharged African-American sportswriter on a Chicago newspaper and a female TV anchor in Kansas City fired for improper age-based reasons—the potential conflict between the normal remedy of reinstatement and the sensitivity of the news media context has lurked just below the surface, awaiting the case in which it cannot be avoided. When that time comes, it should be apparent that some aspects of the news business—even what seem to be business aspects—need to be treated with greater sensitivity than comparable issues elsewhere in the workplace.

One respect in which the media are not exempt is that of trespass, a point well illustrated by the *Food Lion v. ABC* case. If the *PrimeTime Live* camera crew had forced its way into the store, much less broken in at a time when the store was closed, even the most laudable of missions would have availed them not the least. Nor would their journalistic calling or the particular quest have exempted them from legal consequences if their assigned jobs at Food Lion had confined them to the open retail areas and they had taken their concealed cameras and microphones into the meat locker or the manager's office or anywhere else in the store that would have been off-limits to legitimate holders of the jobs they obtained.

Even more clearly, they could not have claimed immunity if they had damaged controls on the locker or the counters or caused the spoilage of perishable produce or if they had caused harm to legitimate fellow employees (for example, by bringing about the dismissal or discipline of a regular worker by induced or coerced complicity with the clandestine news-gathering operation). To that extent the federal court in *Food Lion v. ABC* was on familiar and solid ground in entertaining a trespass claim; what made the case troubling and different was that the ABC camera crew, having committed no physical trespass, were treated as trespassers only because the court first ruled they had breached the duty of loyalty the court felt they owed an employer under North Carolina law.

From this point on, the guidelines become less clear. When it comes to the gathering of news, the Supreme Court has spoken several times. Each time, the justices have stopped just short of recognizing a First Amendment right to obtain information. In the early 1970s, the Court was asked to protect a reporter's right to withhold the identity or location of a confidential source — something that the "shield laws" of many states do protect, but with widely varying scope and effect. The majority ruled in *Branzburg v. Hayes* that a reporter who has been called as a witness before a grand jury is no different in this respect from any other citizen who possesses information vital to a criminal inquiry.

The high Court acknowledged that, in the abstract, "news gathering [qualifies] for First Amendment protection; without some protection for seeking out the news, freedom of the press could be eviscerated." On the other hand, "the First Amendment does not guarantee the press a constitutional right of special access to information not available to the public generally." Thus, "the press is regularly excluded from grand jury proceedings" and "newsmen have no constitutional right of access to the scenes of crime or disaster when the general public is excluded." The specific duty which the Court imposed in this case—being required to divulge the identity of a source to whom confidentiality or anonymity has been promised—was simply part of the general obligation a journalist bears to respect the legal norms and sanctions of the larger society.

Six years later, the justices would revisit these issues and would reaffirm what *Branzburg v. Hayes* had denied to the news media. A San Francisco public television station brought suit in federal court after being denied camera access to a series of scheduled tours of a county detention facility. Once again the status of news-gathering was crucial, the more so because members of the general public had been included on such tours, albeit without cameras. The appeals court had ruled in the station's favor, finding that access was appropriate in such a situation. When the case reached the highest Court, four justices shared the view of the circuit court: "Information gathering," they insisted, "is entitled to some measure of constitutional protection" so that a prison policy of "arbitrarily cutting off the flow of information at its source abridges the freedom of speech and of the press protected by the First . . . Amendment."

This was, however, a minority view. The majority in *Houchins v. KQED* clearly reaffirmed the rejection in *Branzburg v. Hayes* of a First Amendment–based right to obtain government information as a means of gathering news in order to inform the reading and viewing public: "There is no discernible basis for a constitutional duty to disclose, or for standards governing disclosure of or access to information. We reject the Court of Appeals' conclusory assertion that the public and the media have a First Amendment right to government information regarding the conditions of jails and their inmates and presumably all other public facilities such as hospitals and mental institutions."

This is where matters remain essentially to this day. The Supreme Court never came any closer to recognizing a First Amendment right of media access or news-gathering. In a few special situations, some measure of access has been recognized—most notably in the coverage of criminal trials—but there it is the right (acknowledged since ancient times) of the *general public* to attend, from which no citizen could be barred solely because he or she happens to be a reporter.

One other Supreme Court case bears even more directly on the current discussion, and it is no more helpful to the news media. Political reporters for the *Minneapolis Star-Tribune* received from a prominent Republican adviser, named Dan Cohen, an offer no journalist could easily refuse—promise not to mention my name as your source, and I'll give you an exclusive set of documents about an opposing candidate for high office in the imminent 1982 elections. The reporters agreed to protect Cohen's anonymity and wrote stories on the basis of his disclosures. But their editors (who knew the identity of the unnamed source) took a different view and insisted that Cohen be publicly cited as a key to the credibility of some rather startling revelations. The reporters protested, but to no avail. When the story appeared, Cohen was fired. He brought suit against the newspaper and the reporters for breach of a promise that had been made and, to his obvious detriment, had then been broken.

The Minnesota courts declined to impose such an obligation on a reporter, even though ordinarily a person who made and broke such a promise would be legally liable. Here, however, "enforcement of a promise of confidentiality . . . would violate the defendants' First Amendment rights." The Supreme Court majority soundly rejected that view and reversed the state courts in *Cohen v. Cowles Media Company.* To those justices, this was not a

First Amendment case but one that involved nothing more than a routine breach of contract, for which damages were appropriate if the promise and the breach were established. Since Minnesota's doctrine of promissory estoppel, on which the claim rested, was a law of general applicability which in no way targeted or singled out the news media, "the First Amendment does not forbid its application to the press." Four justices dissented, lamenting the majority's readiness to impose civil liability for the publication of truthful information that held obvious public interest.

Of the Supreme Court's rulings in this area, it is undoubtedly *Cohen v. Cowles Media Company* that bears most closely on potential media liability for the gathering of news. And it was the Cohen case on which the courts in *Veilleux v. NBC* and *Food Lion v. ABC* relied most heavily in holding that certain otherwise actionable conduct—fraudulent misrepresentation in one case and breach of an employee's duty of loyalty in the other—would subject journalists to civil damage liability under general state tort law. We will revisit the conclusions of both those federal courts of appeals after bringing into the equation several other recent and highly relevant cases that raise related issues of potential news-gathering liability.

So much for the bad news. There is a brighter side to the picture. Optimists may find little to celebrate in recent rulings about news-gathering, but they do invoke other sources to support a more hopeful prospect. The Supreme Court has consistently recognized that the news media serve a vital public interest by gathering and disseminating information and has strongly suggested that such a role warrants protection under the First Amendment. Typical is this statement, albeit not in a directly applicable context: "The First Amendment goes beyond protection of the press and the self-expression of individuals to prohibit government from limiting the stock of information from which members of the public may draw." The Court has also occasionally taken note of the "newsworthiness" of material in or on its way to the press as a mitigating factor in close cases of potential media liability. And even as the justices were about to reject a journalist's plea to shield the identity of confidential sources, they noted in *Cohen v. Cowles Media Company* that "without some protection for seeking out the news, freedom of the press could be eviscerated."

There is even support for the view that where a claim of freedom of the press is sufficiently compelling, it may not matter how the news was gathered. Specifically, in overturning the injunction which a district judge had issued to bar the *New York Times* and the *Washington Post* from publishing the Pentagon Papers excerpts in 1971, the Court treated as legally irrelevant the fact that the copy of that highly classified document used to prepare the stories had actually been stolen. Of course this was the very rare case in which government had sought to gag the press through a prior restraint—an abhorrent reminder of British colonial rule, which is almost never tolerated under our

First Amendment. Indeed, several of the Pentagon Papers justices thought the situation would have been different if it had reached them on the basis of post-publication criminal charges rather than a on the basis of a pre-publication order. It is widely assumed, even by the most ardent First Amendment champions, that the unauthorized use of properly classified government documents entails legal risks that might well include criminal sanctions. To this day we do not know how the Court would treat such a case arising after the fact, though we do assume it would be substantially less appealing—and that the theft of a classified document would be far more troublesome—than it was in the actual Pentagon Papers case. Suffice it to say, as the optimists remind us, that occasionally the free press interest is so strong that it may not be trumped even by the use of unlawful means to gather the news.

A much later case reaffirms this principle. In 1993, an employee of a South Dakota beef-processing plant wore a hidden camera to work one day and videotaped various suspect practices in the preparing of meat products. The tape was given to CBS for use on a 48 Hours segment. The company found out about CBS's planned broadcast and went to court seeking an injunction. A state trial judge granted the order, noting that only "calculated misdeeds" had made possible the prospective airing of this highly damaging material. The South Dakota Supreme Court affirmed. The case then reached Justice Harry Blackmun, who had responsibility for cases from that part of the country. Since the state courts had imposed a classic prior restraint, he immediately dissolved the order, noting that "if CBS has breached its state law obligations, the First Amendment requires that [the beef producer] remedy its harms through a damages proceeding rather than through suppression of protected speech." While this ruling left open the possibility of subsequent redress, the segment was broadcast later that very day and no later legal proceedings seem to have followed.

Beyond the doctrine of prior restraint, the media and their lawyers derive some comfort from the Supreme Court's treatment of rather different legal claims that could be used to inhibit or deter the gathering of news. The justices unanimously rejected Reverend Jerry Falwell's attempt to hold Hustler publisher Larry Flynt liable for an extremely offensive and demeaning parody of a Campari liquor advertisement. Since Falwell was clearly a "public figure," the Court ruled that he could not recover damages for "intentional infliction of emotional distress," even though private individuals may seek redress for humiliation under similar conditions. That judgment, distinctive though the case surely was, spawned optimism in the media world that any claims against news-gathering practices that resulted in injury to the reputation of a public figure would similarly be barred by the First Amendment.

Another source of media optimism has been the Supreme Court's recognition of a constitutional basis for access to certain sources of news and information. In the case of Richmond Newspapers v. Virginia, the Justices declared that reporters may not be barred from covering criminal trials. Before the mid-1970s, it was unclear whether the constitution gave reporters any basis for access to potential news sources. The Supreme Court's limited answer in the context of the criminal trial relied on a historic Anglo-American tradition of openness which did not necessarily ensure equal access to other public places or events, although in a reassuring footnote the justices suggested that access should also extend to civil trials, which "historically have been presumptively open." In fact, the issue of access to civil trials has proved far more problematic; the Supreme Court's assumption turned out to be unduly optimistic. Some states have not historically treated civil trials as open and claims of access have thus needed to be resolved on their own merits, with results that are not yet uniform.

Finally, we might return *Cohen v. Cowles Media Company* itself for a more hopeful perspective. There, we recall, a seemingly callous Supreme Court majority allowed damages to be awarded against a newspaper for printing the name of a source to whom its reporter had promised anonymity. The dissenters noted with alarm that, perhaps for the first time, liability had been based on the publication of truthful information, not material that had been unlawfully obtained and of obvious and substantial public interest.

A group of seasoned media lawyers recently posited a more benign view of the Cohen case, emphasizing two easily overlooked factors. For one, they observed, the effect of imposing liability in such a case was (as the majority insisted) only "incidental" to news-gathering and dissemination and did not present a direct burden of the type other tort remedies might create. Moreover, "enforcing the press promise at issue in *Cohen v. Cowles Media Company* arguably would promote news gathering over the long term more effectively than would allowing the promise to be broken." Read in this way, despite its unsettling implications, the concept of civil liability for breaching a promise to a confidential source, which was outlined in the Cohen case, may actually enhance the role of a free press.

Suffice it to say, for this as well as many other reasons, the net impact of Supreme Court case law on the current debate about media liability for the gathering of news is mixed and uncertain at best. There is support for the more hopeful perspective we have just canvassed as well as for the bleaker view with which we began.

The record of the lower courts on news-gathering and civil liability has also been more mixed than the initial emphasis on *Food Lion v. ABC* and *Veilleux v. NBC* might suggest. Indeed, one recent case offers an intriguing and potentially hopeful contrast. The Desnick Eye Center, a chain of ophthalmic clinics, became the target of an investigation by ABC's *PrimeTime Live* in the mid-1990s. A network producer contacted the owner, Dr. James Desnick, explained his potential mission, and requested access to the main office. He promised that there would be no "ambush" or "undercover" tactics and that the treatment of the clinic would be "fair and balanced."

Dr. Desnick agreed to allow an ABC crew to film a cataract operation at the central office and to interview doctors, patients, and technicians. Unknown to the doctor, other ABC crews had been sent to Desnick clinics in Indiana and Wisconsin, posing as patients and filming eye examinations which they received. The segment that ultimately aired on *PrimeTime Live* was highly critical of the company, claiming that its practices took advantage of elderly and infirm patients, especially by recommending and performing unnecessary surgery.

Desnick and several employees who had been named in the broadcast sued ABC in federal court, insisting they had been the victims of fraudulent, trespassory, and invasive news-gathering. The district court dismissed their complaint, and it reached the appeals court, where Chief Judge Richard Posner wrote for a panel affirming the lower court's disposition. The actions of the ABC crew seemed not to have amounted to trespass, since they had not gone beyond either the public areas of the clinic or certain non-public areas to which they had been granted access. A similar analysis disposed of the claims of invasion of privacy.

Most troubling to the appeals court were the claims of fraud and misrepresentation. Yet here too the panel ruled in ABC's favor—partly because the applicable Illinois law permitted recovery of damages for such conduct only if it was "particularly egregious" or was part of a pattern of deception that caused a victim to rely, to his or her detriment, on what turns out to have been hollow promises. ABC's activity had not, in Judge Posner's view, risen or fallen to that level, and thus it did not warrant recovery as a matter of state tort law.

The court of appeals also thought this case justified a comment on the larger issue of liability for news-gathering. Recalling the Supreme Court's insistence many years earlier on "breathing space" for media coverage of public issues, Judge Posner noted that the high Court had forged "many safeguards designed to protect a vigorous market in ideas and opinions." Such protections, he noted, apply "regardless of whether the tort suit is aimed at the content of the broadcast or the production of the broadcast." A libel plaintiff who is a public figure, for example, must meet a very high burden of proof, which properly protects the news media even though "today's 'tabloid style' investigative television reportage [is] conducted by networks desperate for viewers in an increasingly competitive television market. . . . [The reports are] often shrill, one-sided, and offensive . . . [and] the tactics used by the networks are surreptitious, confrontational, unscrupulous, and ungentlemanly."

Dr. Desnick did not drop his case at this point but returned to the trial court, where he tried to buttress the libel and privacy claims. The trial judge dismissed the whole suit once again. Judge Posner again affirmed for the court of appeals, ruling in late October 2000 that no actionable claim had been established—chiefly that ABC had not acted "recklessly" in crediting the statements of a hostile informer on whom it had relied in compiling the case against Desnick and the clinics.

Perhaps the best test of how the media may fare in such cases comes from a controversy that never reached the courts, but the facts of which pose the hardest questions of all. It also generated a full-length motion picture entitled *The Insider.* Jeffrey Wigand had for some years been a high-ranking executive of the Brown and Williamson Company, a cigarette manufacturer. He agreed, soon after leaving his job with that company, to an extensive interview with CBS's *Sixty Minutes.* Though he had signed a confidentiality agreement before his employment ended, he talked at length with the CBS crew about cigarette production and marketing practices, including revelations that would be highly damaging to his former employer and to the rest of the tobacco industry. Brown and Williamson learned of Wigand's interview and threatened to sue CBS for interfering with a contractual relationship unless the network canceled the broadcast. After being advised by legal experts on such matters that such a lawsuit might succeed, CBS decided to drop the interview. Most of Wigand's disclosures later appeared in other media.

First Amendment experts have seldom been as sharply divided on any issue as they were over the Wigand interview and CBS's cancellation. P. Cameron DeVore, a Seattle attorney who was CBS's outside counsel, insisted that this case would have been indistinguishable from Cohen's suit against Cowles Communications—a simple tort claim for a breach of contract or promise, for which courts would routinely grant damages without regard to the media status of the entity that committed the breach.

Other experts on freedom of speech and press sharply disagreed. James Goodale, who had counseled the *New York Times* successfully through the Pentagon Papers case, argued that it would have been "very hard for CBS to lose" and that the case would likely have been "a slam dunk for *60 Minutes.*" He and like-minded colleagues relied not only on First Amendment protections but quite as much on the myriad practical problems a plaintiff such as Brown & Williamson would face under New York law in proving a cause of action for a somewhat elusive legal wrong.

Jane Kirtley, former head of the Reporters Committee for Freedom of the Press and now a media law professor at the University of Minnesota, shared Goodale's conclusion. Though she acknowledged that had the network taken a different position, it would have faced a "hard-fought and drawn-out battle" in court, she insisted that "CBS would have prevailed on the merits." She also lamented how clearly the incident "unfortunately demonstrates that even financially powerful news organizations can be vulnerable to self-censorship when the way in which a reporter acquired information is called into question."

Since the Wigand/*60 Minutes* case never reached the courts, we will never know what even a trial judge would have ruled, much less what the Supreme Court might have said if called upon to extend or qualify its decision in *Cohen v. Cowles Media Company* in a different context. The case does, however, nicely illustrate several principles that have shaped our discussion here and will continue to apply to legal claims against allegedly wrongful news-gathering. Two truths emerge clearly at opposite poles—on one hand, the First Amendment protects more than simply the publication or dissemination of the news; it also extends to the process by which the news is gathered or acquired. On the other hand, it is equally clear that the First Amendment does not give the press license to trespass on the property of others in the course of seeking and gathering news.

Several difficult questions remain between these two easy cases. What recognized legal claims, other than trespass, might be applied to the news media with only that "incidental" impact on the press that the *Cohen* Court deemed acceptable? Obviously the applicable state law varies substantially on such issues, as we have seen. Illustratively, the very different outcomes of the similar suits by Food Lion and by Dr. Desnick against ABC for allegedly wrongful news-gathering on the part of *PrimeTime Live* reporters partly reflects subtle but important contrasts between Illinois and North Carolina state tort law, which federal courts are required to apply in such cases.

The status of the person who seeks redress will obviously affect the outcome. Even though the privilege of fair comment about a public official or public figure is technically confined to libel law, the epic dispute between Jerry Falwell and Larry Flynt tells us that its reasoning carries over to such analogous claims as intentional infliction of emotional distress. Since most plaintiffs in such cases are public figures—companies such as Brown & Williamson, Food Lion, or Desnick Clinics as much as individuals such as Rev. Falwell—they incur a legal burden that is substantially greater than does the ordinary private citizen as plaintiff. When the plaintiff is not such a public figure—Raymond Veilleux and his Maine truck drivers would be good examples of private persons outside the limelight—courts are likely to be more sympathetic, especially to legal claims or wrongs other than libel, to which the basic media privilege less clearly applies.

The public or private status of the plaintiff may not be all that will guide a court in close cases. There is some evidence that certain plaintiffs are less favored not only because they are public figures but because they should have known better than to place themselves in such a perilous or vulnerable position. Take the case of Dr. Desnick, for example. Judge Posner, in affirming the judgment against him and his clinics, observed that "Desnick, needless to say, was no tyro, or child, or otherwise a member of a vulnerable group." Such a person ought, said Judge Posner, to realize that "investigative journalists well known for ruthlessness always promise to wear kid gloves" and that "they break their promise, as any person of normal sophistication would expect." In stark contrast, the California appeals court that upheld the claims against the Sacramento television station was quite consciously protecting plaintiffs who literally were children, and who would surely fall within Judge Posner's rubric of "vulnerable group." Less dramatically, the first circuit court's view of Raymond Veilleux and his truck drivers seemed also somewhat more sympathetic. Though the degree of naiveté or skepticism to be expected of a particular source is hardly dispositive, these are bound to be close cases in which such a factor could be helpful in resolving otherwise intractable issues.

The relative "wrongfulness" of the accused media conduct is also likely to play a role, even though courts are loath to rank news-gathering transgressions. The courts' discussion of the activity targeted in each of these cases dwelled at least briefly on its factual, as well as its legal, status. The courts seem to have had greater conviction in some cases than in others that the accused journalists were bent on pursuing a story regardless of consequences, or (as in the case of the children confronted by the Sacramento TV camera crew) "making news, not gathering it." Thus, the level or degree of "wrongfulness," including the extent of departure from established news-gathering norms, may play a part in the equation.

Certainly the potential impact upon the news media of a particular judgment is likely to be relevant. In the most extreme case, that of an injunction or prior restraint, we know from the Pentagon Papers case that even the theft of information will not undermine or defeat the free press claim. At the other end of the scale, where the impact of liability seems merely "incidental" (as the money damages awarded against the newspaper seemed to the Court in *Cohen v. Cowles Media Company*) the lesser impact of the sanction may weigh in the plaintiff's favor.

Finally, some consideration should be given to the larger impact that any such judgment may have upon basic First Amendment values. Those such as Jane Kirtley and James Goodale who condemned CBS for canceling the Jeffrey Wigand interview argue that freedom of the press may have suffered much more from such seemingly voluntary action than it would have from an adverse court ruling. A good lawyer can almost always find some basis for distinguishing an unfavorable precedent—if only because the facts of no two cases are identical—and, save for judgments of the U.S. Supreme Court, a court decision has no binding force beyond the state or federal district or circuit within which it was rendered. Yet an action such as that of CBS may turn out to be far more damaging to news-gathering and freedom of the press than the worst consequences of the feared legal judgment it was designed to forestall.

7.

Defective and Dangerous Products?

One afternoon in April 1992, Texas state trooper Bill Davidson stopped a suspicious car on a highway in Jackson County. The car, it turned out, had been stolen, although that was not the reason for the stop. The driver was a young man named Ronald Howard. Soon after he had been pulled over, Howard turned a 9-millimeter pistol on the officer and fired a fatal shot. Investigators soon learned that when he had been stopped, Howard was listening to a tape of rap songs performed by Tupac Shakur entitled *2Pocalypse Now.* At his trial, Howard sought mercy by pleading that the anti-police lyrics had caused him to shoot Officer Davidson. The jury apparently disregarded this claim and sentenced him to death.

The Davidson family soon retained a lawyer and filed suit in federal district court against the performer (Tupac Shakur), the manufacturer (Time Warner), and the distributor (Interscope and Atlantic Records) of the tape. Though it was not known just which song Howard was listening to when he was stopped, the tape contained several lyrics that were openly and notably hostile to law enforcement, one ending with the line "and even cops got shot when they rolled up." It loosely described killings carried out with the very brand of handgun that Howard used to shoot the trooper.

The Davidsons' lawsuit advanced several theories by which they argued that creators and distributors of such lyrics could be held legally liable to victims or their families. They claimed that the lyrics were obscene, though it was clear that the technical legal definition of obscenity could not be met in such a case, however offensive and vulgar the words might be. The plaintiffs also tried to bring some of the rap lyrics under the heading of "fighting words," but here too the narrow and specific criteria simply did not fit. Libel of police officers also found its way into the complaint, although it would have been impossible to prove such a claim without a far more focused set of accusations than those in Tupac Shakur's verses. The Davidsons also argued that some material on the tape was volatile enough to be deemed "incitement to imminent lawless action," and thus forfeited free-speech protection under the First Amendment.

The most intriguing of the Davidsons' allegations, however, was none of the above, but rather the claim that such a tape was a defective and inherently dangerous product, the maker and distributor of which could be held liable to a third party who had been harmed through its use. That element of the case sets the stage for the focus of this chapter, the merits of which we shall return to shortly. Meanwhile, in federal court, the Davidsons' case did not fare well. Tupac Shakur and Time Warner were promptly dismissed as defendants since neither did enough business in Texas to be subject to the jurisdiction of courts in the Lone Star state. The claims against the remaining defendants were almost as easily disposed of by applying relevant Texas tort law principles to each of them and finding the facts legally insufficient to warrant any civil liability. The Davidsons decided not to appeal, and the case thus came to rest in the trial court where it began. This outcome left open an intriguing array of issues that might well come before another court, even though it would be hard to imagine another situation more emotionally appealing from a plaintiff's perspective.

In fact, strikingly similar issues were soon to recur. Eight months after the dismissal of the Davidsons' suit, a 14-year-old student named Michael Carneal carried six guns to his McCraken County, Kentucky, high school one morning. Without any warning, and apparently without reason, he turned one of the guns on and fatally shot three fellow students (Jessica James, Sabrina Steger, and Nicole Hadley) as they gathered to form a pre-class prayer group on the school grounds. Five other students were seriously wounded.

Police immediately seized Carneal's computer and inspected the contents. They found that Michael was an avid Internet user who had downloaded a considerable amount of sexually explicit and violent material. He was also, the police soon discovered, a heavy user of violent video games. He had a passion for violent motion pictures, most especially and recently the film *Basketball Diaries*. That movie contained a particularly graphic scene in which a student kills several classmates with a shotgun. A child psychiatrist who examined Carneal after his arrest concluded that he had been "profoundly influenced by his exposure" to *Basketball Diaries*. She also observed that "the media's depiction of violence as a means of resolving conflict and a national culture which tends to glorify violence further condones [Michael's] thinking."

Soon after Michael Carneal had been convicted of second-degree murder and sentenced to twenty-five years in prison, a second phase of the saga began. The parents of the three deceased children retained an attorney and filed suit in federal court against the producer and distributor of *Basketball Diaries*, the operators of several Internet Web sites that Michael had accessed regularly, and the makers and distributors of violent video games which he had used. Those games were characterized not only as bloodthirsty in content but also as catalysts to the massacre in the school yard — "games which [in the words of the victims' families legal complaint] made the violence pleasurable and attractive, and disconnected the violence from the natural consequences thereof, thereby causing Michael Carneal to act out the violence . . . [and which] trained Carneal how to point and shoot a gun in a fashion making him an extraordinarily effective killer without teaching him any of the constraints or responsibilities needed to inhibit such a killing capacity."

The families' case relied upon two distinct legal theories. On one hand, the parents claimed that the movie and video game manufacturers and distributors and the Web site operators had been negligent—that is, they owed a legal duty to children who might be harmed by a user's violent acts, and that they had breached that duty (by failing to take cautionary measures) to a degree that made them legally liable for the predictable consequences. In such a case, however stark and grim the facts, it would have been virtually impossible to establish any such legal duty for reasons that reflect the reluctance of our legal system to hold one person liable to another, except where an obligation has been voluntarily undertaken or where the relationship between the two people is so close that it naturally creates or imposes such an obligation.

The second theory seemed more promising and recalled the Davidson suit. The Kentucky parents claimed that the video games, and even the film *Basketball Diaries*, were inherently dangerous products, for the harmful or lethal use of which the producers and commercial distributors might be held legally accountable to totally innocent victims such as Jessica James, Sabrina Steger, and Nicole Hadley.

The plaintiffs faced a daunting set of obstacles from the start. Kentucky law is about as unfriendly to such claims of product liability as is the law of any jurisdiction. Moreover, the judge to whom the case was assigned, a senior district judge well versed in Kentucky law, was reputed to be especially unsympathetic to such claims of accountability, however emotionally appealing may have been the parents' plea for redress. Thus, not surprisingly, the entire case was dismissed in April 2000. As with the Davidsons in Texas, the first ruling seems also to have been the last; the Kentucky parents either could not, or chose not to, pursue an appeal to a higher federal court which might have proved more receptive.

While neither case garnered any judicial support, both evoked considerable popular interest and widespread media coverage. They also aroused grave concern and anxiety within the entertainment industry. Though its lawyers and executives remained confident that they could dodge the bullet in particular cases, they could hardly avoid uneasiness about the risks and costs of having to defend against such novel claims of products liability against those who create movies, video games, the lyrics of a rap song, or an Internet Web site. Despite the failure of such claims in the Davidson and James-Steger-Hadley suits, the case that may yield a different result is waiting somewhere in the wings—almost certain to be filed in a state where the law is more congenial to such claims than that of Texas or Kentucky or pleaded before a judge more sympathetic to such claims or, for that matter, a judge openly hostile to violent media. Thus it is vital at this stage to probe the potential for such a claim while it remains a hypothetical but eminently plausible prospect.

These cases occur at the intersection of two seemingly settled and familiar doctrines. On one hand, if you are hurt by a dangerous or defective product, you assume you can sue the maker and seller and recover damages. On the other hand, published words and images have never been thought to be "inherently dangerous" products simply because someone who has seen those words or images then harms, or even takes the life of, another person. We begin with the first of these maxims and then address the second.

Actually, the belief that one may recover damages for serious injury by suing the maker of a defective product has surprisingly recent origins. Through the end of the nineteenth century, and well into the twentieth, a person who had been harmed by the use of a product had to prove negligence to recover damages from the manufacturer or distributor. If the particular item was defectively made, and that defect caused injury, recovery might be possible. But if the source of harm was an *inherently* dangerous (though properly made) object or device, there could be no negligence, and hence no potential for redress. Moreover, it was virtually impossible to bring such a suit against anyone other than the immediate seller, typically a retail store with limited resources. The manufacturer, and even the wholesaler, who had far deeper pockets, remained largely immune from suits by injured consumers, protected behind the doctrine of "privity."

By the 1920s, all that began to change, as courts became increasingly aware of the hazards of manufactured products and of the inequity of denying any recovery to the retail consumer or user—the one person most likely to be at risk in the use of a dangerous product. The great Judge Benjamin Cardozo, then on New York state's highest court, explained thus the rationale of such a departure: "We have put aside the notion that the duty to safeguard life and limb, when the consequences of negligence may be foreseen, grows out of contract and nothing else. We have put the source of the obligation where it ought to be." Starting with New York, and spreading across the country through the twentieth century until it became nearly universal, this view of products liability law marked a dramatic change both for producers and for consumers.

Even so, the products liability doctrine stopped well short of imposing absolute or strict liability. An injured plaintiff must still prove some sort of defect in the product—in its manufacture, in its design, or in the maker's or distributor's failure to warn consumers of a problem of which they should have been made aware. The products liability concept contains several other limitations. There must have been a "sale" in order to trigger the doctrine; harm caused by what was clearly a "service" would not suffice. For the most part, proving that a sale occurred is not difficult in the typical consumer transaction; when it comes to expressive material, as we shall shortly discover, such proof may be problematic.

Other obstacles may confront a products liability plaintiff, reflecting the influence of general common law tort principles. Any such lawsuit must also establish that the alleged defect actually "caused" the harm. Proof of such causation is usually easy enough in the typical case of a physical object that inflicts injury on a user or bystander.

Finally, among the obstacles that such a suit would encounter, it is not always clear that every person harmed by a defective or dangerous product may recover damages in every state. The law varies considerably with regard to the range of eligible plaintiffs. In the less liberal states, recovery is limited to the actual user of the product, thus excluding even predictable bystanders. Elsewhere, some but not all bystanders may recover, while the most liberal states permit recourse even by unlikely bystanders, so long as they can demonstrate a causal link to the product and therefore the defect. Such variations create problems even for those who have been injured by ordinary tangible consumer products; such difficulties are not likely to diminish in the attempt to impose liability on producers of intangible material alleged to have caused serious harm.

If products liability claims are this complex for injured users of conventional consumer items, the prospect of suing publishers and media distributors might appear wholly fanciful. That turns out, however, not to be the case. In fact, there have been a fair number of such suits against publishers of books, newspapers, and other media. Though very few such claims have succeeded, a handful of them have survived in the courts despite the odds. Basic guidelines have emerged from a rather surprising volume of relevant litigation. A diner who suffers severe indigestion from a meal prepared from a printed recipe may think he or she could sue and recover from the cookbook publisher, but such persons invariably learn that that is not the case. Students who are injured when an experiment in a textbook causes disaster may harbor similar expectations, but they soon realize that the courts have a quite different view. Even victims of flawed or incomplete instructions in a manual or "how-to" book have found the courts surprisingly unsympathetic to their quest for redress of harm which they believe is directly attributable to an error in the text.

The pattern for denying recovery in most such cases was set by an Illinois state court ruling in 1937. That court ruled confidently that a reader who became ill after using a dandruff formula featured in the local newspaper had no cause of action against the publisher, even in a state that had fully accepted the products liability concept. Most later cases have reaffirmed the soundness of this ruling and have concurred. In short, one should normally forget about products liability as a source of relief in situations of this type. The printed word may not be totally immune from liability claims, although it surely enjoys a strong presumption against civil liability for unintended consequences.

In addition to the burdens that any products liability plaintiff faces, those who seek damages for allegedly defective words and images encounter four additional hurdles. First is the need to convince a court that the harm has been caused by a "product" at all—a term that easily suits an automobile, tool, or machine but far less readily encompasses a book or magazine, much less a motion picture or a video image. Many courts have been acutely uncomfortable with extending the term "product" to such material and have declined, at least partly on that basis, to impose liability or even submit such a claim to a jury.

The second hurdle is establishing that the transaction was in fact a "sale" —an essential element in a product liability claim by a consumer. To return briefly to the Kentucky suit brought by the families of Michael Carneal's victims, the showing of a motion picture to a theater audience almost certainly would not create the requisite "sale" and thus would not trigger a products liability claim even in a state more friendly to consumer claims than Kentucky. The sale and purchase of violent video games from a store, or through an on-line transaction, would by contrast quite clearly meet that element of the products liability test.

Access to and downloading of material from an Internet Web site would fall intriguingly between the movie display and the video game sale. As University of Kentucky professor Richard Ausness notes in a recent article on these issues, "nothing tangible changes hands" when such digital material on a Web site is received and stored. But he also cautions that "it is hard to characterize this sort of transaction as a service" even where no charge is made for such access. Where there is a charge, either for general access to the site or for particular material, the "service" analogy seems even more strained. It probably will not be long before this precise issue comes before a court that would be ready to consider a products liability claim if it were persuaded that a "sale" had occurred.

A products liability plaintiff must also, as we noted earlier, establish that the injury can be traced to an alleged "defect" in the "product." Courts are quite familiar with that process in conventional consumer product cases. But this task may prove far more difficult in the case of less tangible items. It is especially problematic with respect to literary or entertainment materials, where courts usually conclude that an intervening act of will thwarts a causal link between the producer and the ultimate victim. To be sure, some behavioral science evidence suggests that a nexus exists between certain types of "violent" material and rising aggression levels, if not overt acts. Suffice it to say that the need to prove causation would hamper not only the "copycat" plaintiff but also one who seeks to invoke products liability against a producer or distributor.

Finally, such technical complications in the fit between products liability law and expressive material have been buttressed by judicial concerns about the very nature of the media in which the alleged "defect" is said to be present. When a court imposes liability on the manufacturer of a conventional consumer product, there is no risk of chilling protected speech or of inviting self-censorship within an expressive medium. Yet any damage award against a publisher or media distributor inevitably creates such a risk and thus immediately raises First Amendment concerns. Courts have been understandably reluctant, even where there clearly has been a "sale" of a "product" with a "defect," to allow redress against publishers and distributors. Even where all these elements are present, such claims are all but barred by the First Amendment, and that is often the end of the case.

Illustrative of this dominant view is a leading federal court of appeals decision in 1991 that dismissed a suit by two people who had relied to their detriment on what turned out to be inaccurate information in an encyclopedia of mushrooms and had ingested a poisonous variety. They sued the publisher, G.P. Putnam's Sons, claiming that the misleading classification made the book a "defective product." The plaintiffs cited a recent case in which a French court had imposed liability on the author and publisher of a guide to edible fruits and plants which contained a photograph of a wild carrot that was misleadingly like a poisonous hemlock the plaintiff had eaten with harmful results. In the case of *Winter v. G.P. Putnam's Sons*, the injured plaintiffs claimed that such a work was indeed a "product" that had "defects" for which the publisher should be no less liable than would be the producer of a tainted or poisoned food product that caused similar intestinal injury.

The appeals court declined to accept this analogy and dismissed the mushroom suit. The judges were troubled in part by the attempt to extend products liability beyond the tangible objects and devices for which it had been fashioned and into a realm of intangible materials. Such an extension to the universe of words and ideas could, the court feared, "seriously inhibit those who wish to share thought and theories." The plaintiffs had tried to avoid such a ruling by distinguishing the encyclopedia from literature of other types, for which they could hardly gainsay constitutional protection.

Specifically, the mushroom ingesters sought to analogize their claims to one of the few situations in which plaintiffs have managed to hold publishers legally liable. Damage claims have been brought with some success against producers and distributors of inaccurate or misleading aeronautical charts by victims of crashes that could be traced to navigational errors. Like these maps, the argument ran, the mushroom encyclopedia was a type of work that contained "representations of natural features [and was] intended to be used while engaging in a hazardous activity." Thus, said the plaintiffs, one could impose liability in such a case as this without risking serious damage to free expression.

The appeals court was still not impressed. Charts and maps might be one thing; general books, even relatively didactic ones like a mushroom encyclopedia, were another. Thus, concluded the appeals court, "We decline to expand products liability law to embrace the ideas and expression in a book." And, the panel added, "We know of no court that has chosen the path to which the plaintiffs point."

That concluding comment may slightly overstate the degree of consensus for no-liability. Most courts have indeed reached the same conclusion— in suits against publishers of chemistry texts that contained experiments that could cause explosions, claims against cookbook publishers by victims of indigestion and worse caused by eating meals prepared from recipes in the book, redress sought for disastrous effects of following to the letter guidance set forth in diet and weight-loss manuals, and so on. Two rather striking, but ultimately unsuccessful, suits against travel-guide publishers reflect this dominant view. In one case, the plaintiff had been assured that a particular beach in Hawaii was safe for surfing, which in fact it was not. In the other, a user of the guide sued the publisher for having recommended a hotel in the parking lot of which her husband was shot. These cases reflect the factors we noted earlier—concern that a book is not a conventional "product," that erroneous or misleading words are not a "defect" like a mechanical flaw, and that imposing liability against authors, editors, and publishers may threaten freedom of expression to a degree unlike any other form of civil liability. Characteristic of that latter concern is the conclusion of the western New York court which declined to impose liability on the publisher of a science textbook for injuries that were suffered by a student while correctly performing an experiment described in the book. Most important in barring liability "is the chilling effect [such a burden] would have on the First Amendment." "Would any author wish," the court inquired rhetorically, "to be exposed to liability for writing on a topic which might result in physical injury, e.g., how to cut trees; how to keep bees?" An Illinois judge added that even if the potential chill upon free expression could be avoided, "the adverse effect of such liability upon the public's free access to ideas would be too high a price to pay."

Despite the broad consensus that such statements reflect, two notable exceptions remain, to which we will return shortly. In several other situations, courts have at least seriously considered the prospect of product liability based on published words and have required the publisher's or author's insurance company to defend a products liability lawsuit. In one such case, the insurer had to appear in court to defend the publisher of a separately sold manual for an electrical saw against a claim brought by a reader who had been injured while using the saw. In another such case, a federal appeals court ruled in the mid-1980s that insurers had to defend, and might eventually have to indemnify, a physician who wrote a diet book which one dozen readers followed with serious harm to their health. While such judgments are of course limited to an insurance company's responsibility for representing a beleaguered client and do not imply any final judgment on an author's or a publisher's liability, they do at least represent a foot in the door. For those who watch ominous portents, they cannot be wholly discounted.

There are at least two other situations in which liability might conceivably occur. In the late 1960s, a California court upheld a products liability claim against *Good Housekeeping* magazine based on harm suffered by a reader who used to her detriment a product that had received the magazine's "Consumer's Guaranty Seal." The court stressed several unusual factors in finding the publisher liable. *Good Housekeeping* had actually inspected the injury-causing product and had pronounced it consumer-worthy. The reader had clearly relied on the magazine's "seal of approval" in buying and using the product, and had used it in exactly the way the magazine envisioned. Thus, the publisher had not simply described or even commended the product but had, in the California court's view, created an express warranty about its safety. The courts of many other states would not have been quite so protective even in such a case of specific reliance. California has long been a national leader in imposing strict liability in order to protect even remote users who suffer injury from defective products. Though there appear to be no similar cases elsewhere, courts will occasionally note, as an exception to the rule of non-liability, the situation of a publisher that "expressly guarantees the contents of its publication"—an obvious reference to the *Good House-keeping* case.

Finally, there is one other exception that cannot so easily be explained away. The navigational chart cases represent a curious anomaly. Courts that have held publishers liable for harm resulting from errors in aeronautical maps have focused on two arguably distinguishing factors: the publisher has both "created" and disseminated the harmful information, and the risk of injury or death inheres in the actual use of the charts for the very navigational purpose for which they were designed. These courts have had no difficulty, unlike courts dealing with other types of publications, in classifying the charts and maps as "products" for liability purposes. Apparently meaningful was the fact that such navigational aids are "simply mass produced" and reach every user "without any individual tailoring or substantial change in contents." One federal appeals court which sustained such a claim ruled that a chartmaker owed to pilots "a special responsibility . . . to insure that consumers will not be injured by use of the charts; [the defendant] is entitled—and encouraged—to treat the burden of accidental injury as a cost of production. . . . This special responsibility lies upon [the publisher] in its role as designer, seller and manufacturer."

The few scholars who have pondered these issues have not been kind to the navigational-chart rulings. Professor Lars Noah of the University of Florida argued in a 1998 article in the *Oregon Law Review* that the distinction on which such rulings rely "makes little sense" because "purchasers read and rely on the information in such charts in much the same way that they use the instructions in mass-produced textbooks, cookbooks, field guides, and similar 'how to' manuals, though pilots may enjoy less of an opportunity for reflection than other readers." Professor Richard Ausness, the other current analyst in the area, agrees: "Frankly," he has written, "it is difficult to see how an aeronautical chart is so different from a book that the former item can be classified as a product while the latter is not" (*Florida Law Review* 2000).

Professor Noah is especially critical of a Texas court's tortured effort to distinguish the navigational chart cases in the course of ruling that a magazine could not be held liable for superficially similar content. The Texas judges thought they understood the difference: "The charts were physically used in the operation of the aircraft at the time of the accident. The inaccurate data directly caused . . . the accidents in question in the same manner in which a broken compass or an inaccurate altimeter would have caused a plane to crash." Such an analogy, insists Professor Noah, is indefensible because navigational charts are hardly part of the aircraft's operating equipment.

Logical or not, this anomalous exception to the general rule of publisher non-liability persists. Courts dealing with magazines, newspapers, books, and other media still go to considerable lengths to distinguish the navigational chart cases. Thus, anyone contemplating the future of products liability claims like those in the recent Texas and Kentucky cases should at least bear this special doctrine in mind.

In the interest of completeness, one other legal principle should be briefly noted. Traditional tort law recognizes that one person may sometimes owe to another a duty to warn of known risks or hazards and may be liable for the failure to do so. This is especially the case if the person sought to be held accountable has taken any steps that might either embolden the victim or might deter others from averting disaster by warning the victim or taking other appropriate measures. Such liability may, in rare situations, extend to expressive conduct. In the early 1980s, a Massachusetts federal district judge refused to dismiss a claim that had been filed against a textbook publisher by a junior high school student who had been permanently scarred as a direct result of an experiment involving methyl alcohol. The substance was highly inflammable and did in fact catch fire during the experiment. The student's claim was that the publisher failed, both in the textbook and in an accompanying teacher's manual, to include appropriate warnings about the potential hazards of such experiments. The complaint also alleged that the "design" of the text was deficient. The case came to trial, although it was soon settled for slightly over $1 million. The judgment which kept the case alive to that point in the proceedings was never reported, although it has been noted in other cases and in the legal literature. The clear implication was that this publisher, unlike most others, had implicitly assumed a responsibility to warn users of the text of hazards they might otherwise overlook—a notable contrast to the view that courts have typically taken of publishers of textbooks, cookbooks, travel guides, encyclopedias, and the like.

While no other court seems to have followed this novel ruling, one legal commentator has argued that liability should be imposed on publishers in such cases, at least if a duty to warn exists and an inexcusable failure can be established. Under that view, to take the classic example of non-liability, where a cookbook publisher fails to warn readers of the superficial similarity among natural ingredients and a hapless diner is stricken by the presence of a poisonous mushroom, liability might be imposed on the publisher. According to Lisa A. Powell, the legal rationale for such a result would be "that a publisher can completely avoid all liability by exercising reasonable care to warn of any dangers associated with reliance on the published material" (*Indiana Law Journal* 1983). Most courts, as we have seen, reject any such notion because of its potential scope and the innately chilling effect on authors and publishers. Even Powell, clearly a proponent of stricter accountability for published words, acknowledges hers to be a minority view.

Let us return now to the two cases with which we began and ask whether any plausible basis might exist for imposing products liability on Time Warner for violent rap lyrics or on the producers and distributors of *Basketball Diaries* or gun-toting video games for their inflammatory content. In so doing, we should assume the existence of two ingredients that seem as plausible as they are essential—increasingly creative and resourceful plaintiffs' attorneys and judges who are either inherently sympathetic to hapless victims of violence or are simply more hostile than in earlier times to those who make and market violent media. Even with these two elements in the equation, making a case for products liability against the media is a daunting task at best.

At the start, there are several rather serious definitional or conceptual issues. Television programs and motion pictures, at least when viewed in a theater or over the air, simply could not be brought within the scope of the term "product" for this purpose. Other media are more likely to be covered; the sale of video games, and certainly of books and magazines, do constitute the distribution of products, and even providing for the downloading of software from the Internet may fit, especially if a charge is made for access to such digital material. While some courts have declined to characterize as "products" even such tangible items as newspapers, books, and magazines, that approach seems a rather simplistic way of avoiding liability. We should probably assume that most such materials could be characterized as "products," but that conclusion merely poses the harder issues of potential liability.

Much harder for plaintiffs in such cases is convincing the court that the "product" contains a "defect." Again, an expressive item might be deemed "defective" or "inherently dangerous" if some physical attribute had caused injury—if, for example, a noxious ink made readers nauseous or even stained their clothing, or if the pages had been cut in such a way as to inflict cuts on the fingers of those who turned them. But when the focus is on the message and not the medium, the situation is very different, as most courts have noted in refusing to treat books, magazines, and films as defective products.

None of the several exceptions we have noted in this chapter seem capable of overcoming the powerful presumption that favors authors, editors, and publishers. Unlike the practice of *Good Housekeeping*, editors and publishers do not normally warrant any specific element within the works they have produced—as witness the two fascinating travel-guide cases, which come about as close as any to a potential basis for liability. Nor can most producers and disseminators of expressive material be compared to the producers of the erroneous navigational charts, who represent about the only group of publishers ever to face liability because of the content of the material they have created and disseminated.

Finally, there is the "duty to warn" doctrine, which may deserve a bit more deference than the single case in which a Massachusetts judge found it plausible. If there is an opening for future cases brought by victims or families of victims of material like that on which the Texas and Kentucky suits focused, this is almost certainly it. We should revisit and reassess its potential before concluding that all publishers are always home free. The basis for any such duty to warn would have to be found in state tort law, since that branch of the common law is always the source of such claims. Both the Texas and Kentucky federal judges who ruled against these plaintiffs carefully examined state tort law and failed to find any basis for a legal duty owed by the producer and distributor to anyone—much less to those innocent bystanders who became victims of violent acts committed by people who had been exposed to and arguably influenced by its content. It seems unlikely that the tort law of any state would reach that far, regardless of the state's level of commitment to redress for victims of defective physical products.

Such a theory would encounter deeper difficulties. Even if some sort of duty to warn could be derived from state tort law, how might a producer or distributor of expressive material possibly fulfil that obligation? Suppose Time Warner's lawyers had told the top executives in the recording division that they now owed a duty to warn that certain of Tupac Shakur's rap verses conveyed militantly anti–law-enforcement sentiments. Could one look to warning labels of the sort that several states have recently required to flag violent or explicit lyrics? Can one conceive of any other form of cautionary notice that might deter an impulsive youth with a handgun from threatening or taking the life of a police officer who stopped him on the highway? To pose such questions is to make clear the illogic, indeed the impossibility, of applying the "duty to warn" theory to media of this sort. Textbooks, instruction manuals, navigational charts, and cookbooks, conceivably, but rap lyrics, movies, and video games, definitely not.

Finally, even if tort law could be made to fashion such a claim, freedom of expression should, as most courts considering such issues have ruled, bar recovery of damages in any event. However dubious may be the literary merits of much material which is the focus of liability claims, its protected status under the First Amendment is beyond dispute. It was with a rock concert in mind that the Supreme Court declared in the late 1980s: "Music is one of the oldest forms of human expression; . . . Music, as a form of expression and communication, is protected under the First Amendment." The same has been said of motion pictures, Internet Web sites, and, very recently, by two lower courts with regard to video games, though the Supreme Court has yet to address that medium. Thus, whatever remedies might emerge from a creative or aggressive recasting of products liability law, the prospect that a victim of media-inspired violent acts might recover damages from the producer or distributor of such material seems as remote as ever under the Constitution's free-speech guarantees, and properly so.

8.

The Risks of Advertising

Michael Sakon was an active, athletic 14-year-old in central Florida. While watching television one afternoon, he was intrigued by a commercial for the soft drink Mountain Dew. The ad showed a happy group of teens riding their bikes down a path and then up a ramp. Just beyond the ramp lay a small pond. The bikers rode off the ramp, sailed over the pond, and landed safely on the far side—right next to a frosty and inviting cooler of Mountain Dew, the contents of which they proceeded to savor.

For Michael, who was an avid biker, the exercise seemed too inviting not to emulate. He found a ramp not far from home and built on an embankment ten to twelve feet above a small body of water. Recalling what he had watched the teens do on television, he biked down the path and up the ramp. In real life, however, the experience proved somewhat more daunting than it had seemed in the commercial. After taking off from the ramp, Michael went sailing over the handlebars. He landed, head first, in deceptively shallow water, the bottom having been obscured by its murkiness. The impact broke his neck.

Soon after the severity of Michael's injuries became apparent, his parents retained a lawyer and brought suit in federal court against Mountain Dew's producer, PepsiCo, as well as the TV station and the advertising agency that had created the enticing commercial. The Florida courts have an unusual arrangement by which difficult or uncertain issues of state law that arise in federal litigation may be certified immediately and directly to the state supreme court for a definitive answer, rather than, as is the case in other parts of the country, requiring federal judges to guess how the state courts would have ruled on the issue. So the core issue of the Sakons' case quickly ended up in the Florida Supreme Court. The justices recognized the question of law that had been referred to them by the federal judge as a novel and difficult one of what is called "first impression"—that is, a legal issue that no other court has yet addressed.

There had been a handful of other cases in which venturesome young people imitated stunts they saw on television or read about in magazines. But no case had yet probed the issue of potential liability for inviting such emulation through advertising or commercial messages. The parties were poles apart as they addressed the Florida Supreme Court. For the Sakons, the basis of legal liability seemed clear: PepsiCo had advertised its widely marketed soft drink in a way that created a grave risk of severe injury for impressionable teens who were, after all, its intended viewers and prospective consumers.

For the company, however, the case was one not only of first impression, but one to which, they argued, First Amendment free-speech principles fully applied. In fact, the federal district judge who first heard the case agreed with PepsiCo's position and dismissed the suit—not only because, in his view, the Sakons could not prove the existence of the vital causal link between the commercial and Michael's injury but equally because he believed that imposing civil liability on an advertiser in such a case would violate the free-speech and press guarantees of the Bill of Rights.

The Florida Supreme Court proved to be far less sympathetic to PepsiCo's position. The justices began by rejecting the company's extravagant First Amendment claims. Commercial speech, after all, was fundamentally different from political and other forms of "pure" speech. Advertising had already received some protection from the U.S. Supreme Court but was still not considered fully analogous to political or literary expression. Thus, the proper issue for Florida's high court was whether, under that lower level of protection, PepsiCo enjoyed some degree of immunity from such a damage claim.

On the other hand, the Florida court was not persuaded that advertising claims were simply open season for regulators and juries. The Sakons had cited a host of cases in which draconian curbs on commercial advertising had been upheld by appellate courts. Most of those cases involved direct forms of government regulation, such as the Federal Trade Commission's oversight of fraudulent and deceptive advertising—a far cry from what was now before the Florida court. There had been nothing inherently false, misleading, or deceptive about the ad. The most one could say was that the young models who performed in the commercial were apparently more experienced bikers or had checked the water level before they leaped or had chosen a less dangerous path or perhaps were simply luckier than Michael Sakon. "PepsiCo's commercial," observed the Florida court, "has done nothing more than portray young people engaged in a sporting activity which can be dangerous if not done by skilled persons under proper conditions."

Finally, and most centrally, the Sakons argued that PepsiCo had a legal duty to warn young people who might, to their detriment, seek to emulate the televised stunt. Here the court found ample basis for ruling in the company's favor in settled principles of state common law of torts (or legal wrongs), which made it unnecessary to reach potential free-speech issues. The ad never expressly urged anyone to undertake the daring stunt portrayed on the screen. In fact, it was highly unforeseeable that any young viewer would imitate the leap—that was no more probable, said the Florida court, than that "persons

attending the circus would undertake performance of acts done by the enter-
tainers, whether on high wires, playing with animals or swallowing a sword."
The justices then asked, rhetorically: "Should advertisements of water ski areas warn that water skiing is dangerous, and that one should not attempt to
ski over a ramp? To be sure, there is danger of injury in these sports by one
inexperienced, but does the failure to warn in the advertisement constitute a
breach of duty to one who observes it?"

The Florida judges also wondered whether, if any sort of caution was
needed, "what warning would really suffice in order to avoid liability?" If the
concern were the depth of the water—clearly a contrast between the pond in
the commercial and the puddle that became the site of Michael's real-life
tragedy—then any such warning would need to alert potential imitators to the
risks of water that was too shallow or, for that matter, too deep. And, with
reference to the leap itself, "must he be warned how to prevent the bicycle
from injuring him?" The court's uniformly negative answer to such questions
now resolved the case in favor of PepsiCo and against the Sakons. The family
had no choice but to return to the federal court for the entry of a final judgment dismissing their lawsuit.

Before its final ruling, in *Sakon v. PepsiCo, Inc.*, the Florida Supreme
Court added an intriguing observation: "The product being advertised had
nothing to do with the activity. The advertisement was not directed toward
encouraging others to undertake the sport but only to drink." The suggestion,
which seems to have occurred to no other court dealing with similar issues,
appears to be this: If the sponsor of the exact same ad had been a *bicycle maker*
rather than a producer of *soft drinks*, maybe it could be held liable for injuries
of the kind that Michael Sakon suffered. At least there would then have been
a plausible question about whether a bicycle manufacturer owed some legal
duty to include cautionary language which might deter an unwary teen from
seeking to emulate such hazardous activity—even if the bike itself posed no
special risk.

Had the case involved a bicycle commercial, even though aimed at exactly the same viewer market and posing precisely the same risk of imitation,
the argument runs, the advertiser might conceivably have been held liable on
the theory that bike-makers owe a duty to potential users that carbonated-
beverage producers do not owe to bikers. Had such a different case brought
about a judgment against the advertiser for damages that would in Michael
Sakon's case have been very substantial, courts could no longer avoid the
issues of freedom of speech that the actual suit against PepsiCo had artfully
managed to avoid for non-constitutional (i.e., state tort liability) reasons. It is
now time to enter the world of commercial speech, one of the most perplexing and malleable fields of First Amendment law.

When the Supreme Court first looked at commercial advertising in 1942,
it ruled unanimously that such communication deserved no protection as

"speech" but could be fully regulated, or even totally banned, as "conduct." New York City could, for example, forbid the display of any commercial message but the owner's on the sides of trucks. In practical terms, this meant that the operator of the largest fleet of trucks in the city could proclaim in bold letters that covered the vehicle's entire side "Ship By Railway Express," but it could not, as it wished to do, exhort others to "Smoke Camels." The rationale for such a selective ban, which was fully acceptable to the justices in the 1940s, was that non-owner ads might create traffic problems and cause accidents that owner-based ads would not.

There matters remained for many years. Occasionally the Court was asked to revisit its insensitive view of commercial speech, but it consistently declined to do so. Once in the late 1950s, Justice William O. Douglas dissented alone from the Court's refusal to take such a case; he was ready at least to consider whether advertising deserved some solicitude. Along the way, the Court did confer First Amendment protection on "editorial advertisements"; specifically, a full-page paid civil rights appeal in the *New York Times*. But the very act of defining so narrow an exception for one type of paid message only reinforced the notion that run-of-the-mill advertising remained beyond the range of constitutional "speech."

It was not until 1975 that a new view of commercial speech emerged. That year the Supreme Court struck down Virginia's ban on ads for a New York abortion clinic; at the time the case arose, abortion was lawful in New York but had not yet been legalized in Virginia in the era just prior to *Roe v. Wade*. The justices were not quite ready to overrule the old cases which had denied protection for advertising; instead, they distinguished the earlier rulings on the basis of the content or message. "The advertisement [for the clinic]" noted the Court, "did more than propose a commercial transaction. It contained factual material of clear 'public interest.'" Moreover, the Virginia law imposed a criminal sanction on an editor or publisher for informing readers about abortion services. It also sought impermissibly to extend Virginia's public policy with respect to abortion into other states in ways that were harmful to the free flow of commerce and information. So the abortion-clinic case was an easy one with which to raise doubts without scuttling precedent.

This tenuous distinction would not, however, last even a full year. By the following term, the Court was ready to confer at least partial protection on paid messages that do no more than "propose a commercial transaction." In striking down another Virginia law—one that forbade pharmacists from advertising the retail prices of prescription drugs—the Court signaled that it was ready to confer significant protection on commercial expression of the ordinary everyday type, no longer confining its solicitude to messages such as those that apprised Virginians of the availability in New York of abortion services.

For commercial speech, however, there remained a basic difference in rationale. Most First Amendment rulings primarily protect the speaker's interests, though courts may occasionally stress the value of a listener's or reader's or viewer's interest in receiving information. In the commercial speech setting, the balance has always been reversed. Though challenges to advertising bans are invariably initiated by manufacturers and marketers, the Court has always stressed that its concern is for consumers (who are essentially the readers or viewers in this communicative process).

The basic purpose for protecting the free flow of information about commercial products and their prices has always been to enable consumers to make intelligent and well-informed judgments. "To this end," the Court has stressed, "the free flow of commercial information is indispensable." So, in a curious way, advertisers have become the indirect, though obviously the most substantial, beneficiaries of an expressive right created for the benefit of their consumers. In that sense, the protection of commercial speech is markedly different from recognition of other forms of expression.

Protection for advertising is more limited than for other messages in other respects. In *Virginia State Board of Pharmacy v. Virginia Citizens Consumers Council*, the case in which the Court invalidated the Virginia law that forbade pharmacists from advertising the retail prices of prescription drugs, the justices signaled that they were ready to confer four significant exceptions, which to this day substantially qualify the status of commercial speech. First, the product or service being advertised must not be unlawful; if government had banned the product it could also ban the advertising of it. Second, a commercial message must not be "false or misleading" or "deceptive"—a vital difference between the status of commercial speech and other forms of expression which are not made more regulable on the basis of truth or falsity. Third, the Court left open the "special problems of the electronic broadcast media."

Finally, although much the same could be said of non-commercial expression, the justices reminded us that the government may regulate the "time, place and manner" of commercial messages. Despite these qualifications, even partial protection for commercial speech represented a major shift in First Amendment thinking and created the type of conflict that troubled the courts in the Sakon case and in others we shall shortly examine.

The commercial speech doctrine has had its ups and downs in the past quarter-century. Only two years after *Virginia Pharmacy*, the Justices sustained the ban in Texas on the use of generic trade names by licensed optometrists. The Texas Optometric Board had argued that those who sought eyeglasses might be misled by signs that read "Lone Star Optometrists" or "Alamo Eyewear" but would be reassured by the presence of individual names, whether or not any such names were widely known for professional competence. Such a tenuous rationale sufficed to sustain the ban under the "deceptive and misleading" rubric. In many situations, and this addresses the darker side of the legal profession, regulation of "ambulance chasing" or aggressive solicitation by attorneys has consistently been upheld, including unseemly attempts to gain legal business from vulnerable victims of accident and disaster or their families.

The template which guides commercial speech even today was fully formed in the 1980 case brought by the Central Hudson Gas & Electric Corporation against the New York Public Service Commission. The Commission had sought to ban, on energy conservation grounds, advertising by utilities that was designed to increase use of air conditioning. The Supreme Court majority accepted the state's claim that energy conservation might constitute a valid regulatory interest, thus satisfying the initial inquiry in such a case. But the majority went on to rule that the relationship between that interest and the specific measure which the Commission had chosen to implement it— the "fit" between the means and the end—was so imperfect and imprecise that the ban on utility advertising failed to satisfy the First Amendment.

As the matrix or template for *Central Hudson Gas & Electric Corporation v. Public Service Commission of New York*, the Court articulated what has become the guide to all commercial speech challenges: "At the outset, we must determine whether the expression is protected by the First Amendment. For commercial speech to come within that provision, it must at least concern lawful activity and not be misleading. Next, we ask whether the asserted governmental interest is substantial. If both inquiries yield positive answers, we must determine whether the regulation directly advances the government interest asserted, and whether it is more extensive than is necessary to serve that interest." This formula is still regularly invoked as the Central Hudson test and provides the formula for analysis of all commercial speech challenges.

The Central Hudson case also revealed a nascent split among the justices regarding their views on commercial speech, five years after the doctrine's debut. A comfortable majority was in the middle, firmly convinced that such a standard preserved vital differences between advertising and unprotected speech on one hand, but also between advertising and political or literary expression on the other side. But that balance no longer fully satisfied two groups within the Court. Justices Harry Blackmun and William Brennan, on one side, were troubled that the Central Hudson formula might prove to be underprotective, even though it had seemed to work well enough in that case. They warned that with a better "fit" between means and end, New York could have banned utility advertising for a reason no more urgent than to reduce wasteful use of electricity to cool homes during the summer. "I seriously doubt," Justice Blackmun warned, "whether suppression of information concerning the availability and price of a legally offered product is ever a permissible way for the State to 'dampen' demand for or use of the product."

On the other end of the spectrum, Justice (not yet Chief Justice) William Rehnquist felt the Central Hudson test was dangerously overprotective. He argued that this standard "elevates . . . commercial speech . . . to a level that is virtually indistinguishable from that of noncommercial speech," and that by conferring even limited protection upon advertising the Court had "unlocked a Pandora's Box." Yet the basic constitutional standard had been established in this case by a clear majority in the middle, and with variations over the years it has shaped the resolution of myriad commercial speech cases.

Those variations have occasionally threatened to swallow the rule. At one point in the late 1980s, the Court went so far as to rule that Puerto Rico could shield its residents from casino advertising while permitting such messages to reach off-island tourists. In that case, a bare majority hinted that government might also ban advertising for other "harmful" though lawful products such as cigarettes and alcohol—that the "greater" power to forbid the sale of the product included the "lesser" power to regulate advertising of such products. Such a suggestion, however, proved remarkably short-lived.

By the mid-1990s, the pendulum had swung all the way back. By that time, a solid majority was ready to reaffirm basic principles of commercial speech protection. The Court ruled that Rhode Island could not combat alcoholism through the "paternalistic" solution of denying its residents any information about retail liquor prices—especially in the absence of any credible evidence that such a ban directly and substantially served the arguably valid goal to reduce drinking. The Court was highly critical of the notion that the "greater power includes the lesser" that had been advanced in the Puerto Rico casino case. The justices also reaffirmed their central premise that "the First Amendment directs us to be especially skeptical of regulations that seek to keep people in the dark for what government perceives to be their own good."

The current Supreme Court reflects three rather different, though usually concordant, views about commercial speech. Several of its members feel, as Chief Justice Rehnquist once did, that even partial protection for advertising conforms uncomfortably to First Amendment values and that commercial speech should be kept quite separate and distinct from other forms of expression. At the other end of the spectrum, Justice Clarence Thomas has emerged as the prime proponent of the view that the dominant standard is underprotective—that, even if advertising is not completely analogous to political speech, it nonetheless deserves greater deference than it has received from the courts.

The middle group, for whom Justice Stevens has been the consistent spokesman, finds the current formula sound, workable, and adequately protective; they insist that while consumers need to be fully informed, advertising is still not pure speech and should continue to be regulable in ways and to a degree that non-commercial messages are not. Future cases will undoubtedly bring minor variations on the basic Central Hudson paradigm, but in the near term, at least, they will not likely depart substantially from the principles that have evolved in the quarter-century since commercial speech first received limited First Amendment protection.

Among the genuinely untested issues, as the court recognized in *Sakon v. PepsiCo, Inc.*, is that of potential civil liability. All the Supreme Court's commercial speech cases, and most of those in the lower courts, have involved public agency regulation, not private remedies. *Sakon v. PepsiCo, Inc.* was clearly one of first impression for the Florida Supreme Court, even though the commercial speech doctrine was by that time fairly well developed. The Florida court was conveniently able to avoid the First Amendment issue by finding that the asserted basis of liability did not pass muster under Florida tort law principles, thus leaving difficult and novel constitutional questions for another day and a different forum.

A fascinating pair of cases involving the same publication provides the best insight we have into the conflict between civil liability and commercial speech. *Soldier of Fortune* magazine is not the average airport newsstand monthly. Founded by a retired Air Force colonel in 1975, the same year the Supreme Court gave initial protection to advertising, *Soldier of Fortune* focuses on military exploits and adventures, weapons, and the like. The founder-editor (described by one reviewer of the twenty-fifth anniversary issue as "an egomaniacal macho bumbler" [Peter Carlson, "Still Standing by His Guns," *Washington Post*, October 10, 2000, C1]) appears prominently in every issue, usually in the process of planning or fantasizing about bold and dangerous forays in perilous places.

Soldier's readership has, from the outset, been overwhelmingly male and military oriented and includes a high proportion of owners of powerful guns and camouflage uniforms. The magazine also contains ads, which for some readers evoke greater interest than the news and editorial sections. The quarter-century reviewer recently noted that "the ads are even more delightfully wacky than the articles," covering such matters as "guns and combat knives and ammo 'Cheaper than Dirt!' and multi-page epic ads that tout esoteric hand-to-hand combat systems." Commercial copy in one recent issue promoted a "steroids alternative" that its manufacturer claimed would "raise testosterone levels up to 300 percent." Clearly such messages would be likelier to draw the attention of readers than those lackluster classifieds that fill the back pages of most specialized monthlies.

Soldier also runs personal classified ads on occasion, and it was such a placement that brought its editor to court in the late 1980s and early 1990s. In the October and November 1984 issue, there appeared an ad which read: "EX-MARINES—67–69 'Nam Vets, Ex-DI, weapons specialist—jungle warfare, pilot, M.E., high risk assignments, U.S. or overseas. (404) 991-2684." The person who had placed the ad and could be reached at the listed phone number in Atlanta was John Wayne Hearn.

Robert Black, a Texan who was at that very moment seeking a means of disposing of his wife, saw the ad and called Hearn. After a series of discussions—covering a variety of non-lethal subjects such as the sale of a gun collection—Hearn eventually agreed to carry out the assignment that had attracted Black's initial interest in the ad. A few months later, Hearn did kill Sandra Black, as well as his own girlfriend's husband and her sister. Hearn was soon thereafter arrested and charged with several counts of homicide. At the time of his conviction, Hearn had an honorable discharge from military service and no prior criminal record. The information contained in the ad, including the telephone number, was absolutely accurate and current.

When this sordid saga emerged during Hearn's trial, Sandra Black's son and her mother, Sandra Eimann, retained an attorney to seek whatever legal redress might be available. Hearn, now serving consecutive life sentences, was hardly a promising defendant. *Soldier of Fortune* magazine and its publisher were, however, quite a different matter. So the victim's family filed suit against *Soldier*, advancing the novel claim that it had breached a legal duty by publishing so suggestive an ad, which in fact had led directly to the death of Sandra Black. In the federal district court, the plaintiffs offered extensive testimony describing both the abundance of similar solicitations in *Soldier*'s classified section and the implications for an average *Soldier* reader of the import of the cryptic phrases and other oblique references contained in Hearn's ad.

While such references might be innocuous or even meaningless in most magazines, the Eimanns' expert witness insisted that in the context of *Soldier of Fortune* and its readership, cryptic references such as those in the Hearn ad would invite precisely the sort of interest that brought Black and Hearn together. The jury was asked to answer in its verdict two specific questions— whether the ad was a proximate cause of Sandra Black's death and whether *Soldier of Fortune* had been "grossly negligent" in running the ad. Affirmative answers to both questions yielded a judgment in the Eimanns' favor of $1.9 million in compensatory damages and an additional $7.5 million in punitive damages.

Soldier of Fortune found a far more receptive audience awaiting them in the Federal Court of Appeals, which eventually reversed the damage award. The appeals court found no need to address the First Amendment claims that *Soldier of Fortune* had advanced, buttressed now by an impressive array of media organizations who filed friend-of-the-court briefs. Nor was there any need to probe the countervailing claim, which the Eimanns had pressed in their brief and oral argument, that such protection was inappropriate for a mere classified ad. As in *Sakon v. PepsiCo, Inc.*, this suit eventually was resolved on dispositive common-law tort principles; the appeals court simply found an insufficient nexus between the ad and the murder to warrant civil liability.

Applying relevant rules of Texas law (the murder took place in Texas), the court of appeals concluded that such a criminal act simply was not a foreseeable result of running the ad and that the publisher had breached no legal duty by doing so. Even assuming that a magazine publisher bears some general duty to the reading public, and even recognizing "the appreciable risk that ads such as Hearn's will cause harm," such a prospect did not warrant (as a matter of general tort law) imposing liability on the publisher when tragic results ensue.

Though the basis of the judgment was clearly non-constitutional, the *Eimann v. Soldier of Fortune* court could not wholly disregard the setting of the case and the novelty of the concerns that *Soldier of Fortune* and its friends had pressed. The well-established First Amendment protection for commercial speech (which the ad clearly was) could not be totally disregarded, as the Eimanns had urged. Recalling an earlier case of a very different nature, the appeals court had noted that "the possibility of illegal results does not necessarily strip an ad of its commercial speech protection." A bit later, the court cautioned that "the commercial speech doctrine would disappear if its protection ceased whenever the advertised product might be used illegally. Peanut butter advertising cannot be banned just because someone might someday throw a jar at the presidential motorcade." And, at the very close of the opinion, the appellate judges offered a reprise of the same concern: "The range of foreseeable misuses of advertised products is as limitless as the forms and functions of the products themselves."

Soldier's fortune enabled it to dodge the bullet once, but not twice. Soon after Hearn's notice appeared in *Soldier of Fortune*'s classified section, one Michael Savage submitted, and the magazine published, this ad: "GUN FOR HIRE: 37 year old professional mercenary desires jobs. Vietnam Veteran. Discrete [*sic*] and very private. Body guard, courier, and other special skills. All jobs considered. Phone (615) 436-9785 (days) or (615) 436-4335 (nights) or write: Rt 2, Box 682 Village Loop Road, Gatlinburg, TN 37738." This message caught the eye of one Bruce Gastworth, who had set his mind on killing his business partner, Richard Braun. After collaboration with another business associate produced only three botched attempts on Braun's life, Gastworth saw Savage's ad and felt he had found his means. After brief negotiations, Savage and an accomplice went to Braun's suburban Atlanta home and, while Braun's two sons watched the brutal attack, killed the father in cold blood on his own driveway. Savage and the accomplice were charged with and convicted for the crime.

The Braun family, like the Eimanns, found an attorney who perceived the potential of *Soldier of Fortune* as a defendant; it had pockets substantially deeper than those of the incarcerated assassin. Such a suit was soon filed, and after several years it came to trial. After lengthy testimony, the jury was instructed in great detail (substantially more elaborate than the charge in the Eimann case) on the parameters of tort liability which might encompass liability in such a case.

The jury did return a finding, on each essential element of the charge, in the Brauns' favor and awarded many millions in damages. *Soldier of Fortune* now appealed to a federal court different from the one to which the Eimann case had gone; historically they had both been part of the old fifth circuit, but in the early 1980s Congress created a new eleventh circuit that was based in Atlanta and covered the eastern half of the old fifth circuit. The appeals court was keenly aware that the Eimann case had recently been resolved in the magazine's favor, and it had to give it some deference, though it was not technically bound by precedent from a sister circuit.

The *Braun v. Soldier of Fortune* court stressed two factual distinctions between the cases—distinctions which guided the eleventh circuit to a different result. For one, the nature of the classified message seemed significantly different; where Hearn's notice had been "facially innocuous," Savage's message "conveyed that the advertiser was 'ready, willing and able' to use his gun to commit crimes." Moreover, the trial judge in *Braun v. Soldier of Fortune* had given much more detailed and specific instructions on the relevant issues of tort law. The greater clarity and focus of the judge's charge would make it much more difficult for a reviewing court to reject or overturn a jury's damage award, even in a case with First Amendment implications. Those constitutional implications could no longer be avoided, as they had been in *Eimann v. Soldier of Fortune*, because the *Braun v. Soldier of Fortune* court was prepared to impose a multi-million-dollar judgment on a magazine for material it had published. That was clearly breaking new and hazardous ground, as the *Braun* court readily acknowledged. The court also noted that imposing civil liability in such a case "poses a greater risk than one finds in ordinary commercial speech cases that a state's regulatory regime or tort law will impermissibly chill publishers."

Nonetheless, the court noted important differences between a suit aimed at advertising copy and one aimed at news or editorial content. For one, the publisher of advertising "has a far smaller financial interest" in the advertiser's message or product than in its own. Moreover, since the gist of the judgment was negligence (which the jury had found under impeccable instructions), the Supreme Court had consistently recognized that publishers of *non-commercial* material risked such liability for defamation and similar claims.

Such a ruling would be limited to situations "where the ad on its face, and without the need for investigation, makes it apparent that there is a substantial danger of harm to the public." The jury had been specifically charged that it could hold *Soldier of Fortune* liable *only* if the content would arouse the concern of a "reasonably prudent publisher" that the ad "contained a clearly identifiable unreasonable risk" and that "the offer in the ad is one to commit a serious violent crime." If those conditions were met, a ruling that allowed liability would not impermissibly chill protected commercial speech. That conclusion followed, even though the appeals court clearly understood it was imposing on certain publishers a substantial and extensive obligation to scrutinize advertising copy that might meet such standards.

The decision was not unanimous. Judge Jesse Eschbach, an Indiana federal judge who had recently retired from active duty but continued to sit in other circuits, recognized the case as one on which case law affords "little guidance." He praised his colleagues' "imaginative interpretation of scant precedent," but disagreed with the majority both on the nature of the ad and on the legal adequacy of the trial judge's instructions. For him, the jury had not been charged to find, nor had it unmistakably found, "that this advertisement was a clear solicitation for criminal activity." Nothing less, in Judge Eshbach's view, would warrant "upholding the crushing third-party liability the jury has imposed on *Soldier of Fortune* Magazine."

There is little doubt that commercial messages are quite different from political or literary material, as the contrasting approach of the two courts in the *Soldier of Fortune* cases reminds us. One of those differences—whether an ad promotes an unlawful product or service—was surprisingly muted during the Eimann and Braun litigation, but now it merits closer scrutiny. When the Supreme Court initially gave advertising some First Amendment protection, it made clear that messages which proposed an illegal transaction fell outside that protection. Later, in formulating its Central Hudson test, the justices posed as the first criterion that "commercial speech . . . at least must concern lawful activity."

Suppose the target or focus of an ad is a clearly illegal product or service? In the absence of such a case, we know virtually nothing about how the Supreme Court would treat such a case; none of the commercial messages the Court has reviewed in the past quarter-century have failed to meet the "lawful" standard. The closest the justices ever came was in the Puerto Rico casino case, where they hinted that if an activity such as gambling *could* be criminalized, government might regulate the advertising of that activity as though it were illegal. This notion—that the "greater" power to ban the product includes the "lesser" power to ban the advertising—was to have a short life. The Rhode Island liquor price advertising case in 1996 put any such implication to rest, and it has not resurfaced even in the opinions of its sponsor, Chief Justice Rehnquist.

In the absence of any relevant case law, it is fair to assume that the Court meant what it said—that if a product or service is clearly illegal, an advertisement which promotes it will enjoy no protection under the commercial speech doctrine. Thus, if the *Eimann v. Soldier of Fortune* plaintiffs had established that Robert Black's classified ad in *Soldier of Fortune* could only be read as seeking an assassin, any basis for First Amendment protection would presumably have vanished. The problem was that such a conclusion would clearly apply only to the person who placed the ad and not as clearly to the medium in which it appeared.

Courts regularly differentiate between the individual and the publication for such purposes. Just before the dawn of commercial speech, for example, the Supreme Court upheld the city of Pittsburgh's human-rights law as applied to help-wanted ads in the local daily newspapers; the law barred segregating such ads into "male" and "female" columns, and the justices found this a valid exercise of municipal authority even though it did constrain one facet of editorial policy. Later references to the *Pittsburgh Press* case strongly suggest that the result would have been the same even after commercial speech entered the First Amendment equation.

However, matters were seen quite differently a few years later, when the city and the newspaper were back in court under a different section of the ordinance. This time the law barred the publication of ads containing references to religion, age, and gender—as in "elderly Christian woman seeks position in congenial home" or "young Jewish couple need apartment near Pitt campus." Now, said the Pennsylvania courts, the human-rights ordinance had the effect of curbing protected speech by *individuals* who placed the ads, rather than the *publication* of those ads in the newspaper. The U.S. Supreme Court declined to intervene this time, so the state courts had what seems quite properly the final word.

The distinction between *Pittsburgh Press I* and *II* is crucial and may be helpful in analyzing the presumptive illegality of *Soldier of Fortune* ads. The law violator would be the person who composed and paid for the classified message, not the medium in which it appeared—unless, of course, one could prove that *Soldier of Fortune* or one of its editors had conspired with the individual advertiser or for some other reason the magazine could be linked with the ad's sponsor in a culpable relationship.

Such potential complicity may be difficult to imagine in print, but it seems far more plausible in electronic format. Suppose an on-line magazine includes (as most do) a classified section in its Web edition. And suppose the advertising manager invites interactive collaboration in preparing ads that will most effectively target and attract the attention of the prime audience. Under these conditions, the potential for media complicity seems vastly greater than in the typical print classified situation. No cases have yet raised this intriguing possibility, though interactivity of Web sites and Web editions of publications has begun to play a role in other dimensions of legal liability. Suffice it to say that publishers might be increasingly wary of possible forfeiture of First Amendment protection by assuming a substantive role in the publication of ads that promote an "unlawful product or service."

What about advertising that may not be flatly illegal but skirts the borders? Footwear giant Nike received massive criticism for its commercials (eventually withdrawn) that aired on national television during the 2000 Olympics in Sydney, Australia. One of the ads featured a prominent female runner, who was shown being attacked while bathing in a remote cabin and then being pursued through the woods by a presumptive assailant wielding a chainsaw. The athlete's survival was apparently attributable to her superb condition — and, not trivially, to her choice of Nike shoes for this perilous journey. Though these brutally tasteless ads were pulled long before any legal action could have been taken, serious questions arose about possible liability on the part not only of Nike but also the advertising agency and perhaps even NBC as the Olympic network.

Nike insisted that its ad (a spoof of *The Texas Chainsaw Massacre*) was meant to amuse, but not to terrify, its viewers. A corporate spokesman called the commercial "humane and ironic." Most critics were not the least bit amused. Columnist Ellen Goodman, for one, offered to "explain to [Nike] why a slasher ad is as welcome as a fork in the eye of the Olympic family audience," adding that "this alleged satire of women's fear on a program celebrating strengths didn't strike my funny bone." NBC's decision to cancel the ads after a day or two on the air rendered moot any possible legal proceedings which might have been contemplated against any of the responsible parties.

Had such commercials continued to be shown throughout the Olympics, and had anyone sought legal redress, potential theories of recovery of damages do not come easily to mind — assuming, of course, that the female athlete portrayed as the slasher's intended victim was compensated for the use of her name and likeness. Even if a suit were to be filed by the victim of an attack who claimed her assailant had been inspired by the Nike commercial, courts would routinely decline to impose liability on the basis of legal standards we have already reviewed.

In fact, such an ad would appear to be protected commercial speech, however offensive and unwelcome it was to the vast majority of viewers. The content could hardly be deemed "deceptive or misleading," since the athlete was undoubtedly in far better condition, and fleeter of foot, than her male pursuer. Nor could the message itself be deemed in any way unlawful, unless in some bizarre sense it could have been seen as promoting the illegal use of chainsaws and other potentially lethal devices. This is not to say that the Federal Communications Commission and/or the Federal Trade Commission might not be able to develop policies designed to limit the use of such commercials — perhaps restricting them to hours at which substantial numbers of children would not be watching.

So much for ads of this sort under Nike's sponsorship. Suppose, however, the sponsor had instead been a chainsaw manufacturer. That variation brings us back to an intriguing issue we encountered, but did not pursue, in the case of Michael Sakon and his disastrous bicycle leap over the pond. The Florida court, ruling against the Sakons' claims, posed this distinction: "The product being advertised had nothing to do with the activity. The advertisement was not directed toward encouraging others to undertake the sport but only to drink." This suggestion (not developed in the *Sakon v. PepsiCo, Inc.* case or elsewhere) deserves closer scrutiny.

At least two differences based on the sponsor's relationship to the targeted copy seem to carry potential legal significance. For one, a court might well feel that a manufacturer of bicycles owes a cautionary duty to young people who might use its product in a dangerous fashion—a duty which those who produce and distribute soft drinks do not bear. Though bicycles could hardly be considered inherently dangerous objects, unlike firearms or perhaps even automobiles, there is nonetheless a plausible risk that a venturesome or heedless young biker could misread the feasibility and safety of such a stunt, precisely as Michael Sakon did to his great peril. Such a question might well be submitted to a jury, even though the Florida court properly ruled that no jury should be allowed to consider potential liability on the part of PepsiCo. There seems to be a sufficiently stronger basis from which to infer a bike-maker's duty to warn those who might be influenced or inspired by the very same commercial. Such a ruling might well yield a substantial judgment against the advertiser and perhaps against other parties as well.

Even so, let us not so easily forget that we are dealing with protected commercial speech. Now enter the other legal distinction, which is potentially even more meaningful. It recalls the special treatment by the courts of claims that might be found "deceptive or misleading" in the context of analysis of issues of commercial speech and governmental efforts to regulate advertising. When the sponsor makes and sells soft drinks, the only possible basis for finding the ad to be "deceptive or misleading" is the obvious fact that if you leap over the pond, you may not find the reward on the far side in the form of a frosty cooler containing cans of Mountain Dew. Such potential disappointment hardly makes the ad deceptive or misleading. But when the sponsor makes and sells bicycles, the implication that any healthy young biker could safely emulate the stunt on the screen may assume quite different proportions.

In regulatory matters, an agency's judgment that certain advertising claims could deceive or mislead consumers carries substantial weight with the courts; recall the Supreme Court's exceptional deference to the Texas Optometric Board's view that use of trade names could be inherently deceptive or misleading, even though the optometrist's real name would not likely be a household staple. Thus a court reviewing a *Sakon*-type suit against a bicycle-maker could conclude that the sponsor was unprotected by the commercial speech doctrine—if conditions warranted finding the commercial to be potentially deceptive or misleading.

While we are now well beyond anything that courts have yet encountered, such possibilities are no longer remote or conjectural. It is but one step beyond the actual facts of *Sakon v. PepsiCo, Inc.*—the very same commercial sponsored by a bike manufacturer rather than a purveyor of soft drinks. The result might well be, as the Florida court hinted in a remarkably perceptive dictum, very different in the commercial setting, even though in the non-commercial world the relationship between the speaker and the subject of the message would matter far less , if at all.

It may now be helpful to offer concluding thoughts about potential civil liability for the consequences or effects of advertising copy. The case law is remarkably thin in this shadowy area between commercial speech and civil liability. Yet the several cases we have examined here seem to offer most useful illustrations and variants. The contrasting pair of *Soldier of Fortune* rulings is especially helpful, reaching as they do divergent results that turn only in part on subtle variances in the facts and jury instructions. The starting point in any such case is the substantial difference between commercial and non-commercial expression.

Advertising, which until the mid-1970s was as unprotected as obscenity and child pornography, now enjoys partial, though still far from complete, First Amendment protection. Though all the Supreme Court cases thus far have involved government restriction of advertising rather than private remedies, the principles developed in those cases are not limited to the regulatory sector. The differences between commercial and non-commercial messages are crucial to any legal issues that involve advertising and its consequences or effects.

The premise that free speech does not condone promotion of an unlawful product or service is profoundly important, although its implications remain largely untested in the courts. Non-commercial speech may occasionally be curbed because it promotes unlawful activity—but only, the Supreme Court has stressed repeatedly, if it constitutes "direct incitement to imminent lawless action" and is likely to bring about such action. No such "clear and present danger" test protects commercial speech. If the ad deals with illegal drugs or seeks to sell handguns to minors or promotes prostitution, no more need be said. The potentially limiting effect of this crucial distinction remains to be tested, though the *Soldier of Fortune* cases hint at the significance it may assume in the context of advertising for unlawful services.

The other basic difference concerns the "misleading or deceptive" canon. In the regulatory setting, this factor yields marked contrasts between treatment of commercial and non-commercial messages. Its potential relevance for civil damage suits remains to be tested, even in the lower courts. Our analysis of the Sakon case and its variants should begin to suggest how this distinction might bear on civil-liability judgments. Here, as with the "unlawful" exception, the impact of such a finding cannot be exaggerated.

If advertising is found to deceive or mislead, or simply to create the possibility that consumers might be deceived or misled, then its message is stripped of all First Amendment protection, and it becomes as vulnerable to both public and private remedies as commercial messages were a half-century ago. Whether or not a *Sakon*-type commercial sponsored by a bike manufacturer would be deemed "deceptive or misleading" is a difficult and elusive question, but it is one that surely merits closer attention. The case that will bring this issue to court is probably not too far in the future.

9.

"The Movie Made Me Do It!"

On the evening of March 8, 1995, Patsy Ann Byers had just taken over behind the counter of a convenience store in Ponchatoula, Louisiana, when an armed robbery occurred. The robbers, teenagers Sarah Edmondson and Benjamin Darrus, opened fire in the store, and a shooting spree followed. Byers was seriously wounded and became a paraplegic. She died of cancer three years later. During the trial of Edmondson and Darrus, it became clear that they had been obsessed by a recently released motion picture, *Natural Born Killers*. One scene of the film portrays the armed robbery of a store and the fatal shooting of several people in that store.

Given this information, Byers's family filed suit against Time Warner and its subsidiaries, which had produced *Natural Born Killers*. The suit also named the local chain of movie theaters in one of which the assailants had seen the film. Producer Oliver Stone was later added as a defendant. The family's claim was that "all of the Hollywood defendants are liable . . . for distributing a film which they knew or should have known would cause and inspire people such as . . . Edmondson and . . . Darrus, to commit crimes such as the shooting of Patsy Ann Byers, and for producing and distributing a film that glorified the type of violence [Edmondson and Darrus] committed against Patsy Ann Byers by treating individuals who commit such violence as celebrities and heroes."

The Louisiana trial judge examined the barrage of pleadings, motions, and cross-motions which had come from both sides in this now widely publicized case. He concluded that "the law simply does not recognize a cause of action such as that presented in [Byers's] petition." Accordingly, he dismissed the suit against most of the defendants. The plaintiffs, emboldened by support they had received from victims' rights groups and others who had watched the case, decided to appeal.

By the time the case reached the Louisiana Court of Appeals, a dozen more shootings around the country had been traced to the impetus or inspiration of *Natural Born Killers*. At least one other lawsuit was filed (in a Georgia state court) against the producers and distributors.

The media community was by then acutely aware of, and understandably uneasy about, the potential of such cases, which could significantly alter the legal landscape. For the past thirty years or so, victims of "copycat" crimes had sought to impose liability on those who created and disseminated violent material. They had been almost uniformly unsuccessful in court against a broad range and variety of films, books, television programs, magazines, and other media. Now that comfortable pattern was about to change.

The Louisiana Court of Appeals ruled that the *Byers* case must go to trial. The issues reached that court in a preliminary posture, where every argument the plaintiffs advanced in their complaint must be accepted as true, even though when the case went to trial those allegations would need to be proved. The complaint alleged, for example, that motion-picture producers and distributors owed a legal duty to people like Byers and in this case had breached that duty. The conclusion was that the film industry could be held as legally liable here as, let us say, a theater owner would be liable to injured moviegoers if a faulty ceiling fell on them and caused serious injury. The plaintiffs also claimed that they could prove the producer intended in this case to cause impressionable viewers of the film to emulate in real life the violence they saw on the screen. Accepting for purpose of argument the validity of such claims, the appeals court ruled that the Byers family had a valid case if the evidence brought out at a trial did show that "the Warner defendants are liable as a result of their misfeasance in that they produced and released a film containing violent imagery which was intended to cause its viewers to imitate the violent imagery."

On that basis, however challenging it might be to prove such culpable conduct on the producer's part, the Louisiana court held that the Byers family should have an opportunity to do so. The court considered, but flatly rejected, free-speech claims which the defendants had advanced and which had received substantial (indeed usually dispositive) deference in a host of other "copycat" cases. This case seemed to the appeals judges basically different because here the plaintiffs had alleged—and thus had assured the court they were prepared to prove—that Oliver Stone and Time Warner had actually intended that *Natural Born Killers* should have precisely the effect it apparently had on Byers's assailants. When the case returned to the trial court, the claims against the producers and distributors were dismissed in mid-March 2001, reinstating the judge's initial ruling. Not only could the plaintiffs not establish the degree of intent they had alleged, said the trial judge; even if they could do so, recovery of damages would in his view be barred by the First Amendment. Thus Oliver Stone and the other entertainment defendants were dropped from the suit, leaving in the case only the insurer of one of the killers' families. Plaintiffs' attorney Joe Simpson announced that he would again appeal, a process that would likely prolong further an already protracted case.

The Louisiana court was heavily influenced by another case that was working its way through federal court about the same time. A brutal killing had taken place several years earlier in a Maryland suburb of Washington, D.C. The killer was a professional hit man, James Perry, recruited for this purpose by Lawrence Horn, who wished to eliminate his paraplegic son Trevor and ex-wife Mildred so that (as the only surviving beneficiary) he would control the proceeds of a substantial settlement the son had received after a successful medical malpractice suit. After James Perry had been tried and convicted, it turned out he had ordered from Paladin Press a copy of a book entitled *Hit Man: A Technical Manual for Independent Contractors*. The book contained graphically detailed instructions on how to carry out an execution — though the subtitle suggested one could do so "without being caught" (and that part of the book's promise apparently eluded this reader). The family of the victims sued the publisher in federal court. In a complex pre-trial stipulation, the publisher's lawyers agreed that, solely for purposes of a preliminary ruling, their client had "intended" that the *Hit Man Manual* would be used as it had been by the hired gun in this instance, to kill innocent people.

Despite such a startling concession, a federal district judge ruled in the publisher's favor and dismissed the suit. Recently appointed after long service as a U.S. attorney, Judge Alex Williams was hardly naive about brutal crime. But to him it seemed obvious that "books do not kill; only people kill." Whatever Paladin Press and its lawyers might have conceded in the stipulation, such a suit simply could not go forward. He found legally dispositive both the particular facts of the case and the general state of the law. The circumstances did not impress him as overly favorable to the plaintiffs' claims. The book had been in print for over a decade before the assassin ordered it, and thirteen months had passed between receipt of his copy of the *Hit Man Manual* and the actual killing. Thus, despite striking similarities between his modus operandi and the instructions in the book, the close nexus that tort law would require for such a judgment did not seem present.

Even more persuasive for Judge Williams was the bearing of the First Amendment in such a case. Whatever its lack of literary merit, such a book seemed to him clearly protected expression. It was not obscene, did not contain "fighting words," and was not commercial speech. The only basis on which it could be denied such protection, he ruled, was a finding that it had directly "incited" lawless action. The plaintiffs had creatively sought to apply several cases in which authors and publishers (for example, of manuals on how to evade income taxes) had been held criminally liable for "aiding and abetting." But Judge Williams ruled that whenever the content of the message was "advocacy" (as it seemed to be in the *Hit Man Manual* case), the First Amendment would not permit courts to impose liability, no matter what label such a claim carried. In short, however ingenious the attempt to find a side or back door that might be opened if the First Amendment barred the front door to such a liability claim, the Constitution's guarantee of free speech and press simply did not allow recovery of damages for the effects of advocacy or incitement.

The Court of Appeals for the Fourth Circuit saw the *Hit Man Manual* case very differently. For starters, Judge Michael Luttig, who wrote the opinion, was the son of parents who had been brutally murdered two decades earlier under circumstances so close to those of the *Rice v. Paladin* case he had seriously considered recusing himself but in the end decided he could be objective. The court for which he wrote, in reversing Judge Williams, found that the publisher, through its novel stipulations, had made a nearly fatal concession; in their pleadings, Paladin had acknowledged a degree of intent that would overcome the normally impenetrable First Amendment barrier. That the defendant was a publisher and that the basis of the case was a book were troubling but, in the end, not legally disabling factors.

The appeals court set forth at length the lethal instructions which the *Hit Man Manual* contained and which the killer had followed to a rather striking degree. Those instructions seemed more than merely descriptive or illustrative of how successful murders had been carried out in the past. They seemed to contain a didactic, even hortatory, quality that brought the *Hit Man Manual* within the ambit of the "aiding and abetting" cases (several of which had been decided by this same court). The tone was not simply "Here's how it has been done" but "Here's how you should do it"—a subtle but, to the appeals court, legally significant contrast. The hired killer, said Judge Luttig, had been "readied by these instructions and steeled by these seductive adjurations." He had, from start to finish—from first contact with a client to disposal of the bodies—"followed many of the book's instructions" down to a level of detail unlikely to have been coincidental. Then, as though to confirm such inferences, came the stipulations regarding intent, through which the publisher had virtually conceded every vital element of a plaintiff's case.

Finally, there was of course the First Amendment issue, which had been dispositive for Judge Williams. For the appeals court, the "incitement" doctrine did not occupy the entire field, as it had for the district judge. If state law permitted recovery for "aiding and abetting," as Maryland's law did, then a case could be brought against "speech acts" which caused serious harm. There were still two possible barriers, however. One was the undoubted need for a higher level of intent in a case that targeted expression as this one did—but that very element could be met here through the stipulations to which the publisher had mysteriously acceded. The other possible stumbling block for the court of appeals was the risk that such a doctrine, once applied to speech, could reach genuinely protected advocacy. That prospect took the appeals court back to the novel circumstances of this case (both the facts and the stipulations), on the basis of which the judges felt that the *Hit Man Manual* could be comfortably distinguished from other "copycat" situations in which seemingly similar claims had been uniformly dismissed.

Then the court reminded readers of how it perceived the *Hit Man Manual*—a book with a "declared purpose . . . to facilitate murder," arguably directed at "a discrete group rather than to the public at large" and apparently "marketed directly and even primarily to murderers and would-be criminals." Thus the stipulations were not only fatal to the threshold ruling on the case but might even be within range of potential proof at trial. At least that was an option the plaintiffs ought to have.

Finally, Judge Luttig insisted that the content of this book was far removed from abstract advocacy which the First Amendment would protect, even if inflammatory. The *Hit Man Manual* was, to the contrary, a detailed compendium of specific instructions on how to violate the law or evade detection while committing the most heinous of crimes. Moreover, unlike most protected expression, "ideas simply are neither the focus nor the burden of this book." Thus, the First Amendment concerns that had troubled courts in other analogous cases simply did not rise to a comparable level here.

The appeals court concluded by seeking to reassure the media and entertainment industry about the potential scope of its ruling. Despite the concerns expressed in amicus curiae briefs by publishers and others, such anxiety was unwarranted. The ruling in *Rice v. Paladin* , wrote Judge Luttig, could not properly serve as precedent for imposing liability wherever any redemptive element existed—a "political, educational, entertainment, or other wholly legitimate purpose"—even for depicting homicide or mayhem. Specifically, no comparable inference of actionable intent could be drawn in suits against "almost any broadcast, book, movie, or song that one can imagine" since such material could still confidently claim a First Amendment shield that had eluded Paladin Press.

Such narrowing language may initially have reassured movie producers such as Oliver Stone, who saw *Natural Born Killers* as the sort of entertainment material to which the *Rice v. Paladin* ruling did not apply. Such comfort proved quite premature. Barely six months later, the Louisiana Court of Appeals disregarded the distinction. Without noting either the obvious factual differences or the court's own limiting language in *Rice v. Paladin*, the Louisiana judges simply invoked *Paladin* as persuasive precedent—apparently on a basis no stronger than the presence in both cases of allegations of "intent." It was enough for the *Byers v. Edmondson* court (the *Natural Born Killers* case) that the Fourth Circuit had found the *Hit Man Manual* to be "not protected speech"—a sufficiently broad ruling to give that judgment persuasive force in a case that dealt with markedly different material—indeed, material of the very type the *Rice v. Paladin* court seemed to insist its ruling should never reach.

Thus, within a matter of months, the legal landscape had changed dramatically. The safe harbor that publishers, producers, and distributors had taken for granted for decades had suddenly vanished. The *Rice v. Paladin* decision alone would have been ominous enough, though the initial reaction to the Fourth Circuit's ruling was to take the appeals court at its word and assume it was, as Justice Oliver Wendell Holmes once wrote of a Supreme Court case he wished to confine to its facts, a "ticket for this day and train only." The Louisiana court's ruling on *Byers v. Edmondson* shattered even that comforting assumption. Now, suddenly, the ground rules are very different for those who create and disseminate material that might lead someone, however deranged, to commit mayhem. Though it is too early to tell how far these early precedents may extend, and what other expressive conduct they might possibly reach, it is none too soon to appraise the sea change that has occurred.

Rice v. Paladin and *Byers v. Edmonson* are not quite unique in contemplating media liability for violent acts. There was one early precursor, a California case so far back in time and factually so different that distinguishing it had become routine. The case came to court because one Saturday morning, several youths were in their cars chasing radio-broadcast clues that led them all over the San Fernando Valley in search of a disc jockey who kept himself a mile or two ahead of his nearest pursuer. Eventually, the clues led the youths to a shopping center where the clue-giver had stopped. The first listener to locate him would receive the reward, which was less than $25. On the freeway off-ramp that led to the mall, one of the youths forced a small car off the road which contained an elderly couple named Weirum. The husband was killed when the car rolled over. The widow and her children sued the radio station and its parent, RKO General. The suit, which was filed in California state court, sought damages for wrongful death, claiming that the station had been negligent in promoting so inherently dangerous an activity.

The California Supreme Court, writing on an essentially clean slate in the mid-1970s, agreed with the Weirum family and sustained the damages which a trial judge and jury had awarded. Several factors persuaded the court that recovery for damages was appropriate here: The chase was inherently a high-risk activity, creating a wholly foreseeable risk of the sort of tragedy that actually befell the Weirums. The tantalizing clues were aimed at young radio listeners who had to be willing to take chances in order to track down the disc jockey. The contest was part of a promotional scheme to raise weekend ratings and attract new listeners.

Thus all the essential elements existed to support a traditional tort claim of negligence—in fact, a level of fault that approached intentional harm. The only remaining barrier was the inescapable fact that liability here would be based solely on words. The disc jockey's clues would elsewhere have been protected by the First Amendment. They were neither obscene nor "fighting words."

Even so, the California State Supreme Court dismissed the free-speech claim with uncharacteristic brevity and indifference: "The First Amendment does not sanction the infliction of physical injury merely because achieved by word, rather than act." Finally, the court sought to narrow the scope of what it recognized to be a portentous ruling—especially in the state that was home to the motion-picture industry and produced much of the material seen on television. The facts seemed to the *Weirum v. RKO General* court so exceptional that the media should not worry about the prospect that "they will henceforth be burdened with an avalanche of obligations."

That prophecy proved eminently sound through most of the ensuing quarter-century. The next case to reach the California courts offered a crucial test. It was the classic copycat situation. A 9-year-old girl named Olivia Niemi had been savagely beaten on a San Francisco beach. The manner in which a gang of boys attacked her, including the insertion into her body of a toilet-plunger handle, so closely resembled the modus operandi of a very recent NBC television special entitled *Born Innocent* that the victim's family sued the network for having caused her injuries. When a superior court judge initially dismissed the case, an appeals court sent it back for trial, noting that the material might lie beyond First Amendment protection. That view soon yielded, however, to the network's insistence that "incitement is the proper test here" and that unless the TV program could be shown directly to have incited the attack—which the plaintiff's attorney candidly conceded it could not—that was the end of the case.

One further issue received passing attention. The Niemi family's lawyer had argued that while First Amendment protection clearly covered news broadcasts and documentaries, the status of fiction was less certain. The court rejected this suggestion, finding it "too blurred" to have practical value, and noting the Supreme Court's comment in regard to film that "what is one man's amusement, teaches another's doctrine." Such a distinction seems not to have recurred in later civil-liability cases, though eventual government efforts to regulate violent entertainment in the 1990s foundered in part on the uncertainty and "blurred" nature of that very same line between fact and fiction on the air.

After the initial ruling in *Niemi v. National Broadcasting Company*, no court ever doubted the soundness of this view, until *Rice v. Paladin* and *Byers v. Edmondson*. The constitutional basis for such consistent rejection of civil-liability claims deserves closer scrutiny. Though the First Amendment had theoretically protected freedom of speech and press since adoption of the Bill of Rights in 1791, it was not until World War I that courts began to define the scope of those liberties. In a group of cases that involved anti-war protest and draft resistance, the Supreme Court articulated the earliest standard, that of "clear and present danger." What survived far longer than the formulation itself was Justice Holmes's memorable epigram—"the most stringent protection of freedom of speech would not protect a man in falsely shouting fire in a theater and causing a panic." Marvelous sound bite though it is, this aphorism may have created more problems than it solved. Though we routinely refer to a "crowded theater"(adding an adjective Holmes did not use) and just as routinely omit the "falsely" (which he did include), there are several other complications. The last phrase, "and causing a panic" suggests that the legal judgment must always depend on the result. In fact, however, at the close of the very same paragraph, Holmes largely dispelled that notion, writing that "we perceive no ground for saying that success alone warrants making the act a crime."

Perhaps the gravest flaw in the clear-and-present-danger formula was the ease with which Holmes's less-sensitive colleagues were soon able to invoke his test to sustain convictions based on nothing more than abstract advocacy of subversive doctrine. Justice Louis D. Brandeis joined Holmes in dissent, insisting that "it is only the present danger of an immediate evil or an intent to bring it about that warrants Congress in setting a limit to the expression of opinion." In a companion case of the mid-1920s, where the majority candidly conceded "there was no evidence of any effect resulting from the publication and circulation of the Manifesto," Holmes and Brandeis drew a sharper line: "If in the long run the beliefs expressed in proletarian dictatorship are destined to be accepted by the dominant forces of the community, the only meaning of free speech is that they should be given their chance and have their way."

Toward the end of the decade, still in dissent, Brandeis (joined again by Holmes) codified First Amendment doctrine in language that has a strikingly prescient ring: "If there be time to expose through discussion the falsehood and fallacies, to avert the evil by the process of education, the remedy to be applied is more speech, not enforced silence. Only an emergency can justify repression." Curiously, that view governed Supreme Court rulings in the decade of the 1930s, one seldom noted for liberal views on such issues as federal power or economic legislation. The convictions of several radical labor organizers and other agitators were reversed by a strict application of clear and present danger.

By the outbreak of World War II in 1941, the Court had fully accepted the Holmes-Brandeis view of political speech. The formulation suggested how far the dissenters of the 1920s had carried the day: "The substantive evil must be extremely serious and the degree of imminence extremely high before utterances can be punished." As proof of the Court's acceptance of this stringent standard, contempt citations issued during a bitter labor dispute against a newspaper and a union leader were set aside, even though one could have found, as the lower courts did, that their menacing words directed against a California trial judge might appear to compromise the fairness of justice at an extremely tense time.

Two decades later, the court went even further, refusing to allow a trial judge to gag a deputy sheriff for making similarly unsettling statements about a grand jury inquiry. The guiding principle was by now firmly cast: "In the absence of any showing of actual interference with the undertakings of the grand jury, this record lacks persuasion in illustrating the serious degree of harm to the administration of law necessary to justify exercise of the contempt power."

The Supreme Court did waver in several internal security cases of the 1950s, seeming to revert to the less protective view of the 1920s. By sustaining criminal charges for conspiracy to advocate and teach the violent overthrow of the government, the justices seemed once again to accept the view that if the danger was sufficiently grave, a criminal charge based solely on words might suffice, however remote the prospect that such words would produce violent action against the government. The test which the majority adopted had come from Judge Learned Hand, writing in the Communist conspiracy case for the court of appeals: "In each case [courts] must ask whether the gravity of the 'evil,' discounted by its improbability, justifies such invasion of free speech as is necessary to avoid the danger." With the benefit of a half-century's perspective, the Communist conspiracy cases today seem a tragic, if wholly understandable, aberration. Moreover, the majority in these cases acknowledged that, although never overruling the callous judgments of the 1920s, "subsequent opinions have inclined toward the Holmes-Brandeis rationale."

The stage was thus set for the current era of First Amendment doctrine. In 1969, a unanimous Court adopted the test that still governs: "The constitutional guarantees of free speech and press do not permit a state to forbid or proscribe advocacy of the use of force or of law violation except where such advocacy is directed to inciting or producing imminent lawless action and is likely to incite or produce such action." The facts of the case declaring this doctrine confirmed the Court's commitment to this standard. Charges had been brought against a Ku Klux Klan organizer named Ernest Brandenburg on the basis of a highly inflammatory speech to followers and partisans in a field in southwest Ohio. The crux of the charge was violation of a state law that was virtually identical to a federal provision which the Court had earlier sustained. But the prosecution never proved there was an "imminent" threat of lawless action or that the speech contained "direct incitement" or that violence was likely to ensue. Such a failure or omission was now fatal to any charge against advocacy.

One minor refinement was to complete the Brandenburg test a few years later. It came in a classic street-corner agitation case from Bloomington, Indiana. Gregory Hess had worked up a crowd of passionately anti–Vietnam War protestors near the Indiana University campus. While fanning the flames of hostility against the Indochina war, Hess said either "we'll take the fucking street later" or "we'll take the fucking street again." After being charged with a breach of the peace and convicted in state courts, Hess sought Supreme

Court review under the recently announced Brandenburg standard. There he prevailed, a clear majority of the justices finding his speech to be protected by the First Amendment.

Two factors proved dispositive: First, Hess did not openly advocate imminent law violation; "at worst, [his statement] amounted to nothing more than advocacy of illegal action at some indefinite future time." Because there was no proof that Hess's "words were intended to produce, and likely to produce, *imminent* disorder, those words could not be punished by the State on the ground that they had 'a tendency to lead to violence.'" The other flaw in the case against Hess has even more direct bearing upon our discussion of civil liability, to which we shall shortly return: "Since the uncontroverted evidence showed that Hess' statement was not directed to any person or group of persons, it cannot be said that he was advocating, in the normal sense, any action." The clear import of this ruling is that under *Brandenburg v. Ohio* and *Hess v. Indiana*, at least for purposes of criminal liability, a statement must have been targeted or directed to an audience where its impact would likely be an unlawful response.

That is a very high standard indeed. It protects a substantial amount of deeply unsettling speech, even some which might result in violence but would not meet the other desiderata. In the United States we set the bar that high because we accept Justice Brandeis's view that "prohibition of free speech and assembly is a measure so stringent that it would be inappropriate as the means for averting a relatively trivial harm to society" and that "among free men, the deterrents ordinarily to be applied to prevent crime are education and punishment for violations of the law, not abridgment of the right of free speech and assembly."

So much for criminal sanctions on speech. What about civil liability, the very different prospect of imposing money damages against a speaker whose words lead to some sort of harm, injury, or damage to property? It could be argued that the circumstances are wholly different, and that the Brandenburg-Hess principle constrains only the prosecutor, not the private plaintiff. As early as 1964, the Supreme Court ruled that civil suits for libel, at least, were subject to the same First Amendment limits. "What a State may not constitutionally bring about by means of a criminal statute," wrote Justice Brennan for a unanimous Court, "is likewise beyond the reach of its civil law of libel." The issue of how far beyond defamation that doctrine should extend remained a subject of conjecture for nearly two decades.

The justices clarified the issue considerably in a 1982 ruling. A group of civil-rights protestors successfully urged a boycott of retail stores in a Mississippi town, pressing African-American shoppers not to buy where they could not obtain jobs. Though the protest and boycott were mostly peaceful, there were a few violent incidents. There were also some strong threats from the boycott's leaders. After they had suffered substantial loss of business from the boycott, Claiborne Hardware and sixteen other merchants sued the demonstrators for substantial damages. They recovered in the state courts, but the NAACP sought and obtained further review on First Amendment grounds.

The Supreme Court took a very different view of the boycotted merchants' claims. They noted that although there had been some violence and the demonstrators had done more than simply assemble for peaceable protest, the target of the damage suit was a complex mixture of various elements. The First Amendment, cautioned Justice Stevens on behalf of the majority, would not bar recovery for the direct effects of illegal or violent conduct, and if the judgment had been so limited it would almost surely have been sustained. But the scope of the award was far broader, including all losses "resulting from the boycott." Thus some part of the damage award might well have been based not on conduct alone; it may also have included some speech.

Civil liability may not, under the First Amendment, be imposed on the basis of expression that fell short of what the Brandenburg and Hess cases had made subject to criminal sanctions. In measuring the permissible scope of a civil damage claim against the boycott's leaders, Justice Stevens invoked precisely the test that would have applied had this been a criminal prosecution: "When an advocate's appeals do not incite lawless action, they must be regarded as protected speech." Thus *NAACP v. Claiborne Hardware* is appropriately cited for the vital conclusion that speech is as fully protected against civil damages as it is against criminal penalties.

One possibly limiting factor should be noted. The case did involve a civil rights protest, to which the Supreme Court has always given exceptional protection: "Speech to protest racial discrimination is essential political speech lying at the core of the First Amendment," wrote Justice Stevens in *NAACP v. Claiborne Hardware*. Yet nothing said in this case, or in the nearly two decades that have followed, suggests any understanding on the Supreme Court's part that the shield which it had created for speech that did not meet the standards established in *Brandenburg v. Ohio* and *Hess v. Indiana* should be limited to a particular, albeit especially favored, subject matter. Where civil liability in later cases has been imposed—against militant abortion protestors, for example, and racist tormentors—it has been the nature of the charged activity, not the worthiness or unworthiness of the group or its message, that warrants the different outcome.

It is now time to look more closely at how lower courts have treated claims of civil liability against creators and distributors of expressive material. The cases fall broadly into three categories. The largest number of them, like the cases involving the *Hit Man Manual* and *Natural Born Killers*, result from acts committed by a person who has read or viewed violent material and has emulated that material in doing harm to others. A few of the cases, however, seek recovery for harm which the reader or viewer has done to him or herself. There is a third type of case, in which the basis of claimed liability is not so much that the producer and distributor created a model or pattern that was followed in doing harm, but rather that they created an "atmosphere" of violence within which mayhem and carnage are predictable results. Although the results have been remarkably uniform across the three types of cases, each deserves distinct analysis.

The lower federal and state courts entertained in the 1970s and 1980s a host of copycat cases very much like *Rice v. Paladin* and *Byers v. Edmondson*. Judges consistently ruled in these cases that entertainment media may not be held liable for the violent acts of a reader, viewer, or listener. Such judgments rested on two now-familiar premises—first, that state tort law did not impose an actionable duty on the producer and distributor, and second, even if such a duty did exist, civil damages would unduly burden the free expression of those involved in the creative process. The results varied little from state to state, or from one medium to another, and encompassed a wide range of literary and artistic material.

Quite typical was an important judgment of the Supreme Judicial Court of Massachusetts, relieving Paramount Pictures of any liability in a 1989 suit. The case was brought by parents of Martin Yakubowicz, a teenager who was stabbed to death on a subway car by an assailant who had just seen Paramount's *The Warriors* and who turned upon his young victim in a manner strikingly reminiscent of the film's most violent scene. The case was unusually appealing because of several factors. National promotions and previews of the film had featured graphic images of carnage and bloodshed. The Boston release date was chosen to take maximum advantage of a mid-winter public school break.

Paramount had actually learned of the film's darker potential some days earlier when violence erupted after initial screenings in Palm Springs and Oxnard, California. The studio took the extraordinary step of urging local theaters to hire extra security guards while they were showing *The Warriors* and offered to reimburse them for any extra security expenses. The Boston theater had accepted Paramount's offer on the very day the fatal stabbing occurred. The next day, Paramount took the additional, even more exceptional, step of offering to release from contractual liability any theater-owner who felt that exhibiting *The Warriors* might "pose a risk to persons or property." The film's national advertising campaign was canceled that same day.

Even with such a record, the Bay State's highest court wavered not the least from the now-uniform view of such claims. Despite Paramount's undoubted knowledge of the movie's capacity to bring out the worst in some who saw it, the court ruled that the studio had breached no legal duty to the general public. Indeed, since the case reached the high court on a motion to dismiss, the issue was not which party had the better of the merits but whether the Yakubowicz family could present its case to a jury—whether, in short, there was any genuine doubt about the legal boundaries. In the absence of evidence that would show direct incitement to imminent lawless action, and thus satisfy the Brandenburg-Hess test, no such doubt existed.

The court actually screened the movie for itself to be certain that "nothing in it constitutes unprotected incitement." Since the target of the suit was material protected by the First Amendment—the U.S. Supreme Court had given substantial if not complete protection to motion pictures in the early 1950s—nothing less than incitement would suffice, regardless of what might be the proper standard in a suit brought against a brewer or distiller or gunmaker for creating an unreasonable risk leading to the death of an innocent bystander.

Though far fewer in number than the classic "copycat" cases, several lawsuits have sought to hold producers and distributors liable for creating an environment that seems conducive to violence. Two such cases will illustrate both similarities and differences in the "atmospheric" liability area. Florida teenager Ronny Zamora claimed in a federal court complaint he and his father filed in the late 1970s that he had become "involuntarily addicted" and "completely subliminally intoxicated" by massive exposure to television. It was solely for that reason, his family insisted, that Ronny had fatally shot his 83-year-old neighbor—an act of violence for which he had been convicted and was then serving prison time. The suit named the three major commercial television networks (the Fox network had not yet emerged and cable's share of home entertainment was still negligible).

The district court recognized this to be the first—and as it would turn out, also the last—case of its kind. Any attempt to apply traditional principles of liability foundered on the breadth of the alleged broadcaster responsibility. It was not as though Ronny's alleged video obsession could be traced to a single show, or even a series, much less a station or even a network. The culprit was simply television, in the abstract and in its entirety. That was too much for Judge William Hoeveler, a seasoned jurist who would later earn fame when he presided over the trial of Panamanian dictator Manuel Noriega. After the plaintiffs persistently declined his suggestion to narrow or sharpen the focus of their suit, Judge Hoeveler wrote that "the standard demanded is so devoid of guidance and so lacking in a showing of legal cause that the complaint must be dismissed." Before doing so, however, the judge emphasized his concern for the potentially chilling effect of any such recourse upon protected expression such as television programming. Even a far more precise link between cause and effect—for example, a claim that a specific program had caused Ronny Zamora's attack on his aged neighbor—would be deeply troubling. Absent proof of incitement that would satisfy the Brandenburg-Hess standard, the First Amendment simply barred recovery.

The other "climate" or "environment" case was very different. A young woman named Jocelyn Vargas was shot as she walked down a San Francisco street toward a bus stop after leaving a movie theater where she had just seen

Boulevard Nights. In her suit against the producers and distributors of the film, she claimed that her unknown assailant must have been a "member of the general public prone to violence . . . who had been attracted to the Alhambra Theater by the showing of said violent movie." The defendants, she argued, had set in motion a predictable scenario with the highly probable consequence of an attack such as the one which befell this hapless victim. To her and others within and outside the theater, the entertainment producers and purveyors owed a duty of care which they had breached by failing to warn of potential disorder.

The appeals court immediately recognized the novelty of the case. The author of the opinion was Judge Joseph Grodin, a seasoned San Francisco civil liberties lawyer who was later a California Supreme Court justice. The producers and distributors predictably argued they were fully protected by the post-*Weirum* judgments; California courts by this time had confined *Weirum v. RKO General* virtually to its facts. But such a defense was not even in the ballpark, insisted Vargas and her lawyers. As the court summarized the plaintiff's novel claim, "they do not seek to impose liability on the basis of the content of the motion picture—indeed, they suggest that so far as their theory is concerned, the movie might as well have been 'Mary Poppins' rather than 'Boulevard Nights.'" Indeed, Vargas's point was not that the film's *content* had incited the act that cause her injury, but that the *act of showing it* "would attract members of the public who were predisposed to violence."

This was indeed a novel variant upon conventional liability claims, and it gave Judge Grodin and his colleagues some pause. Yet they concluded, after close analysis, that the treatment of such a claim could not differ because the asserted basis of liability was ingenious. If liability could be imposed on a filmmaker because of knowingly creating a climate or context of violence or for showing a film that would attract an unruly crowd, the result would be no less chilling to speech than would a damage award based directly on the film's content. The only warnings a producer or exhibitor could possibly issue "would deter substantial portions of the public from attending" the theater at all.

Moreover, drawing perceptively upon his academic experience, Judge Grodin sensed the relevance of a First Amendment doctrine seldom if ever applied in this area—the "heckler's veto." Courts had long insisted that where a volatile speaker stirs up a crowd, "the first obligation of government is to maintain the peace and enforce the law, and not to silence or punish the speaker." There was a clear parallel to this case. If the arrival of angry gang members could make the creators and exhibitors of the film potentially liable for whatever happened, regardless of the film's content, then those who asserted such claims could "in effect . . . dictate what is shown in the theaters of our land."

Finally, if the focus of such a suit truly was not the *content* of a particular film but the *process* of creating and distributing motion pictures, even incitement theory would give injured persons no recourse, since the *activity* of making and disseminating films was fully protected. In this sense, the Vargas plaintiffs may have been too clever by half. Their ingenious attempt to avoid the frying pan of the post-*Weirum* rulings (which consistently refused to impose liability) may be what forced them into the fire of total First Amendment protection for an unexceptionable creative activity. Such a novel theory of liability might, of course, have fared better at the hands of a less sensitive and learned judge than Joseph Grodin.

Indeed, the U.S. Supreme Court had recently taken a step that now seems quite relevant to and consistent with the outcome of *Bill v. Superior Court* (the Vargas case). While towns and cities may not bar non-obscene films on the basis of their content, the justices ruled in 1976 that municipal zoning powers could be used to regulate the business activity of "adult" theaters, bookstores, and other establishments featuring sexually explicit material. The basis of that and later rulings was concern for the "secondary effect" that such businesses might have on the neighborhood. The Court has continued to insist in such cases that it has not invited communities to restrict or penalize the *content* of what is displayed in these establishments but simply permits regulation of a type of *business*. Somehow the *Bill v. Superior Court* plaintiffs never made the connection between their theory of civil liability and the zoning power over "adult" theaters, or if they sought to do so, they were arguing before the wrong judge. Thus, the "climate" or "environment" theory of civil liability has foundered badly in the two cases that have advanced it. One has the feeling that this approach never had the hearing it may deserve, and that creative lawyers for plaintiffs may someday bring it back to life in a much more lethal form. But for now, we note it here mainly for historic interest.

There is a third type of copycat case—one that effectively argues "the book or movie made me do it to myself." These cases are subtly different, as four examples will indicate. Eleven-year-old Craig Shannon was watching the televised *Mickey Mouse Club* one afternoon in the winter of 1978. The program featured, as the announcer declared, "magic you can create with sound effects." One especially appealing trick involved filling a balloon with air, adding a BB pellet, and then rotating the balloon at increasing speeds to simulate the sound of a tire peeling off a car. Craig did just what he had seen on the TV screen. Instead of hearing a magical sound, he suffered partial blindness when the lead pellet broke through the balloon's wall and landed in his eye.

The Shannon family sued Walt Disney Productions, creator of the Mickey Mouse series, and the channel on which Craig had viewed the "magical sound effects" segment. A trial judge summarily dismissed the case, finding no basis for tort liability and believing that such suits were barred by the First Amendment. The Supreme Court of Georgia recognized, however, that the issue was not so easily resolved. The high court had first to contend with the *Weirum* case from California, recent enough and at least superficially similar enough to warrant its attention. The *Weirum* ruling, wrote the Georgia judges, had been properly confined to situations where the charged message is no less than an incitement to imminent lawless action, essentially the Brandenburg-Hess standard. Thus, *Weirum v. RKO General* was of no help to the Shannon family's claim.

Nor was there any comfort to be gleaned from a series of "pied-piper" cases in which, typically, someone gave a child the keys to a car or an aggressive ice-cream vendor lured heedless children into the path of an approaching truck or bus. Such enticements or inducements also differed from the *Mickey Mouse Club* segment in that the defendant in those cases had usually "provided the child with the instrumentality causing the injury"—something that could not be claimed of a TV demonstration or description. Finally, the Georgia Supreme Court recognized an unavoidable First Amendment risk; allowing recovery for damages, even in an appealing case like that of the Shannon family, would "open the Pandora's box" and "would have a seriously chilling effect on the flow of protected speech through society's mediums of communication."

Not long after Craig Shannon's injury, 13-year-old Nicky DeFilippo was watching *The Tonight Show* on the Providence, Rhode Island, NBC station. Host Johnny Carson was chatting with his guest, a professional stunt man who was about to show Carson how he could drop through a trap door with a noose about his neck and emerge intact. The guest cautioned his audience that "it's not something you want to go out and try." He recalled a friend who had emulated the hanging routine, "just fooling around, and almost broke his neck." Carson himself underscored this warning to the unwary or foolhardy among his viewers. After a commercial break, a blindfolded Carson successfully performed the stunt, to the delight and amazement of the studio audience. Nicky, alone in his basement, tied to a water pipe a noose which he had knotted, placed his neck in it, and let go. Several hours later his parents found him, hanging lifeless from the pipe, the TV set still on and tuned to the NBC channel. Nicky was apparently a devoted Johnny Carson fan, for whom that affection had brought no grief until this moment. Moreover, he was apparently the only person among millions of *The Tonight Show* viewers who suffered any mishap from the daring stunt.

The DeFilippo family sued the local station, the network, and the producers, seeking substantial damages for their son's tragic death. Like the Shannons, they relied heavily on *Weirum v. RKO General*, which remained the only precedent supportive of such a claim. Like the Georgia court, Rhode Island's judges rejected the analogy and ruled in favor of the media defendants. Neither traditional tort law nor First Amendment precepts would warrant recovery in such a case, at least short of proof of incitement which would satisfy the Brandenburg-Hess standard. Such proof would be even harder here to marshal than in *Shannon v. Walt Disney Productions, Inc.* because of the warnings that both Carson and his guest had issued before performing the stunt. To the familiar concerns about potential liability, the Rhode Island Supreme Court added another factor: If liability could be imposed because one child came to grief by imitating what he had seen on television, the result would "invariably [be] self-censorship by broadcasters in order to remove any material that may be emulated and lead to a law suit."

By the mid-1980s, the courts seemed to be of one mind about such cases. There were on the way, however, two other cases of self-inflicted wounds that would test the emerging consensus. John Daniel McCollum was a deeply disturbed youth in his late teens who was living with his parents in a Los Angeles suburb. One night in the fall of 1984, he was lying on his bed listening endlessly to morose lyrics recited by Ozzie Osborne. The unconventional but highly popular singer had earned notoriety not only through live performances, in one of which he bit the head off a bat, but by the morbid emphasis some of his lyrics placed upon the act of suicide. One of those verses (the finale to his "Suicide Solution") would become John McCollum's fixation on that fateful evening. He listened over and over again to Osborne's implied invitation to "get the gun and try it—shoot, shoot, shoot." And that is precisely how McCollum did indeed end his life. His parents found John lifeless on his bed, the Osborne tape still running in his headset.

The family brought suit in a California state court against Osborne's studio and distributor, seeking heavy damages for their son's death, which they alleged was induced or inspired by Osborne's counsel. The trial court quickly dismissed the case. The appellate court recognized that this claim had arisen not many miles from the site of the *Weirum* case, and within the same legal system. But everything that had occurred in the interim had confined *Weirum* to high-risk commercial promotions likely to incite impressionable listeners. Here it could hardly be said that Osborne (much less his record producer or distributor) was engaged in such activity. Apart from the often aimless ambiguity of the lyrics, "there is nothing in any of Osborne's songs which could be characterized as a command to an immediate suicidal act."

Even if such language could have been found on the tape, the California court would have balked for another reason: "Musical lyrics and poetry cannot be construed to contain the requisite 'call to action' for the elementary reason that they are not intended to be and should not be read literally on their face, nor judged by a standard of prose oratory." Finally, the California judges shared the growing concern of other courts about the potential for self-censorship that such claims posed: "Musical composers and performers, as well as record producers and distributors, would become significantly more inhibited in the selection of materials if liability for civil damages were a risk to be endured for publication of protected speech."

The last of the notable self-destruction cases involved not a film or TV program or lyrics on a disc or tape but, of all things, a magazine article. *Hustler* included in its August 1981 issue an article entitled "Orgasm of Death." The text described the practice of "auto-erotic asphyxia," which combines masturbation with "hanging" in order to cut off the blood supply to the brain at the moment of orgasm. Whatever allure the title and details might initially have conveyed, readers were warned that this the routine was "neither healthy nor harmless" and were told very directly that this was "one form of sex play you try only if you're anxious to wind up in cold storage, with a coroner's tag on your big toe."

Nonetheless, one Troy D., a venturesome 14-year-old *Hustler* reader in Texas, did attempt the procedure which the article described and lost his life in the process. The mother of the victim, Diane Herceg, sued *Hustler* in federal court for having caused the death of her son. She was joined in the suit by her son's young friend, who suffered severe trauma when he discovered Troy's lifeless body. The trial judge, applying the Brandenburg-Hess standard, ruled that nothing less than proof of incitement would warrant recovery. Nonetheless, the plaintiffs persuaded a sympathetic jury that the article amounted to incitement, and on that basis they recovered moderate damages. The federal appeals court eventually reversed, ruling as had the other courts in the 1980s that liability could not be based on published material that offered even the marginal literary value of "Orgasm of Death." So long as the Brandenburg and Hess cases supplied the relevant legal standard, that task was virtually impossible. The appellate court strongly implied that a magazine article would never generate a liability claim sufficient to satisfy the First Amendment— and surely not in this case. Moreover, the court noted that, like Johnny Carson and his stunt man, *Hustler's* editors had sought to dissuade readers from taking the path which the article so vividly described.

However, the *Herceg* case sounded the first discordant note in what had been, since *Weirum*, a harmonious judicial symphony of non-liability. Judge Edith Jones dissented sharply from the majority's view of the appropriate standard for such cases. In part, she seems to have been influenced by her low regard for the medium itself: "Hustler," she wrote, "is not a bona fide competitor in the 'marketplace of ideas.' It is largely pornographic, whether or not technically obscene." While perhaps not subject to an outright ban, such publications seemed to Judge Jones far less deserving of First Amendment solicitude than the *New York Times* and others for which the Supreme Court had fashioned full protection. Like other inhabitants of the nether world of "low-value speech"—libel and advertising—"pornographic" magazines made for Judge Jones a modest claim, at best, to Constitutional protection. Thus, the Brandenburg standard simply should not apply in the absence of "public advocacy of controversial political ideas." And even if the Brandenburg case did supply the proper legal test, the Supreme Court had recognized there that "the state's regulatory interest legitimately extends to protecting the lives of its citizens from violence induced by speech."

Beyond her general disdain for the medium, Judge Jones found highly suspect the article that caused the tragedy. That particular piece, she insisted, posed a grave risk for the young and impressionable reader. Despite the disclaimers, the article offered a powerful inducement through its graphic and detailed account of auto-erotic asphyxiation. Emulation was not only foreseeable but highly probable. Thus, she would have allowed a jury to find, as the jury in fact had found in this case, that money damages offered an injured reader proper redress against an irresponsible publisher of marginal material.

Curiously little attention was given at the time to Judge Jones's potentially disquieting dissent. In fact, her words were to prove prophetic a decade later. More cautious observers, or observers less confident that courts would continue to rule summarily in their favor, might have taken closer note of such a discordant voice. But the unanimity of the lower court judgments in the post-*Weirum* period undoubtedly induced a dangerous degree of complacency in the media community that only the reality of *Rice v. Paladin*, the *Hit Man Manual* litigation, would ultimately challenge.

It is now time to return to the most recent period and the reshaping of the legal landscape which seems to have occurred. For the first time in a quarter-century—virtually the entire life span of copycat litigation—there is a very serious prospect that those who create, produce, and distribute expressive material may be held liable for harm that others inflict after having read, viewed, or heard such material.

The basic question we face is whether *Rice v. Paladin* and *Byers v. Edmondson* are aberrations or whether they represent a fundamental change in the way courts and judges view such claims. There is support for both theories. On the "aberration" side, the two recent cases are distinguishable in several significant respects. Both *Rice v. Paladin* and *Byers v. Edmonson* involved truly brutal, heinous crimes—each widely publicized for reasons that were wholly unrelated to the role of the *Hit Man Manual* or *Natural Born Killers*. The savage attacks that led the victim's families to seek relief against Paladin Press and Time Warner were of a very different order from the catalytic events in most of the earlier cases. Not surprisingly, these became the first such cases in which national victims' rights groups weighed in as friends of the court in support of the plaintiff families.

Moreover, the quality of legal counsel pressing the victims' case was also of a different order from most of the earlier copycat suits. In *Rice v. Paladin*, the Rice family had as their advocate in the court of appeals University of Richmond law professor Rodney A. Smolla, author of award-winning treatises and articles on free expression. His commitment to take on the case, fully recounted in *Deliberate Intent*, a book-length analysis of this remarkable litigation, seemed a departure from his lifelong defense of expressive and creative interests. Yet he became convinced that one who profited commercially from distributing material such as the *Hit Man Manual* did not merit categorical First Amendment protection. In that respect, Smolla's may have been a minority view, but surely he is not alone among deeply concerned First Amendment experts.

The source of expert legal counsel for the plaintiffs in *Byers v. Edmondson* was even more remarkable. The day before Sarah Edmondson and Benjamin Darrus, the rampaging teenage killers, entered Patsy Ann Byers's store in Ponchatoula, Louisiana, they randomly shot and killed a cotton-gin operator named Bill Savage in Hernando, Mississippi. Hernando, it happened, was the community in which John Grisham had practiced law before he began writing about it. Bill Savage had been a close friend, news of whose death evoked Grisham's anguish. The author not only comforted Savage's widow, but after the next attack he offered support to Patsy Byers's family. Later, as the police investigation progressed, Grisham learned that Edmondson and Darrus had been obsessed with *Natural Born Killers* and that the film was by now linked to at least a dozen copycat slayings across the country—far more than even the most violent of previous films.

At this point Grisham publicly indicted producer Oliver Stone, who, he charged, "always takes the high ground in defending his dreadful movies." *Natural Born Killers*, Grisham conceded, "was not made with the intent of stimulating morally depraved young people to commit crimes," but he went on to suggest that "such a result can hardly be a surprise." The catalytic role of the film in the killing of his friend and others seemed beyond question to Grisham. Though young people like Benjamin Darrus may never before have exhibited violent behavior, "once he saw the movie, he fantasized about killing and his fantasies drove [him and Sarah Edmondson] to commit their crimes."

Moving to the issue of redress, John Grisham suggested that in extreme cases such as the one that had touched his life, recovery of damages might be warranted, even though both the courts and the entertainment industry had resisted such a prospect. "It will take only one large verdict against the likes of Oliver Stone and his production company, and perhaps the screenwriter and the studio itself, and then the party will be over." Such a judgment would likely occur far from Hollywood, "in some small courtroom with no cameras." In such a setting, "a jury will finally say enough is enough; that the demons placed in Sarah Edmondson's mind were not solely of her making." Some months later, Grisham explained that his initial comments reflected "the heat of the moment." Yet, even after being "roundly criticized" by media lawyers and others, he insisted he "still [had] no regrets," adding of *Natural Born Killers*, "it's been responsible for more killing than any other movie."

Upon learning of Grisham's charge, Stone took umbrage and faulted his critic for maintaining a double standard. The "party" on which Grisham had now blown the whistle was one from which he, too, had benefited. "The fact is," Stone fired back, "Mr. Grisham has become a very rich man off a body of work which utilizes violent crime as a foundation for mass entertainment." But Grisham's resolve to assuage the death of his friend was unlikely to be thus abated.

In fact, Grisham had already taken steps to place the Byers family case in the hands of a respected Louisiana lawyer, Joe Simpson. At the opening legal strategy session, Simpson recalled Oliver Stone's own boast following the premiere of *Natural Born Killers*: "The most pacifist people in the world said they came out of this movie and wanted to kill somebody." Simpson added his own scenario for the lawsuit that he would soon file: "That's the starting point —to delve into Stone's mind." The allegations in the complaint soon to be filed tracked that prospect, claiming that Stone and his colleagues had not simply created and distributed an exceptionally violent film, but that they *intended* the film to cause susceptible moviegoers "to begin, shortly after repeatedly viewing same, crime sprees such as that which led to the shooting of Patsy Ann Byers." It is precisely such evidence which Mr. Simpson insists would warrant keeping the case alive, despite the trial judge's second dismissal of all claims against the producer and distributor. The appeals court (and by implication the state supreme court) have already evidenced their receptiveness to such claims. A further appeal, and the persistence of this case as a challenge to a quarter-century of apparent media immunity from such legal threats, seems inevitable.

Therein lies the third of the distinguishing factors. In both *Rice v. Paladin* and *Byers v. Edmondson*, unlike the earlier copycat cases, the complaint alleged that the material had been produced and marketed with a clear *intent* to cause harm to innocent victims. Indeed, in the *Hit Man Manual*, the publisher actually *stipulated* that such intent existed—conceding, for the purpose of initial rulings, a vital element of the case that would have had to be proved in court if the case had ever gone to trial. The issue of intent plays out similarly in *Natural Born Killers*, though for a different reason.

When a defendant files a motion to dismiss, and argues, as did Stone, Time Warner, and the other defendants, that the case against them could not prevail under the law even if were fully proved, any factual issues are resolved in the plaintiffs' favor. All the factual allegations in the complaint, however implausible they might seem, are assumed to be true. Thus, in both cases the defendants were willing to assume that, even if such an intent could be proved (however improbable that may have been), no legal liability could have been imposed. Thus, the legal posture of these two cases, at the point where the crucial rulings were made, differs markedly from prior copycat suits.

To summarize the "aberration" theory before moving to the "sea change" view: The facts of both *Rice v. Paladin* and *Byers v. Edmondson* are far worse than those of most cases in which media defendants have avoided liability.

The defendants in both cases are, for that and other reasons, undoubtedly less appealing than the networks and other more familiar targets of civil-liability claims. Advocacy on behalf of the victims' families is of a substantially higher quality, and both cases have received unprecedented support from victims' rights groups. And, as we have just seen, these cases uniquely reflect a concession by the defendants that they were not only careless, or even callous, but that they actually intended that their material be used to kill innocent people.

One could simply put these two judgments aside and assume that the law will soon resume its normal course. Modest support for so comforting a conclusion comes from the trial judge's dismissal of the suit brought against the producer of the movie *Basketball Diaries* and video-game makers on behalf of the victims of Michael Carneal's Kentucky schoolyard shooting. Yet it seems risky to dismiss *Rice v. Paladin* and *Byers v. Edmondson* as pure aberrations or to assume that the legal landscape remains essentially unaltered. If only because of the direct impact of the former case upon the latter—the Louisiana court's heavy reliance on the fourth circuit's judgment on *Rice v. Paladin* as a major basis for refusing to dismiss the Byers family's suit—such an assumption would be unduly complacent.

Moreover, once victims' groups and plaintiffs' lawyers taste media blood, as now they clearly have, life will never be the same. Those who plead such cases on behalf of victims and their families have learned an invaluable lesson. It took a British columnist, writing in the fall of 1999, to capture the portent of the initial rulings in the *Natural Born Killers* case: "For the Hollywood lawyers a nightmare was unfolding. Step by step a court system is moving towards the unthinkable—making the producers and distributors accountable for the copycat violence resulting from their movies." Under such reasoning, one might dismiss *Rice v. Paladin* alone as an aberration but not *Byers v. Edmondson* as well.

How much of a sea change has occurred? Though it is too early to predict with confidence, a few base points emerge. First, we should recall how the copycat cycle began a quarter-century ago. The starting point was the California Supreme Court's declaration in *Weirum v. RKO General* that words uttered by a radio talk-show host were not absolutely protected against civil liability by the First Amendment. The circumstances were unusual there, to be sure—a radio station's commercial promotion designed to boost Saturday-morning ratings, an inherently dangerous activity induced by the announcer's "clues," and a tragically predictable accident befalling a blameless elderly couple. However often this case has been distinguished, and it has become increasingly easy to do so over the years, it remains on the books as a reminder of what were once the views of a court which, in later judgments, would be probably viewed as most sympathetic to media defendants. Should the same or a very similar case return to the California courts, it seems unlikely that *Weirum v. RKO General* would be overruled.

Second, even before reaching First Amendment issues, most of the post-*Weirum* cases foundered on the grounds of state tort law. Plaintiffs, with surprising persistence, advanced a basis for liability that simply could not be proved—typically, that a publisher or producer or distributor owes not only a general duty of care but specifically owes such a duty to an innocent bystander. Courts either find no such duty in the law of the state or conclude that the intervening act of a third party (or of the victim in the self-wounding cases) creates a fatal break in any possible chain of legally actionable obligation. The posture of the *Hit Man Manual* and *Natural Born Killers* suits changes all that, since a claim of *intent* to harm bystanders essentially bypasses or avoids the need to prove a duty and its breach. While it seems unlikely that another media defendant would concede such intent, as Paladin Press did through its stipulations, the lawyers for plaintiffs will almost certainly allege intent, as the Byers's attorney did in the *Natural Born Killers* complaint.

Such an assertion in the initial complaint presents the publisher or producer with a kind of Hobson's choice—either concede the claim for purpose of argument by entering a motion to dismiss (as Oliver Stone and Time Warner did in the Louisiana courts) or risk going directly to trial on a set of facts likely to arouse the sympathy for the plaintiffs (as happened in the trial court in the *Herceg v. Hustler* case, where only the intervention of a divided court of appeals eventually saved the day for publisher Larry Flynt). Thus, when it comes to state tort law, media defendants can still confidently expect early dismissals if the case is based on negligence. If, however, culpable intent is alleged, the implications may be very different indeed.

Third, even the most sympathetic courts have never held that media defendants are categorically entitled to First Amendment protection from any and all civil liability. Rather, judges have for the most part invoked the Brandenburg-Hess incitement test and have then ruled that the facts before them could not possibly satisfy that rigorous standard. To some degree, the plaintiffs and their lawyers bear the onus for what amounts to a self-inflicted wound. With surprising consistency, they have assumed they had to prove incitement and then, too late in the litigation, have found (and sometimes conceded in court) that they could not possibly do so. Here too, the rules may have changed; at least no victim's attorney is likely ever again to make such an assumption or concession.

Two basic questions now merit our attention: Could a copycat claim ever amount to "incitement"? and May liability be imposed on a media defendant without meeting the Brandenburg-Hess standard? The federal appeals court gave affirmative answers to both questions in the case of *Rice v. Paladin*, and without separate analysis the Louisiana appeals court concurred. On the first issue, whether a copycat claim could ever constitute "incitement" as the Supreme Court defined that term, the conventional wisdom would reject such a prospect on at least two grounds. The opinion in *Brandenburg v. Ohio* defined regulable advocacy as "*direct* incitement of *imminent* lawless action." Both terms would be difficult, if not impossible, to satisfy in such a case. The facts of *Rice v. Paladin* suggest how far from "imminent" was the activity for which Paladin Press was said to be culpable. The book had been on the market for a decade before the assassin ordered it, and his copy remained on the shelf for over a year before it could have played a part in the killings.

On the other hand, Professor Smolla argued, and the court of appeals seemed to agree, that "imminence" need not be confined solely to the time between purchase and crime but may envision a more gradual process during which the effect of the catalytic words operate to produce a harmful result. So relaxed a view of "imminence" seems wholly at variance with the Supreme Court's rigorous view, dating back well before *Brandenburg v. Ohio*, indeed to the much earlier insistence of Justices Holmes and Brandeis, that suppression of speech may occur only if "the incidence of the evil apprehended is so imminent that it may befall before there is opportunity for full discussion."

The same is true of the "direct" requirement. In the case of *Hess v. Indiana*, the justices reversed a speaker's conviction because even though he addressed a live audience before him, the charged words were not clearly "directed to any person or group of persons." If that constitutional criterion is not met even in such a face-to-face situation, it would be hard to imagine a book, magazine, movie, or TV program ever being sufficiently "direct" to satisfy the standard.

A plausible variant may suggest the scope of the doctrine. If Paladin Press had operated an interactive Internet Web site, on which it invited prospective assassins to provide specific details and in response to which the publisher delivered specially tailored assassination plans, civil liability resulting from the execution of such a plan would presumably meet the "directness" standard. (There might still be issues of "imminence," but that would be a different question.) Nothing less "direct" than a communication of that type would appear to be what the Supreme Court had in mind in imposing very rigorous criteria on legal sanctions for speech of the type these cases present.

The final issue, of course, is whether the Brandenburg-Hess doctrine provides the sole avenue of civil liability, or whether speech of a similar type that causes harm might be reached by other means. The appeals court in *Rice v. Paladin* insisted that in states such as Maryland, where "aiding and abetting" was actionable, speech so defined could be made the basis of civil liability (or recovery of damages) regardless of the "clear and present danger" doctrine. That view certainly has a more than superficial appeal. As we saw in Chapter 1, not all words are protected by the First Amendment. Not only are obscenity and child pornography unprotected, but words used to further a conspiracy, to solicit or induce a crime, or to carry out the role of an accessory before or after a crime may be punished or made subject to a civil suit without abridging the speaker's First Amendment freedoms.

Several paths might lead one to such a conclusion. For one, there is a lingering uncertainty about whether *Brandenburg v. Ohio* applies as fully to entertainment as to political advocacy and as completely to civil as to criminal liability. The Supreme Court has directly addressed the civil/criminal issue only once, in *NAACP v. Claiborne Hardware*; the majority opinion created as many problems as it solved, though it seemed to say (and most lower courts have assumed) that civil and criminal sanctions were subject to the same constitutional standards. Even the *Rice* and *Byers* courts seemed to accept that equation, and we should not be less willing to embrace it. The more troubling concerns involve the nature of the material and the theory of legal liability.

It could be argued, as Judge Edith Jones did in her dissent in *Herceg v. Hustler,* that some material of the type that is targeted in copycat cases differs so profoundly from the "political advocacy" on which *Brandenburg* and *Hess* focused that comparable protection is not warranted. Similarly, the fourth circuit's characterization of the *Hit Man Manual* as "an instruction book on murder" sought to avoid the Brandenburg shield by citing both the mechanistic nature of the contents and the exclusive focus of the text on illegal activity.

The second distinction is clearly dubious. Apart from the fact that even the *Hit Man Manual* contained some passages that one could not fairly disparage in this way, virtually the same claim had been made about Ernest Brandenburg's racist rantings to a volatile Ku Klux Klan rally, which formed the basis of the prosecution. One does not even reach the "clear and present danger" issue unless one is dealing with speech that urges or promotes unlawful ends; the analysis begins, not ends, at that point.

The other issue is inherently more difficult—whether some speech is so *didactic* or *prosaic* that it simply does not qualify for protection under the Brandenburg-Hess standard. None of the other relevant cases recognize such a distinction, and for good reason. Nor can such a line be drawn with any clarity or comfort—as the casual application of the rationale in *Rice v. Paladin* to Oliver Stone's violently fictional film reminds us. If calling a book a "murder manual" served to deny it First Amendment protection, it would then be virtually impossible to distinguish from the *Hit Man Manual* some novels of Robert Clancy and other popular authors, or for that matter the 1907 Joseph Conrad novel which Theodore Kaczynski once said he used as a guide to making the Unabomber's lethal explosive devices. Most other observers simply lack the confidence of the Fourth Circuit Court that any such line can be drawn with clarity or certainty. Thus the firm insistence of the appeals court that no other copycat suit is "factually analogous to this case" suggests a degree of precision or clarity that simply does not exist in real life.

Finally, does "aiding and abetting" provide a viable alternative to "clear and present danger" as a means of making creators of violent material more accountable to innocent victims? Such a theory assumes that one would be able to prove all the essential elements, including the requisite degree of intent—to which Paladin Press may have stipulated, but the actual demonstration of which at a trial would have been difficult if not impossible. Even so, such a theory suggests that one might reach otherwise protected expression by a side or back door when the front door is firmly barred by the First Amendment is a deeply troubling notion. The entire force of Supreme Court adjudication, and a virtually unanimous line of lower court decisions, forecloses such a prospect.

10.
What's Next?

Whatever complacency about civil liability the entertainment industry may have brought into the new millennium should have been dispelled by a suit that reached California courts in January 2001. Elyse Pahler, a tenth-grader in San Luis Obispo, had been brutally murdered as a satanic sacrifice. Her killers were three male teen devotees of the rock band Slayer. That group had pioneered the so-called "death metal" sound through albums bearing titles such as *Show No Mercy, Hell Awaits,* and *Reign in Blood.* After the youths had been charged with Elyse's murder, one of them explained that listening to Slayer's music "started to influence the way I looked at things." In admission statements which they filed with the criminal court, all three assailants declared that they were following instructions found in Slayer songs such as "Altar of Sacrifice," "Kill Again," and "Necrophiliac."

It turned out that the three young killers had formed a band of their own, which they named Hatred and through which they aspired to Slayer status. They contrived a nefarious plan to advance that cause. They would murder a virgin in order to consecrate their belief in and bond with Satan. An investigator who helped solve the case eventually theorized: "It [the killing] was to receive power from the devil to help them play guitar better. By making this perfect sacrifice to the devil, it might help them go professional." It was Elyse Pahler that the three youths chose as their victim, abducting and torturing her before taking her life. She was simply listed as missing until, eight months later, her decomposed remains were discovered in a eucalyptus grove near her home. The three killers pleaded no contest and were sentenced to 25-year terms in separate California prisons.

David and Lisanne Pahler soon brought suit in state court, charging that Slayer, Columbia Records, Sony Music, and others involved in the production and distribution of "death metal" should be held liable for their daughter's death. Her father explained the impetus behind their case: "There's a whole generation of children out there that are being fed this music. It's like feeding a child a little poison every day. We're saying, 'enough is enough.'" The family's lawsuit requested not only money damages but also a court order to restrict the sale of violent music to minors.

Although the Pahlers realized that similar claims had routinely been dismissed in the past, they felt that their suit was different in several respects. For one, the family was now represented by a large and powerful law firm which had successfully sued R.J. Reynolds for damages for its use of Joe Camel in cigarette-marketing campaigns. Lawyers in this firm were now convinced that a theory of accountability which had worked so well against big tobacco could also bring the music industry to account.

On the Pahlers's behalf, the suit claimed that recording companies which intentionally market lyrics glorifying violence and death—especially where such marketing is aimed at susceptible teen audiences—can be legally held to have incited violent acts which follow exposure to such material. The complaint leaves little doubt about its premise: "The distribution and marketing of this obscene and harmful material to adolescent males constituted aiding and abetting of . . . criminal acts. None of the vicious crimes committed against Elyse Marie Pahler would have occurred without the intentional marketing strategy of the 'death metal' band Slayer."

The Pahlers's suit had one other unique feature. Instead of relying on common-law theories such as negligence and products liability, as had most of the earlier anti-entertainment suits, this one invoked a specific California statute which targeted certain marketing methods as "unfair business practices." Thus, explained David Pahler, "this case isn't about art; it's about marketing." The record companies, he continued, "couldn't care less about what their fans did to our daughter. All they care about is money."

This case may differ from its antecedents in one further and crucial respect. As we have seen time and again in the earlier chapters, many a plausible and emotionally appealing claim has foundered on the plaintiff's inability to establish a causal link between entertainment material and injury or death. Where some evidence bearing on that nexus exists, its credibility has been highly suspect; typically any such proof comes in the form of a desperate defendant's exculpatory plea that "the movie [or the song] made me do it." In the Pahler case, however, the statements by the killers about the influence of Slayer lyrics on their thought and actions were apparently untainted by such motives. The crucial evidence bearing upon causation may thus carry a degree of credibility that has not existed in any of the previous cases.

Finally, there was evidence that Slayer and its distributor seemed almost to revel in, and to glorify, the link between violent lyrics and brutal acts as a virtue in promoting the discs. The jacket of a recent Slayer release contained a photo montage that included newspaper clippings such as the headline "Rap Song Blamed in Texas Trooper's Death" and a picture of a bloody corpse near another clipping about a widow who sued a record company after her husband was murdered by three skinheads who were obsessed by heavy-metal music. Such promotional material would tend to undermine any claim of innocence on the part of those responsible for producing and distributing Slayer's music.

Despite these special features, the entertainment industry was not without its champions. Eminent New York media lawyer Floyd Abrams represented several of the defendants and made a commitment of time and energy to this case that is uncommon for proceedings in a state trial court so remote from a lawyer's home base. He insisted that Slayer's music and lyrics were fully protected by the First Amendment, though he conceded that invoking the California unfair business practice law "makes it easier to get into court . . . than in many other states." Eventually the California Superior Court judge agreed with Abrams and dismissed the Pahlers's complaint. Even with the unique twists, the allegations seemed to him insufficient to establish a basis for liability and damages. But the lawyers who filed that complaint, sensing a promising parallel between the marketing of cigarettes and of "death metal" music, have simply redrafted the complaint, hoping that it would eventually get them over the threshold on which many other plaintiffs in similar suits have stumbled. They feel that the prospect of recovery for damages seems realistic for the first time in many years if they can get such an emotionally compelling case to a jury.

The case went almost unnoticed until the trial judge's ruling. It then received substantial attention, both in the industry media and through a major story in the *Washington Post*—significantly, now featured as the lead item in the *Post*'s Business section, no longer relegated to Style or Weekend. The *Post* reporter, after surveying the earlier cases and assessing the potential of this latest development, offered this sobering comment: "The centuries-old debate testing the limits of free expression against the norms of a free society is laid out in hundreds of pages of legal briefs. And right now it's anyone's guess which way the case will go."

As recently as five years ago, one could not fairly have described the prospect for such a case as "anybody's guess." With the sole exception of one highly unusual California case in the 1970s, courts had consistently refused to allow such claims to proceed beyond the initial pleading stage. Even the most emotionally appealing suits were dismissed, invariably on both common law and First Amendment constitutional law grounds. Yet the landscape has changed dramatically since the mid-1990s. This seems an appropriate point to take stock of these changes, before probing the implications for each of the major players in this rapidly evolving drama.

Recall what has recently happened to alter the once-easy assumptions about media immunity from civil liability:

• A publisher has been held potentially liable by a federal appeals court for a murder committed by one among thousands of readers of one of its books, even though he bought the book more than a year before the killing. While the particular case (that of *Rice v. Paladin Press*) turns partly on the novel stipulations of publisher intent, the court of appeals opinion strongly implies a readiness to permit a jury to impose liability for "aiding and abetting" a homicide. It was surely no coincidence that the Pahlers's suit against

Slayer and its producers invoked "aiding and abetting" as the theory by which targeted and "unfair" marketing practices might lead to civil liability.

• Producers and distributors of a motion picture have been held, by a state appeals court, potentially liable in damages to victims of a slaying spree committed by teenagers who had viewed the film repeatedly and were apparently "obsessed" by its most violent scenes. In *Byers v. Edmondson*, the way in which the claim arose may have increased the risk, since allegations in a complaint, including those of specific intent, must be taken as true. Yet the court's approach to the issues strongly suggests sympathy to the merits. The state's highest court and the U.S. Supreme Court declined to intervene at this stage.

• An organization that posted militantly anti-abortion material on an Internet Web site was held liable by a jury for more than $100 million in damages to physicians and other clinic staff members, some of whom were targets of threats posted on that site, but others of whom were never even named in that medium.

• A television network has been held liable in damages for the acts of their reporters and camera crews in misrepresenting their employment applications to a retail food store, in which they discovered, filmed and broadcast serious violations of safe food-processing standards.

• Another network has been held liable to truck drivers and owners for breaking a promise not to include in a final broadcast an opposing viewpoint presented by an organization highly critical of the trucking industry.

• Television reporters have been held liable for invading the privacy of homeowners and automobile accident victims, even without any physical trespass or invasion, to accurately capture images and words in essentially public places.

• Another TV producer lost a major damage award for filming (though never broadcasting) a "secret admirer" segment in which a gay man trustingly revealed his affection for another man who, upon learning of such feelings, sought out and killed his previously unknown "admirer."

It is not always the cases one loses that set bad precedents. The ones that the media choose not to contest can be equally troubling. Along with the cases just noted, each of which brought an adverse ruling or judgment, one might mention other claims that were filed in court but were settled before going to trial, under conditions that undoubtedly reflect growing media anxiety about the prospects of taking such issues before a jury. Notable among such concessions was the decision by CBS television not to broadcast the interview with sometime tobacco executive Jeffrey Wigand when his former employer threatened to sue the network for "tortious interference with business relations." As many media lawyers observed, this would have been a difficult claim to prove even against Wigand himself, much less against the network to which he had recounted truthful information about activities (some of them surely unlawful) in the industry about which he was an expert.

Yet the lawyers advised, and the network concluded, that the potential legal risks outweighed whatever benefit might result from broadcasting such material. Eventually, this whole sorry saga reached Hollywood in the form of an award-winning film, *The Insider,* and the Wigand interview eventually aired elsewhere. But the decision not to call Brown & Williamson's bluff by putting Wigand on the air may have done far greater damage, and may have set a much more ominous precedent, than would losing the case in court and paying substantial damages.

The reasons for so dramatic a change in the climate or environment that affects such judgments—both in the front office and in the courts—are far from clear. In his recent book, *Don't Shoot the Messenger,* Washington First Amendment lawyer and seasoned litigator Bruce W. Sanford traces recent public disenchantment with the news media, both print and broadcast. He identifies a number of possible catalysts for such a condition—media concentration and seemingly increased focus on the bottom line at the expense of public service, increasingly aggressive news-gathering methods that reflect both "investigative reporting" and more sophisticated equipment, and a general decline in public confidence in the news media as a reliable source of accurate information about issues and developments most vital to their lives and fortunes.

In his opening chapter, Sanford laments what he sees happening to the media, which becomes the focus of his book: "It is about how the public's anger toward the media is being played out in the nation's courts, where judge after judge is limiting the public's right to receive information all in the name of controlling the 'profiteering' news media." This introductory chapter concludes: "The consequences of the growing canyon of distrust between the public and the media are already discernible and should worry us even more than the knowledge that we understand the situation poorly. For the result of the public's misplaced fury has been a palpable willingness to silence the media—to curtail its ability to gather and report the news, and to make us more dependent than ever on the government for our understanding of human events. There is no more certain road to the loss of freedom."

What Bruce Sanford says of the news media may be even more true for the entertainment industry. In a comment prompted by the Pahlers's suit against record companies over the brutal slaying of their daughter, Southern California ACLU lawyer Peter Eliasberg cautioned, "We're kidding ourselves if we don't think the cultural climate affects judges and their decisions." Then he added, "We're getting to the point if we let these cases go forward, that someone can say 'Shaft' glorifies vigilantism. There is a really serious danger [that creators will decide] to not make a movie or not write a book." Concerns and perceptions similar to those Bruce Sanford cites in the news context seem largely to account for the rising tide of anger and hostility toward the entertainment industry.

Recall, as representative, author John Grisham's bitter remarks about movie producer Oliver Stone, after his close friend was fatally shot by the teenagers on a spree inspired by Stone's *Natural Born Killers:* "[Stone] takes the high road in defending his dreadful movies; [even if it] wasn't made with the intent of stimulating morally depraved young people to commit similar crimes, such a result can hardly be a surprise." Such an indictment is especially harsh, coming as it does from one who is both an experienced lawyer and himself an author of books and films dealing with crime and occasional violence. Yet Grisham's views accord closely with those of many others affected by violent media—not just those who have lost family members or friends to what seem to be media-inspired rampages but many who have been touched less directly as well.

What is to be done? Proposing solutions to so seemingly intractable a problem may be either presumptuous or naive, though this seems an appropriate place at which to begin. First, we might look to the courts, which are almost certain to see a steadily rising caseload of similar lawsuits, if only because the courthouse doors, which for so long seemed barred and locked to such claims, have now been partly opened by the judgments we noted earlier. Without trying to assess blame—for example, to determine whether the courts have somehow caused the current situation or are simply responding to new and stronger claims of liability—several guiding principles emerge from our review of recent cases.

Perhaps most basic, it seems beyond question that virtually all the material which has been the target of civil-liability lawsuits remains fully protected by the First Amendment. The few exceptions are notable for their rarity—for example, advertising for an unlawful product or service (which may explain one of the *Soldier of Fortune* cases) or the posting of "true threats" on an Internet Web site. Despite the liberal use by critics of terms such as "obscenity," none of the charged material is legally obscene or contains "fighting words" or constitutes child pornography or fits into any of the several other niches that would categorically deny it any claim to constitutional protection. The most that may be said is that such material might, in a particular context, be said to forfeit First Amendment protection—notably if it involves direct incitement to imminent lawless action. If, under the proper standard, speech is found to pose a "clear and present danger" of that type, the speaker or publisher might be legally liable for harmful results that can be attributed directly to the material.

This comment introduces two further qualifications which are usually dispositive. Even in the most appealing of cases—*Rice v. Paladin, Byers v. Edmonson,* or the Pahlers's suit against Slayer and the record companies—it would be impossible, without setting tort law of causation on its head, to establish the essential link between such a catalyst and a third party's criminal act. Judge Alex Williams said it best in dismissing the *Hit-Man* suit: "Words don't kill; only people kill."

Even if causation could be proved—the Pahlers's lawyers think they have an airtight case against Slayer based on the killers' statements—the First Amendment simply does not permit courts to impose liability on the creator of such material without establishing that there has been "direct incitement to imminent lawless action." A record, book, or motion picture that is made available to the entire world simply cannot meet that standard, most clearly because its content has not been directed or "targeted" to a specific listener in the way the Supreme Court has required. Whether one calls it "aiding and abetting" (or anything else) ought not to lower the standard one bit; liability (civil or criminal) for provocative or hortatory speech may rest only upon a showing that the incitement test has been met.

Such a showing is not impossible, nor is the standard illusory. If a person were to operate an interactive Web site and invite would-be killers or robbers to share the activities and lifestyles of intended victims, providing in return a designer blueprint for the "perfect crime," there would be little doubt about the proprietor's potential liability for crimes carried out according to the blueprint. But that is a far cry from the actual facts—reminding us just how far the Fourth Circuit Court of Appeals actually strayed from well-settled First Amendment jurisprudence. However damaging the stipulations on publisher intent may have seemed in the actual case, they would not elsewhere serve to cancel out First Amendment protection for material that fits no other exception to free expression. On that theory, the ruling in *Rice v. Paladin* could be seen as a pure aberration, wholly at variance with a half-century of free-speech jurisprudence. Yet, as *Byers v. Edmondson* makes painfully clear, limiting to its facts a legal judgment that one fears or dislikes may be hazardous to one's financial health and well-being.

We turn from the courts to the media and entertainment industries. Surely they do not help their own causes, or the efforts of those who defend them, by pushing the envelope to its limits. Bruce Sanford is quite right in viewing some part of the wounds he recounts and laments as self-inflicted. While the ABC *PrimeTime Live* camera crew that surreptitiously filmed spoiled meat and fish in a Food Lion store may in one sense have been doing a public service, using a subterfuge to obtain employment and then bringing hidden cameras to work every day involved a practice almost universally condemned by other news media. CBS's outside counsel advised against airing the Jeffrey Wigand interview in part because *60 Minutes'* own hands may not have been entirely clean in the matter. The NBC *Dateline* producer subjected his network to liability at the point he assured the trusting Bangor truckers that their nemesis would play no part in the broadcast, when in fact he knew that lengthy interviews with Parents Against Tired Truckers had already been filmed and almost certainly would go on the air. Producers of the *Jenny Jones Show* ended up on the wrong side of the Amadure family's lawsuit only because they heedlessly incited a relationship between two people of whose emotional vulnerability they should have known something. The record company that produces and distributes Slayer discs is in court partly because it had the questionable taste to adorn a disc jacket with headlines from the most gruesome media-inspired killings such as that of Texas state trooper Davidson. *Soldier of Fortune* not only got itself in trouble, but to some extent it penalized the entire magazine industry, because it accepted and printed ads from people who were seeking to hire assassins or who wished to offer their own services for that purpose.

To return to our cause célèbre, Oliver Stone is still in court in Louisiana not only because he had the misfortune of having an obsessed viewer of *Natural Born Killers* shoot an old friend of John Grisham's. Quite as clearly, Mr. Stone is still a defendant because the plaintiff's very able lawyer knows that he had said before making the movie that he "just want[ed] to do something that is completely nihilistic." That lawyer also knows that Stone proclaimed proudly, after the initial screening of the completed film, that "the most pacifist people in the world said they came out of this movie and wanted to kill somebody."

Thus, it is not hard to understand why many critics of media and entertainment excesses agree with Elyse Pahler's anguished father that "enough is enough" or echo John Grisham's hope that "the laughing will soon stop [in Hollywood]" or share former drug czar Bill Bennett's belief that "it's a good thing for the public to look the entertainment companies in the eye and say, 'we've had it.'" While such views may not be wholly objective, we should recall that it was no less a friend of the media than Medill School of Journalism dean and former PBS news host Ken Bode who observed at the time of the Amedure/*Jenny Jones* case that if "the way to get [the industry's] attention is the checkbook, perhaps [damage awards] will restore some propriety." In short, if some sectors of the news and entertainment media sense a substantial loss of support in recent years, they may well look in part to their own conduct for explanations. To the extent that they seek a more favorable reception in the courts of both law and public opinion, they might do well to look more often at their own practices and ask whether pressing free expression to its limits is always helpful.

Finally, something should be said about those who regulate expression — lawmakers and administrative agencies. In the realm of broadcasting, both Congress and the Federal Communications Commission have substantial authority over the content of what is carried by licensed stations (though they have far less authority with respect to cable channels.) Federal law forbids "indecent and profane" language on the air, and the FCC has for many years enforced the "seven dirty words rule," which was once tested and upheld by the Supreme Court in the context of George Carlin's creative and provocative monologue of taboo and vulgar language.

In other areas, regulation has been tempting but elusive — most notably when it comes to "violent" material. Congress did recently impose the "V-chip" requirement, under which makers of TV sets must install software that informs viewers (mainly parents) of the network's own assessment of content on several criteria at the start of each program, so that sets may be turned off or channels changed if the rating is unacceptable.

The record to date is far from satisfying. It relies entirely on network self-assessment of content, with clear indications that objective viewers might find more to fault in some programs than the network's own icons would indicate. Moreover, the reach of the system is incomplete. NBC has elected to treat the V-chip as voluntary, which technically it is, and to provide its own version of viewer warnings. Yet there will not be any direct governmental regulation of violent content until and unless the FCC declares the V-chip a failure. Then, and only then, would we reach the daunting task of defining "violence" in ways that would cover certain bloody and gory dramas (while exempting news and sports segments and, of course, Shakespeare plays, which may contain an objectively comparable amount of "violence").

Because the regulation of violence on licensed broadcasting has proved so difficult and elusive, it seems highly unlikely that Congress or state legislatures will ever undertake to create a civil cause of action by which a victim of media or entertainment violence could recover damages from the creator of the allegedly culpable material. This is not to say that such a prospect has never been contemplated. In fact, in midsummer of 2000, a "Parents' Empowerment Act" was proposed when H.B. 5045 was introduced in the U.S. House of Representatives. The bill would have provided an individual right of recovery for a minor harmed by exposure to an entertainment product containing material that is "harmful to minors." The creator and disseminator of such material would be potentially liable if "a reasonable person would expect a substantial number of minors to be exposed to the material, and the minor as a result of such exposure is likely to suffer personal or emotional injury or injury to mental or moral welfare."

Not surprisingly, H.B. 5045 went nowhere even during a presidential campaign that faulted media violence to a greater degree than ever before. Apart from a fairly effective industry lobby, there is the inherent difficulty of defining the core concept on which such a law would focus. And there is abiding respect for the most basic of First Amendment values, even when it comes to material that may seem far removed from what the framers envisioned when they wrote the Bill of Rights—a fact that is not trivial among congressional concerns, even in these cynical times. Thus it seems likely not only that H.B. 5045 and its progeny will make little headway in Congress but that similar measures at the federal and state level will probably not make their way into law as the platform for claims of civil liability. Anything, to be sure, is possible, but this prospect has been and remains relatively remote.

sources and references

Although detailed footnotes seem incompatible with a book of this sort, familiar though they are to most legal scholars, some references are appropriate and essential. It is the goal of this brief section to identify major sources and citation for court decisions and other significant developments. References to treatises and law review articles are also included, in the hope that readers with deeper interests may be guided to more detailed sources. Increasingly, the best sources for current information are the web pages of organizations that follow relevant events—the Freedom Forum (www.freedomforum.org), the American Civil Liberties Union (www.aclu.org), People for the American Way (www.peoplefor.org), and more specialized groups such as the Electronic Frontier Foundation (www.eff.org), and the Electronic Privacy Information Center (www.epic.org) with regard to Internet issues and cases. The author's own organization, the Thomas Jefferson Center for the Protection of Free Expression (www.tjcenter.org) maintains active information about current cases, chiefly those in which the Center has been involved, but others of interest and importance as well.

1. First Principles and Basic Tensions

The two major treatises cited in this chapter and in later sections of the book are Zechariah Chafee, Jr., *Free Speech in the United States* (Cambridge, Mass.: Harvard University Press, 1920, 2nd ed. 1942), and Thomas I. Emerson, *The System of Freedom of Expression* (New York: Random House, 1970). Many other recent books have focused on various facets of free expression—for example, Rodney A. Smolla, *Free Speech in an Open Society* (New York: Alfred A. Knopf, 1992). An especially useful early history is David Rabban, *Free Speech in Its Forgotten Years* (New York: Cambridge University Press, 1997). More specialized works cited and quoted in this chapter are Franklyn S. Haiman, *Speech Acts and the First Amendment* (Carbondale: Southern Illinois University Press, 1993), and Stanley Fish, *There's No Such Thing as Free Speech . . . and It's a Good Thing, Too* (New York: Oxford University Press, 1994). Among the myriad law review articles that have addressed First Amendment issues, the last one to advance and analyze broadly the philosophical and constitutional premises of free expression was Vincent Blasi, "The Checking Value in First Amendment Theory," 1977 *American Bar Foundation Research Journal* 521.

Supreme Court decisions cited in this chapter are, on the original "clear and present danger" test, *Schenck v. United States,* 249 U.S. 47 (1919), and on the more recent "direct incitement" standard, *Brandenburg v. Ohio,* 395 U.S. 444 (1969) and

Hess v. Indiana, 414 U.S. 105 (1973). Extending these standards to private civil damage suits was *NAACP v. Claiborne Hardware Co.*, 458 U.S. 886 (1982). The case that found the public utterance of taboo or vulgar words to be protected was *Cohen v. California*, 403 U.S. 15 (1971). Finding obscenity not to be protected speech was *Roth v. United States*, 354 U.S. 476 (1957), and later, reaching the same result for child pornography, *New York v. Ferber*, 458 U.S. 747 (1982). Other major rulings cited in this chapter are those dealing with "fighting words," *Chaplinsky v. New Hampshire*, 315 U.S. 568 (1942); symbolic non-verbal protest, *Tinker v. Des Moines School Board*, 303 U.S. 503 (1969); freedom of association as a protected First Amendment interest, *NAACP v. Alabama*, 357 U.S. 449 (1958); access to courts for litigating public interest claims, *NAACP v. Button*, 371 U.S. 415 (1963); the expressive nature of flag burning, *Texas v. Johnson*, 491 U.S. 397 (1989); the expressive nature of draft-card burning, and the standard for mixed speech/conduct, *United States v. O'Brien*, 391 U.S. 367 (1968); "indecency on the Internet," *Reno v. ACLU*, 521 U.S. 844 (1997); nude entertainment, *United States v. Playboy Entertainment Group*, 529 U.S. 803 (2000); and caricature or satire, *Hustler Magazine v. Falwell*, 485 U.S. 46 (1988).

2. Libel

For a comprehensive and up-to-date overview of the law of libel and slander, one might consult Bruce W. Sanford, *Libel and Privacy: The Prevention and Defense of Litigation* (New York: Harcourt Brace Jovanovich, 2nd ed., 1999) and *Sanford's Synopsis of Libel and Privacy* (Mahwah, N.J. : World Almanac Books, 4th ed., 1991), or Rodney A. Smolla, *Law of Defamation* (New York: C. Boardman Co., 1986). Professor Emerson's treatment of libel law and the First Amendment, to which this chapter makes extensive reference, is Thomas I. Emerson, *A System of Freedom of Expression* (New York: Random House, 1970), chapter XIV, pages 517–62.

Of the three libel cases with which the chapter opens, two are reported and the third is not. Oprah Winfrey's victory in the suit brought by cattle ranchers is reported in *Texas Beef Cattle Group v. Winfrey*, 11 F. Supp. 2d 858 (N.D. Tex. 1998); a useful comment is in 29 *Texas Tech Law Review* 851 (1998). The ruling that Atlanta park guard Richard Jewell was a public figure was that of a Georgia state trial judge; though the decision was appealed, no further proceedings have been reported. A very helpful comment is Cynthia L. Cooper, "Judges Side with the Media," *American Bar Association Journal*, January 2000, p. 32. Dean Sharon Yeagle's unsuccessful suit against the Virginia Tech student newspaper was resolved by the Virginia Supreme Court in *Yeagle v. Collegiate Times*, 497 S.E.2d 136 (Va. 1998).

The major Supreme Court judgment that recognized a First Amendment privilege of "fair comment" on public officials (and later public figures as well) was *New York Times Co. v. Sullivan*, 376 U.S. 254 (1964). Other cases cited in this chapter are *Beauharnais v. Illinois*, 343 U.S. 250 (1952), upholding a state "group libel" law; *Milkovich v. Lorain Journal Co.*, 497 U.S. 1 (1990), refining the concept of "opinion" in libel cases; *Summit Hotel Co. v. NBC*, 8 A.2d 302 (Pa. 1939), the first reported case of broadcast libel; *Gertz v. Robert Welch Co.*, 418 U.S. 323 (1974), and *Dun & Bradstreet. Inc. v. Greenmoss Builders, Inc.*, 472 U.S. 749 (1985), which limited the scope of the *New York Times* libel privilege in cases brought by plaintiffs who are not public figures; and *Hustler Magazine v. Falwell*, 485 U.S. 46 (1988), which extended the privilege to caricature or satire concerning public officials and public figures.

3. Libel on the Internet

The most extensive and helpful analysis of issues posed in this chapter, arguing that Internet libel should be treated by courts much like print libel, is Michael Hadley, "The Gertz Doctrine and Internet Defamation," 84 *Virginia Law Review* 477 (1998). The contrary view, to which Hadley responds, is found in Michael Godwin, "The First Amendment in Cyberspace," 4 *Temple Political & Civil Rights Law Review* 1 (1994), and Jeremy Stone Weber, "Defining Cyberlibel: A First Amendment Limit for Suits against Individuals Arising from Computer Bulletin Board Speech," 46 *Case Western Reserve Law Review* 235 (1995). The freshest perspective on the status and potential liability of anonymous online critics is Lyrissa Barnett Lidsky, "Silencing John Doe: Defamation and Discourse in Cyberspace" 49 *Duke Law Journal* 855 (2000). Many of the issues explored in this chapter were earlier discussed in Robert M. O'Neil, "The Drudge Case: A Look at Issues in Cyberspace Defamation," 73 *Washington Law Review* 623 (1998).

The major case in the field remains the district court ruling in *Blumenthal v. Drudge*, 992 F. Supp. 44 (D.D.C. 1998), followed by an essentially procedural ruling at 186 F.R.D. 236 (D.D.C. 1999). The case was settled before it reached the court of appeals. The litigation brought by Judge Joan Orie Melvin has not been officially reported, though a copy of the most recent opinion may be found in *Mealey's Cyber Tech Litigation Report*, December 2000, vol. 2, no. 10; and in *Pennsylvania Law Weekly*, November 20, 2000, in the Torts section. For an analysis, see Jeffrey Graham, "Libel Online," 87 *American Bar Association Journal* 28 (March 2001). The early Internet libel cases are *Cubby, Inc. v. Compuserve, Inc.*, 776 F. Supp. 135 (S.D.N.Y. 1991) and *Stratton Oakmont, Inc. v. Prodigy Servs. Co.*, 1995 WL 805178 (N.Y. Sup. Ct. 1995). The case absolving an Internet service provider by a subscriber of highly damaging material is *Zeran v. America Online, Inc.*, 129 F.2d 327 (4th Cir. 1997). Of the cases that involve the "unmasking" of those who post anonymous comments in Internet chat rooms, one has been reported—*Global Telemedia International v. Doe 1*, 132 F. Supp. 2d 1261 (C.D. Cal. 2001); the most recent federal district court ruling, which reflects a return to the earlier reluctance to unmask such critics, is noted in the *Seattle Post-Intelligencer*, April 20, 2001, p. B1.

4. Threats and Incitement on the Internet

The suit by the Curley family against NAMBLA, based on statements posted on the organization's web page, has not yet resulted in any reported rulings. An excellent analysis of the issues may be found in Siobhan Morrissey, "Unsavory Speech: A Pedophile Murder Case Drags the First Amendment Back into Court," *American Bar Association Journal*, January 2001, p. 20. The court of appeals decision in Planned Parenthood/Nuremberg Website case is *Planned Parenthood v. American Coalition of Life Activists*, 2001 U.S. App. LEXIS 4974 (9th Cir. 2001); a petition for rehearing before the full court of appeals is pending. Three separate district court rulings are reported at 945 F. Supp. 1355 (D. Or. 1996); 23 F. Supp. 2d 1182 (D. Or. 1999); 41 F. Supp. 2d 1130 (D. Or. 1999). Several law review articles analyze in depth the lower court issues and rulings—notably Steven G. Gey, "The Nuremberg Files and the First Amendment Value of Threats," 78 *Texas Law Review* 541 (2000); and Melanie C. Hagen, "The Freedom of Access to Clinic Entrances Act and the Nuremberg Files Website," 51 *Hastings Law Journal* 411 (2000).

The case involving threats posted by University of Michigan student Jake Baker is reported (under his real name) as *United States v. Alkhabaz*, 104 F.3d 1492 (6th Cir. 1997). A divided court of appeals affirmed a lower court ruling which had dismissed all criminal threat charges against the student, reported in *United States v. Baker*, 890 F. Supp. 1375 (E.D. Mich. 1995). The case has been widely discussed in legal literature. In addition to the Gey and Hagen articles noted above, see Daniel T. Kobil, "Advocacy Online: Brandenburg v. Ohio and Speech in the Internet Era," 31 *University of Toledo Law Review* 227 (2000). The other Internet threat cases, Machado and Quon, which involved offensive and inflammatory e-mails sent to designated students who belonged to ethnic groups apparently targeted by the sender, are unreported.

5. Privacy

The two cases with which this chapter opens are *Shulman v. Group W. Productions, Inc.*, 18 Cal. 4th 200, 955 P.2d 469 (Cal. 1998); and *Wolfson v. Lewis*, 924 F. Supp. 1413 (E.D. Pa. 1996). The famous early law review article was Samuel Warren and Louis D. Brandeis, "The Right to Privacy," 4 *Harvard Law Review* 193 (1890), in which the authors first advanced a cogent case for legal protection of privacy as an embryonic personal interest of societal value. For a most thoughtful analysis of their position from a mid-twentieth-century perspective, see Harry Kalven, "Privacy in Tort Law—Were Warren and Brandeis Wrong?" 31 *Law & Contemporary Problems* 326 (1966). The most recent and most dramatic implementation of the authors views is the new California privacy law, Cal. Civil Code s 1708.8 (1998). For an explanation and sympathetic analysis by one of the law's drafters, see Erwin Chemerinsky, "Protect the Press: A First Amendment Standard for Safeguarding Aggressive Newsgathering," 33 *University of Richmond Law Review* 1143 (2000). Various efforts to enact such laws in Congress have been less successful; for one such proposal, see H.R. 2448, 105th Congress, 1997.

The Supreme Court's rebuke of media "ride-alongs" is *Wilson v. Layne*, 526 U.S. 603 (1999). Earlier Supreme Court rulings, which consistently refused to allow recovery of damages against the press if the published information was accurate, of public interest and had not been unlawfully obtained, are *Cox Broadcasting Co. v.*

Cohn, 420 U.S. 469 (1975); *Smith v. Daily Mail Publishing Co.*, 443 U.S. 97 (1979); and *Florida Star v. B.J.F.*, 491 U.S. 524 (1989). Recognition of the protected status of caricature of public figures came in *Hustler Magazine v. Falwell*, 485 U.S. 46 (1988), and of a celebrity's unusual right to recover for unauthorized media use of an entire "act" or "routine" in *Zacchini v. Scripps-Howard Broadcasting Co.*, 433 U.S. 562 (1977). The federal appeals court case involving the HIV-positive airline employee is *Doe v. City of New York*, 15 F.3d 264 (2d Cir. 1994). The earlier case, from the same court, providing legal protection against an aggressive paparazzo to the family of slain former president John Kennedy is *Galella v. Onassis*, 487 F.2d 986 (2d Cir. 1973). The Canadian Supreme Court ruling which sustained Quebec's damage ruling against a magazine for publishing without the subject's consent a photograph taken on a public street is *Aubry v. Vice Versa, Inc.*, 1 S.C.R. 591 (Can. 1998).

6. THE PERILS OF NEWS-GATHERING

For a most thoughtful and readable introduction to the issues of this chapter, see Jane E. Kirtley, "It's the Process, Stupid—Newsgathering Is the New Target," *Columbia Journalism Review*, September/October 2000, p. 47. The opening case, involving a TV camera crew's act of "making the news rather than reporting it," is *KOVR-TV, Inc. v. Superior Court*, 31 Cal. App. 4th 1023, 37 Cal. Rptr. 2d 431 (1995). The court of appeals ruling on the suit by the Maine truckers against NBC over allegedly breached promises of favorable coverage on *Dateline NBC*, is *Veilleux v. National Broadcasting Co.*, 206 F.3d 92 (1st Cir. 2000). The most recent stages of the running battle between Food Lion and ABC over the network's methods of obtaining material for the *PrimeTime Live* expose is reported in *Food Lion, Inc. v. Capital Cities/ABC*, 194 F.3d 505 (4th Cir. 1999). There are at least seven other reported federal district or appellate court rulings in this case.

Among many articles in legal periodicals, see Chris Carmody, "Applying a 'Persona Test' for Newsgathering Privilege to Food Lion v. Capital Cities/ABC," 93 *Northwestern Law Review* 1287 (1999); Robert M. O'Neil, "Tainted Sources: First Amendment Rights and Journalistic Wrongs," 4 *William & Mary Bill of Rights Law Journal* 1005 (1996); and an especially perceptive and lengthy analysis, David A. Logan, "Masked Media: Judges, Juries and the Law of Surreptitious Newsgathering," 83 *Iowa Law Review* 161 (1997).

The major Supreme Court cases cited in this chapter are, on the unacceptability of prior restraint against the news media, *New York Times Co. v. United States*, 403 U.S. 713 (1971); on media access to the criminal trial, *Richmond Newspapers v. Virginia*, 448 U.S. 555 (1980); on the absence of a constitutional shield for reporters wishing to keep secret the identity of their sources, *Branzburg v. Hayes*, 408 U.S. 665 (1972); and on the right of a source whose expectation of anonymity has been violated by the news media, *Cohen v. Cowles Media Co.*, 501 U.S. 663 (1991).

The two cases dealing with subjects who sued over aggressive and intrusive newsgathering methods, with contrasting results in the federal appeals courts, are (the plaintiff who prevailed) *Dietemann v. Time, Inc.*, 449 F.2d 245 (9th Cir 1971), and (the plaintiff who did not prevail) *Desnick v. American Broadcasting Co.*, 233 F.3d 514 (7th Cir. 2000), affirming an earlier ruling by the same court at 44 F.3d 1345 (7th Cir. 1995).

7. Defective and Dangerous Products?

Several recent law review articles thoughtfully address the issues which this chapter poses and explores—Richard C. Ausness, "The Application of Product Liability Principles to Publishers of Violent or Sexually Explicit Material," 3 *Florida Law Review* 603 (2000); Lars Noah, "Authors, Publishers, and Products Liability: Remedies for Defective Information in Books," 77 *Oregon Law Review* 1195 (1998); and Jeffrey Haag, "If Words Could Kill: Rethinking Tort Liability in Texas for Media Speech That Incites Dangerous or Illegal Action," 30 *Texas Tech Law Review* 1421 (1999). There is a much earlier, but still helpful, discussion of these issues in Lisa A. Powell, "Products Liability and the First Amendment: The Liability of Publishers for Failure to Warn," 59 *Indiana Law Journal* 503 (1983).

The cases with which the chapter opens are *Davidson v. Time Warner, Inc.*, 1997 U.S. Dist. LEXIS 21559 (S.D. Tex. 1997), involving the unsuccessful effort of the widow of a slain Texas state trooper to impose liability on a record producer and distributor; and *James v. Meow Media, Inc.*, 90 F. Supp. 2d 798 (W.D. Ky. 2000), the suit by the families of the Paducah schoolyard shooting victims against a variety of media defendants.

The early case that set the tone of non-liability for publishers in regard to allegedly defective verbal products was *McKown v. Illinois Publishing & Printing Co.*, 289 Ill. App. 59, 6 N.E.2d 526 (Ill. App. 1937). The mushroom encyclopedia case was *Winter v. G.P. Putnam's Sons*, 938 F.2d 1033 (9th Cir. 1991). One illustrative travel guide case, perhaps most clearly protective of publishers, is *Birmingham v. Fodor's Travel Publications, Inc.*, 833 P.2d 70 (Haw. 1992). The few notable rulings to the contrary involve erroneous navigation charts: *Brocklesby v. United States*, 767 F.2d 1288 (9th Cir. 1985); *Saloomey v. Jeppesen & Co.*, 707 F.2d 671 (2d Cir. 1983); and *Aetna Casualty & Surety Co. v. Jeppesen & Co.*, 642 F.2d 339 (9th Cir. 1981).

Other novel cases which suggest a possible basis for imposing liability are *Hanberry v. Hearst Corp.*, 276 Cal. App. 2d 680, 81 Cal. Rptr. 519 (1969), involving a product which, though harmful to the buyer, had received the publisher's Good Housekeeping Seal of Approval; and *Carter v. Rand McNally*, an unreported Massachusetts case in which the student user of a science textbook suffered serious injuries attributable to instructions in the book.

8. The Risks of Advertising

The prospect of civil liability based on commercial speech is a novel one, which has received remarkably little treatment in scholarly journals. Most of the Supreme Court cases, and the articles and notes that comment on those cases, deal with government regulation of advertising—an issue that has been before the High Court nearly every term since initial recognition of First Amendment protection for commercial speech a quarter century ago. A rare and recent article, which touches tantalizingly on these issues, is Bruce Braun, Dane Drobny and Douglas Gessner, "www.commercialterrorism.com: A Proposed Federal Criminal Statute Addressing the Solicitation of Commercial Terrorism through the Internet," 37 *Harvard Journal on Legislation* 159 (2000).

The early case in which the Justices casually (and unanimously) dismissed the notion of advertising as protected speech is *Valentine v. Chrestensen*, 316 U.S. 52 (1942). Seven years later the Court sustained a city ordinance that regulated advertising in ways that would have been unacceptable as applied to almost any non-commercial message, *Railway Express Agency v. New York*, 336 U.S. 106 (1949). The tide began to turn when in 1975 the Court gave partial protection to an ad for an out-of-state abortion clinic, *Bigelow v. Virginia*, 421 U.S. 809 (1975), and the following year conferred at least partial protection on advertising which "did no more than propose a commercial transaction," *Virginia State Board of Pharmacy v. Virginia Citizens Consumer Council*, 425 U.S. 748 (1976). The basic standard governing regulation of advertising came in *Central Hudson Gas & Electric Corp. v. Public Service Comm'n*, 447 U.S. 557 (1980), recently reaffirmed after some curious turns in *44 Liquormart, Inc. v. Rhode Island*, 517 U.S. 484 (1996).

The several lower court decisions discussed in this chapter are *Sakon v. Pepsico, Inc.*, 553 So. 2d 163 (Fla. 1989), the case which opens the chapter, and the strikingly different rulings, by different federal appeals courts, on factually similar ads placed in the same periodical, *Braun v. Soldier of Fortune Magazine*, 968 F.2d 1110 (11th Cir. 1992); and *Eimann v. Soldier of Fortune Magazine, Inc.*, 880 F.2d 830 (5th Cir. 1989).

9. "The Movie Made Me Do It!"

The two major cases which seem to depart from the consistent pattern of publisher and producer non-liability for imitative or "copy cat" crimes are noted at the start of the chapter. The case against the producers and distributors of the film *Natural Born Killers* is *Byers v. Edmondson*, 712 So. 2d 681 (La. App. 1998), which both the Louisiana and United States Supreme Courts declined to review at an early stage of litigation. The other case, seeking to hold the publisher of the *Hit Man Manual* liable for a brutal crime committed by a reader of that book, is *Rice v. Paladin Enterprises*, 128 F.2d 233 (4th Cir. 1997) (reversing a district judge's dismissal of the suit against the publisher), which the Supreme Court also refused to disturb.

Despite the near unanimity of non-liability case law throughout the latter part of the twentieth century, there has been a rising chorus of contrary views from scholars and commentators. The case is best and most forcefully stated in a book entitled *Deliberate Intent* (New York: Crown Publishers, 1999) by Professor Rodney A. Smolla, who successfully represented on appeal the families of the *Hit Man Manual* killing. Other statements of a similar sort, urging a re-examination of the premises of non-liability, are found in Laura W. Brill, "The First Amendment and the Power of Suggestion: Protecting 'Negligent' Speakers in Cases of Imitative Harm," 94 *Columbia*

Law Review 984 (1994); David R. Dow and R. Scott Shieldes, "Rethinking the Clear and Present Danger Test," 73 *Indiana Law Journal* 1217 (1998); and S. Elizabeth Wilborn Malloy and Ronald J. Krotoszynski, Jr., "Recalibrating the Cost of Harm Advocacy: Getting Beyond Brandenburg," 41 *William & Mary Law Review* 1159 (2000).

The major Supreme Court cases on which the doctrine of non-liability rests begin with *Schenck v. United States,* 249 U.S. 47 (1919), in which the Justices first announced the "clear and present" danger test. *Bridges v. California,* 314 U.S. 252 (1941), and *Wood v. Georgia,* 370 U.S. 375 (1962), rigorously applied that standard to out-of-court comment on pending cases. *Brandenburg v. Ohio,* 395 U.S. 444 (1969), and *Hess v. Indiana,* 414 U.S. 105 (1973), sharpened and recast this test in its current form, to bar liability for advocacy less than "direct incitement to imminent lawless action . . . likely to incite or produce such action." Finally, *New York Times Co. v. Sullivan,* 376 U.S. 254 (1964), and *NAACP v. Claiborne Hardware Co.,* 458 U.S. 886 (1982), make very clear the applicability of such stringent standards as much to civil as to criminal sanctions.

The lower court decisions cited in this chapter are *Weirum v. RKO General, Inc.,* 539 P.2d 36 (Cal. 1975), the one precedent for media liability in such a situation, followed by a consistent line of non-liability judgments—*Olivia N. v. NBC,* 178 Cal. Rptr. 888 (Cal. App. 1981) (the *Born Innocent* assault case); *Yakubowicz v. Paramount Pictures Corp.,* 536 N.E.2d 1067 (Mass. 1989); *Zamora v. CBS,* 480 F. Supp. 199 (S.D. Fla 1979) (the suit against all three major networks by the allegedly television-obsessed teen); *Bill v. Superior Court,* 187 Cal. Rptr. 625 (Cal. App. 1982) (suit by the victim of an attack by theater-goers who had just seen *Boulevard Nights*); *Walt Disney Productions, Inc. v. Shannon,* 276 S.E.2d 580 (Gas. 1981) (claim filed by the youth who lost an eye as the result of a TV-invited experiment); *DeFilippo v. NBC,* 446 A.2d 1036 (R.I. 1982) (suit by the parents of a youth who lost his life by emulating a "hanging" stunt seen on a Johnny Carson program); *McCollum v. CBS, Inc.,* 249 Cal. Rptr. 187 (Cal. App. 1988) (suit by parents of teen whose suicide was allegedly inspired by lyrics to which he was then listening); and *Herceg v. Hustler Magazine,* 814 F.2d 1017 (5th Cir. 1987) (suit by mother of teen whose accidental death occurred while following instructions for a dangerous stunt in a magazine article.)

10. WHAT'S NEXT?

A very recent and provocative discussion of many of the themes of this concluding chapter is Bruce W. Sanford, *Don't Shoot the Messenger: How Our Growing Hatred of the Media Threatens Free Speech for All of Us* (New York: The Free Press, 1999).

The suit brought by the family of Elyse Pahler, victim of a savage attack that had allegedly been inspired by "death metal" band music and lyrics, has not yet resulted in any reported judgment. The background of the case, and contrasting views of the central legal issues, can be found in Sharon Waxman, "Did Death Metal Music Incite Murder?" *Washington Post,* January 23, 2001, p. E1. An Associated Press account appeared the next day, January 24, 2001, on the Freedom Forum webpage, at www.freedomforum.org/news/2001/01/2001-01-24-03.htm.

index

ROBERT M. O'NEIL

became Director of the Thomas Jefferson Center for the Protection of Free Expression in 1990, after serving as President of the University of Virginia (1985–1990) and the University of the University of Wisconsin System (1980–1985). He taught constitutional and commercial law at both institutions, continuing a teaching commitment that began in the early 1960s at the University of California-Berkeley after a year-long clerkship with Supreme Court Justice William J. Brennan, Jr. He lives in Charlottesville, Virginia, where he continues to teach law and where his wife is a secondary school teacher and administrator.